THE IRISH TIMES

BOOK

of the

YEAR

2001

EDITED BY

PETER MURTAGH

Gill & Macmillan

Gill & Macmillan Ltd
Hume Avenue
Park West
Dublin 12
with associated companies throughout the world
www.gillmacmillan.ie

© 2001 *The Irish Times*
0 7171 3329 X
Design by Identikit Design Consultants, Dublin
Print origination by Carole Lynch
Printed by Butler & Tanner Ltd, Frome, Somerset

*The paper used in this book is made from the wood pulp
of managed forests. For every tree felled, at least one tree
is planted, thereby renewing natural resources.*

A catalogue record is available for this book
from the British Library.

1 3 5 4 2

Contents

Introduction

Images of events that are seared onto the memory are few and far between. Their essential characteristic is that they last, frozen in time, capable of being recalled in an instant. The Liverpool toddler Jamie Bulger being led to his death, hand in hand, by two older children; the NASA space shuttle Challenger exploding in the blue skies over Florida; the crumpled wreckage of Princess Diana's car in a Paris underpass ...

As this year's *Irish Times Book of the Year* was nearing completion, the truly horrific acts of terrorist mass murder in Washington and New York exploded onto television screens and across page after page of our newspapers.

The Irish Times was fortunate, if that is not an inappropriate word, to have Conor O'Clery and Elaine Lafferty in New York at the time of the disaster. O'Clery, living just a few blocks from the World Trade Centre, actually witnessed what happened, watching as the second plane smashed into the second tower. His report of that event and what happened next — people leaping to their deaths from the upper floors and the eventual collapse of both towers — was written under extreme pressure: pressure of time to meet deadlines back in Dublin; the need to overcome the paralysing effect the event had on almost everyone else as, everywhere, people stood, transfixed, watching TVs; and the pressure that comes with having to set aside personal emotional reactions having witnessed such an appalling event.

O'Clery overcame all these and wrote a fine record of what he saw. It is included in these pages. On the same day, Elaine Lafferty captured the feelings of other New Yorkers. 'This is how we live now ... we will watch as our fellow Americans ... emerge from the catastrophe of downtown Manhattan ... their faces, all of them, regardless of race or ethnicity, are now a ghostly light grey ...,' she wrote. Her other report, also included here, was written two days after the tragedy. It pieced together, in harrowing detail, the last moments of some of those on board the doomed planes.

On the other side of the world, Miriam Donohoe captured the unfolding human drama affecting the exiles of Afghanistan's Islamic fundamentalist Taliban regime. These were the people who had already fled the strictures of a government that harboured the chief suspect for the atrocity in America, Osama bin Laden.

By the time this book is published, President Bush's retaliatory action, in what he termed America's first war of the 21st century, will have become apparent. Whatever it is and wherever it happens, *Irish Times* journalists around the world will be there covering events.

In comparison with these events, much of what happened in the little over 12 months reflected in this book pales into insignificance. Nonetheless, many events were indeed milestones in Irish life: the reality of the global economy and global economic downturn, as exemplified by the Gateway closure in Dublin; the jailing of Liam Lawlor; and the revelation that the population was growing at a rate of 50,000 people a year and that we were no longer, in the words of Gerry O'Hanlon, director of the Central Statistics Office, 'an emigrant country'.

In selecting these and other pieces for inclusion in the book, I have as last year been guided by my own liking for good writing, for humour and wit, for opinions strongly held and well expressed, and for carefully crafted words recording memorable occasions. I want to thank everyone in Gill and Macmillan — especially Deirdre Greenan — for all their assistance in producing this edition. Thanks also to the many friends and colleagues in *The Irish Times* who helped me cull material from the hundreds of photographs and articles that are written and published in the paper, six days a week. The final selection, including flaws and omissions, was mine alone.

Peter Murtagh
The Irish Times
Dublin, September 2001

What Is Journalism?

The late Nicholas Tomalin, who was killed covering the Yom Kippur war for the *Sunday Times* in 1973, once suggested that the essential qualities for success in journalism were 'rat-like cunning, a plausible manner and a little literary ability'. As a description, this appeals to many journalists' rather self-depreciative view of what they do. Indeed, for years, the quotation from Tomalin was stuck to a filing cabinet in the pre-computer Irish Times newsroom. And yet, there is a lot of truth in this axiom. Rat-like cunning is useful for ferreting out and publishing that which some people do not want published; a plausible manner can be helpful in both obtaining and presenting the story; and the importance of literary ability is, one hopes, obvious.

So what is good journalism? First and foremost, journalism is about facts; it presents a story, grounded in real events and, in the words of the late Martha Gellhorn, good journalism is 'serious, careful, honest'. It can effect great change in society, give meaning to events, filter the deluge of information, prioritise and make understandable that which is complex. At its best it offers context and, alternately, entertains, is funny and does not take itself too seriously.

If, on this side of the Atlantic, English-speaking journalists tend to dissemble, denigrating their role in journalism and its central role in democracy, that is not so in the US. The journalist, editor and novelist, Pete Hamill, for example, is considerably less coy. In a lecture to graduates of the celebrated Columbia Journalism School on the wider purpose of journalism, he declared the job of the journalist 'is to urge public figures to be as truthful as possible, because, eventually some pain-in-the-ass reporter will discover the truth. No people, not here, not anywhere, can live in a system that is wormy with lies.' Even if it is only the fear of such exposure that causes less venal behaviour, freedom of expression in journalism is to be vaunted.

Although Hamill's journalistic life was spent, not in the newsroom of the *New York Times* or *Washington Post*, but in the tabloid environment of tough New York newspapers, such as the *Post* and the *Daily News*, he insists that journalists are also 'conscious of the writing, as well as the facts, and choose careful transitions and deliver concrete nouns and active verbs.' Above all, journalists exult in what William Maxwell of the *New Yorker* once described as 'the happiness of getting it down right'. Good journalism is, moreover, about something new, something we did not know, leading to an understanding we did not have before. It is about the best possible explanation in the time and space available. 'Big story or small,' Hamill concludes, 'the reporter adds to human knowledge and thus to change itself. He or she is, in fact, in the knowledge business, not the entertainment business, and while good stories can be funny or amusing they must always be news, even when the news is a simple expansion of vision.'

The publication of an anthology of journalism, such as this, is an opportunity to look at the current position of journalism in Ireland. Before the next *Irish Times Book of the Year* is published, a debate will be underway concerning the inclusion of the European Convention of Human

Rights into Irish law. That debate should include the media because the European Court of Human Rights has made a number of landmark rulings, fundamental to the role of journalists and journalism in Irish society. Along with a wide range of rights, the Convention offers protection to both freedom of expression and to privacy. The Court has ruled in favour of freedom of expression, which has given journalists a number of rights which our Courts will have to consider. These include the right to refuse to name an anonymous source; acknowledge that awards in libel cases can be such as to limit freedom of expression; and establish that the media has a right and a duty to publish and broadcast material, despite national courts ruling to the contrary.

Such rulings, however, have also brought responsibilities. In a 1995 judgment, the Court declared that: 'Not only does the press have the task of imparting such information and ideas [of public interest] the public also has a right to receive them. Were it otherwise, the press would be unable to play its vital role of public watchdog.'

Analogously, in 1992, the judges ruled that: 'The pre-eminent role of the press in a state governed by the rule of law must not be forgotten. Freedom of the press affords the public one of the best means of discovering and forming an opinion on the ideas and attitudes of their political leaders. In particular it gives politicians the opportunity to reflect and comment on the preoccupations of public opinion: it thus enables everyone to participate in the free political debate which is at the very core of the concept of a democratic society.' How the Convention will be incorporated into our law should move the debate about the media to a new level of sophistication that includes privacy, responsibilities and the role of the media within a modern democracy. Without newspapers, such debate is inconceivable.

That the media has a central role to play in a democracy does not mean it must present its news, views and opinions in a manner that will drive the reader away. Part of the responsibility of the media is to ensure that important issues are presented in a way that is sceptical, challenging, intelligent and, where appropriate, entertaining, funny and irreverent. Even more importantly, then, a good newspaper must draw the reader in.

On a daily basis, reporters, news editors and sub-editors select, prioritise and present. In publishing some stories and not others, newspapers inform readers that one story is more important than another. But such decisions are made quickly, often very quickly. Although editors sometimes get it wrong, once in every 24-hour cycle editors say, in effect: 'that's it; that's how we see it'. The *Book of the Year* is a reminder of how the editors at *The Irish Times* called it, how events were recorded, analysed and debated. It is also an opportunity to re-examine the significance of some events, in the light of others, over a 12-month span. The value of an annual newspaper anthology is that it allows one to revisit the year, to re-savour and, occasionally, to re-evaluate how one newspaper defined that year. In this context, the publication of an anthology, such as this, should be seen as a brave endeavour, in so far as it allows readers not only the opportunity to reconsider the events of the year for themselves but to assess how they were served by *The Irish Times* in particular. Scrutiny of *The Irish Times*, therefore, occurs not only on a daily basis, as the news unfolds but, in such a volume, sequentially and retrospectively through the harsher lens of time. *The Irish Times Book of the Year* is, therefore, demonstrative of reader inclusion at its most sophisticated.

An anthology is also a reminder of the value of newspapers in general, aside from *The Irish Times* in particular. Since the invention of the radio, soothsayers have predicted the demise of the newspaper. And, of course, the development of the World Wide Web was to kill off newspapers permanently. Not for nothing do on line journalists speak disparagingly of the traditional newspaper as the 'dead trees edition'. The inference is that the web-based news organ is more democratic, and even that readers can become their own journalists, by linking to the press release, the court judgment, the very records the journalist uses to write the story. But newspapers cannot be so easily replaced. Newspapers give unique meaning to events. The best of them additionally offer colour, passion and atmosphere when written in an informed, engaged and persuasive manner.

Not many newspapers, however, have the confidence to suggest, let alone warrant, the proposition, that an accurate picture of a year could be culled from its own pages. *The Irish Times* not only reflects the changes taking place at home, with its ever-expanding coverage of contemporary issues, but is unusual in expanding its foreign coverage, when so many other newspapers are cutting back. In addition to reflecting changes in lifestyle, at its most serious, *The Irish Times* conveys and balances the importance of social, political, cultural and religious issues, to the extent that its range of coverage and its quality of analysis constitutes a uniquely wide-angled, account of the making of contemporary history. In this, Irish readers are fortunate in *The Irish Times*. This anthology offers its readers the opportunity to relive those events and to reassess the important issues of the last 12 months. That those stories can withstand a second reading is testament to their authority.

The serendipitious qualities of newspapers cannot be replicated in any other medium. In an increasingly predictable media world, where marketing people are replacing journalists, it is the very unpredicatabilty of newspapers which makes them so compelling. At the end of the day, newspapers will survive because reading a newspaper is one of life's great pleasures. When away, what do you miss most? A pint of Guinness? Brown bread? No, the newspaper.

Michael Foley
September 2001
Michael Foley is a lecturer in journalism at the Dublin Institute of Technology and a former Irish Times journalist.

Journalists and Photographers

Arthur Beesley is a business reporter.

Alan Betson is an *Irish Times* staff photographer.

Rosita Boland is features writer with *The Irish Times*.

Brian Boyd is an *Irish Times* journalist, writing mainly on music and comedy.

Suzanne Breen is a reporter in the Belfast office of *The Irish Times*.

Vincent Browne is a weekly columnist with *The Irish Times* and also writes the Vincent Browne Interview, published on Saturdays.

Cyril Byrne is a freelance photographer whose work appears regularly in *The Irish Times*.

Joe Carroll was Washington Correspondent of *The Irish Times* until his retirement early in 2001.

Tom Conachy is a freelance photographer based in Co. Louth.

Kevin Courtney is a freelance journalist, specialising in rock music.

Siobhán Creaton is Finance Correspondent.

Judith Crosbie is a freelance sub-editor and reporter with *The Irish Times*.

Paul Cullen is Development Correspondent. He has also been covering the Flood Tribunal since it began proceedings.

Deaglán de Bréadún is Foreign Affairs Correspondent.

Eithne Donnellan is a staff reporter with *The Irish Times*.

Miriam Donohoe is Asia Correspondent.

Drapier is a member of the Oireachtas who writes a weekly insider's guide to politics.

Keith Duggan is sports journalist who specialises in Gaelic games.

Garret FitzGerald writes a weekly column on the Opinion Page each Saturday.

Brenda Fitzsimons is a staff photographer with *The Irish Times*. She won 1st prize in the News category of the Eircell Press Photography awards for 2000.

Sean Flynn is Education Editor.

Brendan Glacken is a sub-editor and writes a twice weekly humourous column, Times Square. In 2000, he recieved an ESB National Media Award for his work.

Peter Hanan is a freelance caricaturist. His work appears in various sections of the paper and he also illustrates the Saturday Profile.

Mary Hannigan is a sports journalist. She writes the Planet Football each week in the Sports Monday supplement.

Nuala Haughey is Social and Racial Affairs Correspondent. In 2000, she received a Law Society Justice Media award.

Kitty Holland is a staff reporter.

Joe Humphreys is a staff reporter. He has been covering the Lindsay Tribunal since it began proceedings.

Tom Humphries is a sports writer with *The Irish Times*.

Róisín Ingle is a staff reporter. She has been based in Belfast for the past year.

Matt Kavanagh is a staff photographer with *The Irish Times*. He won 2nd in the Arts category of the Eircell Press Photography awards for 2000.

Colin Keegan is a photographer with the Collins Photo Agency of Dublin.

Elaine Keogh is a freelance reporter based in Co. Louth.

Frank Kilfeather was an *Irish Times* reporter until his retirement in 2001.

Elaine Lafferty writes for *The Irish Times* from New York and Los Angeles.

John Lane is a freelance sub-editor and rock critic.

Pat Langan was an *Irish Times* staff photographer until his retirement in 2001.

Hugh Linehan is editor of *The Ticket*.

Eric Luke is a staff photographer with *The Irish Times*.

Sean MacConnell is Agriculture Correspondent.

Dara Mac Dónaill is a staff photographer with *The Irish Times*.

Justin MacInnes runs a commercial photography company in Dublin.

Alva MacSharry was a sub-editor with *The Irish Times* until she moved to France in 2001 from where she continues to work for the newspaper.

Tom McCann is a journalism student from Chicago, Illinois, who was on secondment to *The Irish Times* in 2000.

Frank McDonald is Environment Editor.

Frank McNally is a staff reporter. He also writes a humourous column, The Last Straw, in the Weekend section, published on Saturdays.

Patsy McGarry is Religious Affairs Correspondent.

Brendan McWilliams is a meteorologist based in Darmstadt, Germany, from where he writes a daily column, Weather Eye, which appears on the Bulletin page.

Emmet Malone is Education Correspondent.

Lara Marlowe is Paris Correspondent.

Frank Millar is London Editor.

Frank Miller is a staff photographer. He won 2nd prize in the News category in the Eircell Press Photography awards for 2000.

Seán Moran is Gaelic Games Correspondent.

Gerry Moriarty is Northern Editor, based in Belfast.

Robert Mullen is a freelance photographer based in Arklow, Co. Wicklow.

Clare Murphy is a reporter based at the Belfast office of *The Irish Times*.

Kevin Myers writes Irishman's Diary.

Gillian Ní Cheallaigh is a freelance reporter.

Breda O'Brien is a weekly columnist published each Saturday on the Opinion page.

Bryan O'Brien is a staff photographer with *The Irish Times*. He recieved the Photographer of the Year in the Eircell Press Photography Awards for 2000. He also won 2nd prize in the Political and Features category, and 3rd prize in the News category.

Mary O'Brien is Assistant Readers' Representative.

Conor O'Clery is International Business Editor, reporting from Wall Street, New York, since early 2001. Formerly, he was Asia Correspondent.

Nuala O'Faolain is a columnist in *The Irish Times* Magazine and a novelist.

Pádraig O'Morain is Social Affairs Correspondent.

Noel O'Reilly is journalist who covered the paralympics for *The Irish Times*.

Fintan O'Toole is a weekly columnist and has recently been appointed Theatre Critic.

Marc O'Sullivan is a photographer with the Collins Photo Agency of Dublin.

Emmet Oliver is Education Correspondent.

Gillian Sandford is a freelance journalist based in London. Prior to that, she reported from Belgrade.

Derek Scally is Berlin Correspondent.

Kathy Sheridan is a features writer.

Lorna Siggins is Western Correspondent, based in Galway.

David Sleator is a staff photographer with *The Irish Times*. He won 1st prize in the Sports category in the Eircell Press Photography awards for 2000.

Jamie Smyth is Technology Reporter.

Patrick Smyth is Washington Correspondent.

Jason South is a photographer with the Melbourne Age in Australia. He has been working with *The Irish Times* on exchange for a year. As part of the arrangement, Alan Betson from *The Irish Times* is in Melbourne.

Joe St Leger is a staff photographer with *The Irish Times*.

Jane Suiter is Economic Editor.

Gerry Thornley is Rugby Correspondent.

Terry Thorp works on *The Irish Times* picture desk and is an accomplished rock concert photographer.

Peter Thursfield is Picture Editor.

Martyn Turner is *The Irish Times* political cartoonist.

Time's Eye is written by a distinguished former *Irish Times* journalist.

Michael Viney lives near Louisbourg, Co. Mayo, from where he writes a weekly column, Another Life, which is published in the Weekend section on Saturdays.

Declan Walsh is a freelance journalist based in Nairobi, Kenya.

John Waters is a weekly columnist.

Maev Ann Wren is a freelance journalist and commentator on health matters.

I SEPTEMBER 2000

An Irishman's Diary

Frank Kilfeather

William Henry Harrison heroically refused to wear an overcoat at his inauguration as US President in March, 1841, despite the freezing drizzle. This resulted in a serious dose of pneumonia and he died 30 days later. His was the shortest American presidency and he spent most of it unconscious.

If the man had had any sense he would have worn a heavy coat for the occasion and thereby held office for the full four-year term. But no, he had to prove to the American nation and the world that he was a fine-looking man in a well-cut suit. Appearances count in politics.

I have always been fascinated by the sight of heads of state and senior politicians refusing to wear overcoats at important, but freezing wet, outdoor functions.

Pouring rain

Have you ever noticed that when a head of state is arriving or departing from Dublin airport, the Taoiseach of the day or some senior Minister is there resplendent in his best dark, sombre suit — even if it is pouring rain or if there is snow on the ground? Big drops of rain are hopping off his shoulders; he looks a sorry sight, but he doesn't care; he is observing tradition. Perhaps an aide is running beside him with an umbrella. Why can't the silly man wear an overcoat and hat? It's not going to detract from the occasion to any great extent. The Irish public will probably be able to tolerate one of its leaders wearing an overcoat. God knows, it is able to put up with a lot of other things from them.

I know this is only a small matter, which will probably never be discussed by the Cabinet, but politicians and public figures generally should remember the sorry tale of poor Willie Harrison.

Hot weather, too, can embarrass those in the public eye. Covering a recent graduation ceremony at the Garda College in Templemore, Co. Tipperary, I saw a young female garda collapse on the parade ground, overcome by the heat of a stifling summer day.

She was probably mortified, but it wasn't her fault. It had happened many times before. The 100 new garda were wearing heavy winter uniforms, including white gloves. They had marched up and down the square for about half-an-hour to the beat of the excellent Garda band. A great spectacle.

Ms Natasha Byram wears a Tomás O'Sullivan orange satin backless halter dress, at the Wella Design Centre Autumn/Winter 2000 Fashion Show at the Powerscourt Townhouse Centre. Photograph: Dara Mac Dónaill.

Then they had to stand to attention for another half-hour for speeches and presentations. The sun beat down relentlessly. I stood in the shade of a friendly tree. Their colleagues watched in their short-sleeved shirts and summer uniforms — just what the new garda should have been wearing.

At the end of the ceremonies, the novices were told from the reviewing platform that they were now all free to go and enjoy themselves, to get out of the sun; they had suffered enough. After all, said the senior officer, he and the rest of the dignitaries reviewing the parade were sitting in the shade while the youngsters were strutting their stuff.

Summer uniforms

It was thoughtful of him to mention that he knew they were finding it tough in the sun. But should he not go further and allow the youngsters to wear summer uniforms for summer graduations? I know there is a long tradition that the full uniform must be worn (hence the white gloves), but for 'humane' reasons could this be changed? This would make it a lot easier on the proud new garda. It must be a sad memory, on one of the biggest and proudest days of their lives, to be carried off the parade ground by a rescue unit — which actually seems to be standing by expecting such an occurrence. Their relatives and friends must also be distressed to see this happening to one of their family.

Similar incidents occur in Britain at big police and military parades. How often have we seen a member of the Royal Guard, in his heavy red uniform and high, heavy busby hat, keel over and crumble to the ground? I'm always intrigued that the guy standing to attention beside the fallen one can't do anything except, perhaps, silently thank his lucky stars that it wasn't him.

In addition, the poor unfortunate who collapses will then have the misfortune to see the moment repeated ad nauseum on the evening news in a weather story illustrating the heat of the day. In many professions, dress doesn't seem to matter any more. The so-called white-collar worker now comes to work in casual clothes. Men and women maintain they want to feel 'comfortable'. If they do not, they will not be able to work efficiently. That is the case put forward, and who am I to disagree? A retired banker was telling me recently that 30 years ago the only day when staff were allowed to wear even half-casual clothes was Friday, when they might be allowed to wear a blazer, 'as they could be going off golfing afterwards'. Otherwise, it was the old reliable pinstripe suit and tie.

Snazzy tie

Years ago, a young reporter came into the *Irish Press* newsroom dressed in a very nice sports jacket, a pink shirt and snazzy tie. The news editor, a bit of a tyrant, bore down on him, eyes out on sticks and steam coming from his ears, wanting to know what the hell he meant by coming in dressed so casually. He let it be known they weren't running a holiday camp in Burgh Quay: they were running a serious newspaper and had to keep up standards.

My young companion was quite shattered. He mistakenly thought he was looking a million dollars and representing the paper to the highest standards. He jokingly told me afterwards that he thought he was amazingly well dressed for the salary he was on. But he quickly found out that his sartorial taste wasn't to the news editor's taste and he never wore that jacket to work again.

2 SEPTEMBER 2000

Irish Charm Offensive to Woo the UN

Deaglán de Breadún

There are two versions — shorthand and longhand — of Richard Ryan, Ireland's Ambassador to the UN and a key figure in our campaign for a seat on the UN Security Council. The shorthand version begins with the label he will never shake off, as The Man Who Dined for Ireland. This dates back to the

'Richard Ryan dined for Ireland — now he is dining for the world.'

period in the mid-1980s when he was dispatched to London with the brief of mixing and socialising with the Tory establishment to ensure that Mrs Thatcher could steer the Anglo-Irish Agreement successfully through the House of Commons.

It was a new departure in Irish diplomacy. In the old days, there was a big focus on the Irish community in Britain, our dispossessed emigrants and their demands. But few such people are found on the Tory backbenches and Ryan's Mission Impossible was to persuade these critical elements to see the reasonableness of the Irish case, which just happened to involve giving Dublin an oversight of the affairs of part of the United Kingdom.

In his memoirs, the Taoiseach of the day, Garret FitzGerald, describes Ryan as 'a well-known poet and an excellent shot'. Like many an Irish patriot before him, Richard Ryan was packing a gun, but without any warlike intent since he would use it only for hunting.

The mission was a stunning success, with only 21 Tory rightwingers voting against the agreement in the Commons. The old Etonians and Harrovians

were smitten by the charm of the Christian Brothers boy who clearly demonstrated to them that he was a 'good chap', advancing sound arguments. He was not the only diplomat working behind the scenes and key roles were played by the likes of Noel Dorr, Seán Donlon and Michael Lillis, but when it came to socialising with political intent, Ryan was without peer. The unionists never had a chance.

Mention Ryan to anyone in diplomatic, political or media circles and the 'dining for Ireland' — a bad pun on 'dying for Ireland' — catchphrase immediately surfaces. Sometimes it is said with a grudging air — he was quaffing fine wines while we were nursing pints of stout — but there is no denying that it worked.

However, the label is misleading in that it gives the impression of Ryan as an intellectual lightweight, a *bon viveur* pursuing game across the English moorlands and getting in a plug for government policy over drinks afterwards. There is a deeper side to the man, as seen in his poems, tightly-worded but pregnant with meaning.

Ryan's collections are hard to find. You would have looked in vain this week in the Irish poetry section of a certain leading Dublin bookshop: following alphabetical order, there was nothing between a slim volume by the similarly-named Patrick R. Ryan and the prison writings of Bobby Sands. But you will find him in such anthologies as the *Penguin Book of Irish Verse* and its Faber equivalent.

At University College Dublin in the late 1960s and early 1970s and in literary circles generally, Ryan was often spoken of as the Next Big Thing. If he had published more he would probably be ranked with the likes of Derek Mahon, Paul Muldoon and Ciaran Carson, who are of similar vintage, but it appears the duties of diplomatic service took precedence. Perhaps like Yeats he could claim to have been distracted by 'the seeming needs of my fooldriven land'.

Now Ryan faces an even more daunting task than his 1980s charm offensive among the British establishment. Along with a special unit of the Department of Foreign Affairs in Dublin headed by Assistant Secretary Mary Whelan, he is heavily involved in the Security Council campaign. Three countries are chasing two temporary seats in the Western European and Other Group of States, and our two rivals are Norway and Italy.

Cutting to the chase, Norway is widely regarded as a shoo-in because of its role in the Middle East and strong reputation as a friend of the developing world. This leaves Ireland competing with Italy for second place. Although conducted away from the media spotlight, the lobbying has been intense. Ably assisted by his Korean wife, Heeun, the ambassador has been working his magic on the other member-states. The Taoiseach will be attending the UN Millennium Summit of world leaders next week and he will be followed by the Minister for Foreign Affairs who is due to address the General Assembly.

Between them, Mr Ahern and Mr Cowen will hold bilateral meetings with the UN missions of 60 member-states as part of the Security Council campaign.

Old hands say it is like a Seanad election, with some member-states promising votes to more than one candidate. Only the result of the secret ballot will tell the tale and that is not likely to be held until the end of next month. Ireland has been an assiduous attender at international conferences in the last year as part of its lobbying effort and there has been much glad-handing and gentle persuasion from junior ministers Liz O'Donnell, Martin Cullen, Eoin Ryan and Danny Wallace.

Ask why Ireland is so keen to win the seat and sources lapse into vague generalities. It was a target set out in the White Paper on foreign policy published when Dick Spring was in charge of Iveagh House. There is also a feeling that, with a settlement in the North and the economy booming, Ireland's diplomatic energies need a fresh outlet.

The Italians entered the race comparatively late, which engendered some resentment in Irish circles where it was seen as bad form for one EU state to seek to do down another. Their campaign was led initially by the formidable Franceso Paolo Fulci, a diplomatic legend endowed with charm by the bucketful and considered invincible in elections. The choice of Ryan to spearhead our campaign on the ground becomes more explicable in that context.

'It is a serious prize in terms of our status in the world,' a diplomatic insider said. Winning a seat will mean that Ireland will have to face hard questions about the use of force and on other difficult issues such as the sanctions against Iraq. A senior Government figure told me it would be good for us to have to deal with these issues rather than sitting on the fence. As Joe Louis said about being in the boxing ring, 'You can run but you cannot hide.'

If we are unsuccessful, nobody who knows the UN scene will blame Ryan but it may be a source of quiet satisfaction to some. He does not suffer fools gladly and has proven adept at climbing the greasy pole of diplomatic success. He started his career in Tokyo under the tutelage of Ambassador

Robin Fogarty, dazzling both intellectually and socially, who died before his time in 1995. Ryan served in Brussels and was seconded to the cabinet of Richard Burke on the European Commission. He made his name with the London interlude and this was followed by ambassadorships in South Korea and Spain before he was appointed as Ireland's Permanent Representative (equivalent of ambassador) at the UN in August 1998.

Friends say that, in general, he prefers the company of writers, painters and poets to politicians. However, colleagues say he shares one characteristic with a master practitioner of the political art: like Clinton, he has the knack of 'making you feel like the only person in the world'. Friends say he is hosting two dinner parties a week, trying to drum up support. Who knows what modest impact an Irish victory might have on the forlorn corners of our troubled planet? Richard Ryan dined for Ireland — now he is dining for the world.

5 SEPTEMBER 2000

Review: Tom Jones, RDS

John Lane

Almost 37 years after bursting onto the scene with 'It's Not Unusual', Tom Jones is still performing with the same gusto, the same dodgy dance moves and, amazingly, the same remarkable voice.

He turns 60 this year, yet at the RDS on Saturday he showed all the swagger and vigour of the man who regularly brought the house down in Caesar's Palace more than three decades ago.

As dusk fell, he arrived on stage to the strains of 'The Ballad of Tom Jones' — what else? — and instantly had the near 20,000-strong crowd on its feet.

His band struggled with muddy sound for a short while, but Jones instantly got into his stride, launching 'the voice' from his throat, soaring

Tom Jones in concert in the RDS, Ballsbridge, Dublin. Photograph: Terry Thorp.

above the band, and completely engaging everyone present.

The delighted crowd didn't care about the undertones of domestic violence in 'Delilah', or that the homely 'The Green, Green Grass of Home' is the deluded dream of a condemned inmate. This was a happy occasion — a 90-minute, body-swaying, hand-clapping singalong.

From 30-year-old classics to his last album, Reload, Jones ran through his usual fare of hits and covers — 'Burnin' Down The House', 'Hard to Handle', 'Sexbomb', 'What's New Pussycat', 'Leave Your Hat On', 'It's Not Unusual' — with Lenny Kravitz's 'Are You Gonna Go My Way' and Prince's 'Kiss' for the encore.

His version of 'Walkin' in Memphis' was sung back to him with such force that all he could do was leave the crowd to it.

Aside from his powerful talent, Jones's appeal on the night came from his genuine humility. His iconic persona comes across as personable. He gave pointers to Elvis, but you'd still go for a pint (or a cup of tea) with him after the gig. Onstage was 'The Tom Jones Show', starring the down-to-earth superstar as himself.

7 SEPTEMBER 2000

More Grim Reminders for Omagh as Inquest Begins

Róisín Ingle in Omagh

Omagh Leisure Centre is much like any other such facility in the North. Outside, the façade is dominated by twisting blue and yellow waterslides. Inside, signs direct people to a handball alley and a swimming pool.

But leisure pursuits were the last thing on the minds of the families who filed into the hall — usually the venue for indoor football tournaments — shortly before 11 a.m. yesterday. The sporting space had been transformed into a courtroom for the first day of the inquest into the 29 men, women and children killed two years ago in the Omagh bombing.

On the day the bomb exploded, the same complex served as a centre where relatives of some of the victims, who also included two unborn twin baby girls, endured the agonising wait to learn the fate of their loved ones. Over the next four weeks they will return daily to relive each moment of the nightmare that began on 25 August 1998.

It had been a fine summer day, said the coroner, Mr John Leckey, addressing the courtroom, and Omagh's Market Street was thronged with shoppers. The first person to become aware this small town normality was about to be shattered was UTV programme assistant Margaret Hall. She took the stand as the first of more than 150 witnesses due to give evidence, speaking softly as she recounted the initial telephone bomb warning she received. The chilling notes of the conversation which she tapped into her computer at the time appeared on one of two video screens in the courtroom: IRA … Caller Rang Twice … Bomb Omagh Town. The code word given was Malta, or Martha, Pope, she said.

Another witness was allowed to sit behind a wooden screen as she gave her evidence to protect her identity. She was a member of the Samaritans in Coleraine and had also received a warning call, believed to have been diverted from the organisation's Omagh office. The man said the bomb was 200 yards from the Courthouse, High Street, Main Street, she said.

The families of victims expressed relief that day one of the inquest was now over. Speaking afterwards, Michael Gallagher, whose son Adrian was killed in the bomb, said it had been a difficult day. 'It's been very painful to listen particularly to the bomb warnings … in that very room I spent some of the worst days and hours of my life.'

Even those who concluded their evidence yesterday will take time to get over the experience. Clearly shaken by having to appear at the inquest, Margaret Hall wept as she walked away from the witness box. Hers are unlikely to be the last tears shed at Omagh Leisure Centre over the coming weeks.

11 SEPTEMBER 2000

Overwhelming Spirit Exorcises Kilkenny Ghosts

Keith Duggan

Great teams do not crash. Kilkenny came to Croke Park yesterday facing the demons of recent September history and expelled them all, shooting those ghosts to ribbons.

Five times they singed the Offaly netting, each goal as searing and plain as a redemption cry.

After the last two years of sorrow on All-Ireland final days, Kilkenny hit a perfect note and levelled their neighbours on a scoreline of 5–15 to 1–14. Offaly, ever the wonderful gamblers, knew from early on that this game was up.

'We went up to blow everyone out of Croke Park today and that's what we did,' John Power said afterwards.

And so they hurled as if in a composed fury, on fire from the first whistle. Serious troubles loomed for Offaly as early as the sixth minute.

Philly Larkin, diminutive and unbeatable all day, let fly with a long, arcing ball for the Offaly full back to contend with.

The opposing trio gathered under it and eyed it like it was a descending meteorite. Niall Claffey assumed control and bobbled the catch. The one man on earth he didn't want near him was hovering. DJ time.

Carey snapped up the invite and held the stadium spellbound as he rapped another wonderful goal. Up 1–2 to no score, the goal rush had started.

As the hour wore on, it became apparent that Kilkenny's thirst would be relentless. The celebrated front-trio of Charlie Carter, DJ and Henry Shefflin

shimmered with easy menace, all clearly hell-bent on hitting the back of the net.

Shefflin rifled low and accurate in the ninth minute and, although Niall Claffey half-scrambled the ball off the line, DJ made sure of the goal. Later, he insisted the goal belonged to his colleague. 'Henry doesn't score very many so I better give him that.'

Why not? There were plenty more on offer. Offaly hurled into the maelstrom with typical resolution, hanging in there, waiting for the half-chance.

But, just as they seemed to be making sense of things, mainly through the marksmanship of captain Johnny Dooley, Kilkenny plundered their last line again, with DJ bursting from the pack after a throw-in and shooting from the hip yet again.

Stephen Byrne, the Offaly man facing the torrent, got timber to it, but this time Charlie was there to unwrap the gift. It was 3–8 to 0–7 at the break.

'No matter what sort of team came out in the second half, they weren't going to hurl that back,' observed John Power.

So it went. We learned things about this Kilkenny team yesterday. They speak little, but have great stories to tell. Willie O'Connor hurled for most of the match with broken ribs.

John Power was back swashbuckling and brilliant two years after reckoning his days and black and amber were done. And all season, it was asked if DJ had it in him on the great days.

So gods do not answer letters? 1–4 from play, even if the second goal is credited to Shefflin.

'All this talk about DJ and the rest in All-Ireland finals … you're askin' me, but who do ye think the best hurler you've ever seen is? Answer that if you like,' mused Brian Cody afterwards. 'Hurling should thank God for him.'

Offaly, blindfolded and against the wall in the second half, went for one last glorious stand.

John Troy came in, stirring the faithful in the stands. Brian Whelahan moved up to the front ranks to try and conjure up the heroics of '98.

Charlie Carter, Kilkenny, celebrates his goal during the All-Ireland Hurling Final against Offaly. Photograph: Dara Mac Dónaill.

Johnny Dooley hurled on imperturbably. Memorably, Joe Errity thundered forward and his courage inflamed his team-mates.

Johnny Pilkington cracked home a goal in a crowd after 58 minutes and, even though they trailed by 1–11 to 4–12, their instinct came alive. There are few sights more stirring than this wild bunch charging against the odds.

As ever, their efforts revolved around swift ground stroking and perfect touches. Even yesterday, they made us gasp. Who will ever forget Johnny Pilkington, his team down 1–11 to 4–12, playing a pass through his own legs? Some genius you just can't suppress.

But no team can win them all, not even Offaly. Kilkenny didn't blink and rode out the brief rebellion. Peter Barry picked up where he left off last September.

Eamon Kennedy settled into his crucial centre-half berth magnificently. Willie was Willie, fiery and street-smart. They kept the ball flowing one way.

'Every time that we tried to come back at them, they seemed to get a goal,' sighed Michael Duignan when it was over.

'That's what killed us but that's what Kilkenny have a name for.'

All-Ireland titles are what Kilkenny have a name for. Can any previous wins have been as exuberant as this, the county's 26th? In the last minutes of the game, sunshine spread an amber colour across the field and Brian Cody had his arms raised. They knew, but still they searched.

Eddie Brennan, a star for tomorrow, blazed in for the fifth goal. DJ and Charlie sent over distant signature notes as the party began.

'It was just a spirit, a reaction under pressure,' summed up John Power.

A weaker team might have buckled under the weight, but not this one. This could see the start of the latest Kilkenny cra. They have stared the bad times down and are stronger for it. Who knows when these great neighbours will next meet in September?

Offaly's summers will remain stubbornly unpredictable and all the better for that, but it is not hard to imagine Kilkenny returning to this stage frequently.

After yesterday, the path ahead seemed alight with promise. 'With days like this,' said DJ Carey, 'you'd stay going for ever.'

Amen.

14 SEPTEMBER 2000

Furious Punters Deliver Ringing Message

Arthur Beesley

Eircom's 12 directors and their chairman, Mr Ray MacSharry, strutted on to the podium in the RDS yesterday to the strains of their catchy theme tune which dreamily asserts: 'your love is my love' and 'my love is your love'.

But the punters weren't having any of it. Forget love, they said. Show us the money.

With Eircom stock still far off the flotation rate, 4,000 shareholders were content to express fury, apoplexy, grievance, hurt and pain at the performance of the company they know so well.

Mr MacSharry faced the music and there was definitely no love there. After schmoozing in the lobby before the a.g.m. began, his initial words were greeted — in a sign of things to come — with jeers. 'Could I please ask you to take a moment to establish the location of the nearest exit,' he said.

Given what followed, Ray might have done well to bolt for the door there and then, but he stood his ground. Stood, in fact, for more than 4½ hours and thanked everyone for their remarks. The critiques, comments, booing and slow-handclapping were very bad indeed.

Senator Shane Ross waltzed in with his pal Eamon Dunphy and 28,000 letters of proxy. Wagging a finger at the board with a vitriol he used to reserve for the IRA, he scorned management's share option 'bonanza' and the 'cartel' of institutional investors. Eircom was a dead loss, he said. No other company would touch it. Shareholders greeted the news with a standing ovation.

'Senator Ross has made some points that we can accept fully in relation to the disappointment in the share price,' said Mr MacSharry.

'Resign. Why don't you resign?' cried a member of the crowd.

Yet the former finance minister did not display even an air of resignation, let alone an inclination to stand down. Known as Mac the Knife in the dog days of fiscal rectitude, he was accused of using a guillotine to cut short the meeting.

To be fair, Mr MacSharry seemed keen to let as many shareholders as possible speak — but neatly sidestepped the tricky questions.

A man who said he was in the 'unfortunate position' of being an Eircom worker and shareholder asked whether the firm's chief executive, Alfie Kane, had been censured for stating publicly that its flotation price was too high.

Mr Sharry's response? 'The chief executive expressed a view and there is no point in dwelling on it.'

In the main hall of the RDS, shareholders voted against a share incentive plan and Mr Kane's re-election to the board.

Citing the 'old pals act', shareholder Seán Kelly claimed the board could not care less about Eircom's

Chairman Ray MacSharry during Eircom's AGM in the RDS. Photograph: Frank Miller.

performance. 'You're a thundering disgrace,' he told Mr MacSharry. Laughter.

When board member Dick Spring was asked why he held no Eircom shares, the former Tánaiste and minister for foreign affairs said he 'didn't have cash' to buy the stock. More laughter. Yet Mr Spring's fellow socialists, Tony Gregory and Tomás Mac Giolla, bought shares. In the darkened hall with its elaborate sound system, chaperones wired up with fancy earplugs stood watch throughout while a battalion of six strong-chinned security people guarded the podium.

Some board members sipped their fizzy water and some chewed gum. Nine of the 12 said nothing at all. Mary O'Rourke was nowhere to be seen.

15 SEPTEMBER 2000

Bus Driver Convicted Under Hatred Act

Judith Crosbie

A Dublin Bus driver was yesterday convicted of offences under the Prohibition on Incitement to Hatred Act and of assault at the Dublin Metropolitan District Court.

Gerry O'Grady, a driver for 18 years, had told a Gambian man he should go back to his own country and that 'we don't eat on the buses in this country'.

Two witnesses gave evidence that they over-heard O'Grady use the phrase 'nig-nogs'. O'Grady was also convicted of assault when he threatened another passenger with the cash dispenser from the bus.

Judge Patrick Brady said he was convicting O'Grady of assault because of the evidence and because of his demeanour in court yesterday.

O'Grady will be sentenced next Friday.

O'Grady gave evidence yesterday that Mr Matthew John, originally from Gambia, got on his bus in Maynooth with what he thought was a kebab.

He said he told Mr John he was not allowed to eat or drink on the bus.

He said Mr John walked around the lower part of the bus looking for a sign displaying this rule. O'Grady said Mr John then told him he didn't know how to do his job and wasn't fit to be a bus driver.

'Then he told me: "You are a f...ing racist pig",' O'Grady said.

He said he switched off the bus engine, took the cash dispenser off the bus and tried to call the Garda. However, he saw there were no Garda vehicles in Maynooth Garda station and he contacted the Dublin Bus control room.

Ms Anna Wrynn, who was behind Mr John in the bus queue, approached O'Grady and began criticising him, he said. 'I said to her: "Just stop where you are. I've had enough of this all evening",' he said.

Ms Wrynn gave evidence last week that O'Grady threatened her with the cash dispenser.

O'Grady said when another bus came along the passengers on his bus boarded it and as the bus pulled away, Mr John shouted out at him from a side window.

He said he went into Lucan Garda station and was accompanied by Garda David Byrne on to the bus Mr John was on. When O'Grady showed Garda Byrne where Mr John was on the bus he (O'Grady) tried to go back down the stairs and was prevented from doing so by the garda. He said the garda then hit him in the shoulder.

'I was held against my will. Garda Byrne had his right foot on the upper saloon and his left foot on the stairs,' O'Grady said.

'Mr John then came up to me and said straight into my face that he could buy my job. I told him I was not surprised with the social welfare and £50 socialising money he has,' O'Grady said.

When asked by counsel for the DPP, Ms Claire Loftus, why he said this to Mr John, he replied that he had read the information in newspaper reports on Mr Jackie Healy-Rae's son, Mr Michael Healy-Rae. 'He said they were getting social welfare and £50 socialising money.

Dublin bus driver, Gerry O'Grady, leaving the Richmond District Court in Dublin where he was fined £900 for racially abusing one of his passengers. Photograph: Marc O'Sullivan.

'I never uttered the words "nig-nog" and I never uttered the word "country",' he added.

O'Grady said he did not recollect telling Mr John he should go back to his own country.

Ms Loftus asked him if he was annoyed and agitated during the incident. 'I probably was after being called a racist pig.'

He added: 'I was carrying out part of my duty which the company, I have to say, are not prepared to back me on. They're hanging me out to dry like a turkey.'

The court heard evidence from two of O'Grady's colleagues in Dublin Bus who said they never heard him make racist comments.

(*O'Grady was subsequently sentenced to a fine of £900 and was placed on probation for one year.*)

15 SEPTEMBER 2000

New Recruit Challenged Establishment

Joe Humphreys at the Lindsay Tribunal

Picture the scene. A young woman in a male-dominated profession confronts arguably the two most senior (male) employees in one of the State's largest health agencies over what she regards as its unsafe medical practices.

Imagine, moreover, her confronting the two at their headquarters within weeks of her taking up a new job, having arrived here from outside the jurisdiction.

Not a challenge many would relish.

Yet that is exactly what Dr Helena Daly did in August 1985 when she walked into Pelican House to tell the Blood Transfusion Service Board's national director, Dr Jack O'Riordan, a man regarded as one of the State's leading public health-care professionals, and the board's senior technical officer, Mr Seán Hanratty, that they were failing to take the necessary steps to protect haemophiliacs from becoming infected with HIV.

It is no wonder that she still has vivid memories.

Describing the encounter yesterday on her first day of evidence, Dr Daly said she was 'very surprised' by the reaction she received to her request that all products for haemophiliacs be heat-treated in order to minimise the risk of HIV transmission.

In relation to BTSB Factor 9, in particular, which has been blamed for the infection of seven haemophiliacs with HIV, she said she could not recall being given any technical reason as to why it could not be so treated.

In evidence to the tribunal, the blood bank has cited a fear over thrombogenicity as a reason for the board being slow to introduce heat-treatment.

But Dr Daly said she did not believe the issue was raised. She added that the thrombogenicity risk 'was not a major issue' to treaters who regarded heat-treatment as a basic necessity in spite of potential negative side-effects.

The meeting was arranged on Dr Daly's request shortly after she took up a three-month locum position at St James's Hospital on 1 July 1985.

She had taken temporary leave of absence from the Bristol Royal Infirmary in the UK where she had been employed since 1979, having graduated from UCD in 1975. While in Bristol she had direct experience of one of the first haemophiliac victims of AIDS, and she carried out a study of the case for the *Lancet* medical journal.

Her role at St James's was, in essence, to fill in for Prof. Ian Temperley, director of the National Haemophilia Treatment Centre, while he was on sabbatical leave.

Of the Pelican House meeting, Dr Daly said she left feeling 'very disturbed and very upset' and not convinced that she had conveyed to the board the necessity of heat-treating Factor 9.

She subsequently phoned Prof. Temperley, with whom she had been liaising on the matter and who, she said, agreed wholeheartedly with her demand. Such was her exasperation with the board that she even travelled to see Prof. Temperley in

London, specifically to discuss a strategy for bringing the board round to their way of thinking.

The BTSB eventually agreed to heat-treat Factor 9, but only after the intervention of Prof. Temperley. A start-up date of 1 November was agreed for such treatment. Dr Daly said this was a compromise date and was significant as it was subsequent to Prof. Temperley's return, 'and also after I had gone'.

The intervention was undoubtedly a critical one and it raises the question as to how long the BTSB would have continued issuing untreated Factor 9, and at what cost to the lives of haemophiliacs, if Dr Daly had not acted when she did.

Certainly it does not reflect well on the relevant health professionals that it took someone effectively from outside the jurisdiction to bring about the change.

Dr Daly will continue her evidence today.

23 SEPTEMBER 2000

Girl in the Red Coat

Derek Scally in Berlin

DROEMER

'... Later in the film, Schindler sees the red coat a second time on the ground, its owner presumably dead ...'

Roma Ligocka's first sentence was: 'I want to die with my mother.' Death was nothing special for the three-year-old, nor for any other of the Jews forced by the Nazis to live in the Kracow Ghetto. She felt nothing when her aunt was shot dead before her eyes and saw nothing remarkable in the bodies lying on the street half-buried in the snow. She was too young to know that life in the ghetto was not normal life.

Fifty years later she would realise just how remarkable her experience was. Roma Ligocka was born into a Jewish family in Kracow in 1938 and was 10 months old when the Germans marched into Poland. When she was two, the Nazis rounded up her family and the rest of Kracow's Jews and locked them up in the ghetto. Ligocka is one of the 'hidden children' of the ghetto who, unlike most other children, survived when the ghetto was emptied and its inhabitants shipped to the death camps.

It was as a survivor of the ghetto that the mayor of Kracow invited her, seven years ago, to attend the world premiére of Steven Spielberg's film 'Schindler's List', the story of how businessman Oskar Schindler saved hundreds of Jews from the concentration camps.

The three-hour film was shot in black and white, except for one brief moment of colour when Schindler is transfixed by a small, tired-looking girl of no more than four years old in a red coat.

Ligocka froze when she saw the girl. She remembered the red coat that her grandmother had made her and which she wore during her life in the

'… Ligocka, however, survived.' Roma Ligocka, the 'girl in the red coat'.

ghetto. 'Dear God, that's me,' she thought, unable to speak.

Ligocka met Spielberg two years ago in Berlin when he was awarded the German Order of Merit, the Bundeskreuz; Ligocka was invited to attend the ceremony to represent the survivors of the Kracow Ghetto.

After the ceremony, she walked up to the director and announced: 'I am the girl in the red coat.' She gave the surprised Spielberg a yellowing photo of her taken in 1946 together with her cousin, the film director Roman Polanski. Spielberg was astounded, she says.

'I didn't know the girl actually existed — why didn't I find you?' he asked her. Spielberg's film is based on the book *Schindler's Ark,* which author Thomas Keneally based to a large extent on interviews he conducted with survivors of the Kracow ghetto. 'It may be that someone told him about me, or perhaps I was not the only girl in the ghetto with a red coat,' says Ligocka.

Later in the film, Schindler sees the red coat a second time, on the ground, its owner presumably dead. Ligocka, however, survived. She has never forgotten her coat, nor how safe she felt when she wore it. She says the coat may have saved her life on more than one occasion.

'My mother told me I didn't look so pale when I had it on and that it made my dark hair and eyes less noticeable,' she remembers. Ligocka and her mother were smuggled out of the ghetto and at first lived in hiding with a Kracow family. Had they been discovered, it would have meant death for them and the family. She was very nearly caught by German soldiers more than once and used every trick she could think of to convince them she wasn't a Jew.

'I remember once falling on my knees in front of a German soldier and starting to pray, "Hail Mary, full of grace …"' she says. Living through the war in Kracow with her mother was a daily game of cat and mouse, played in perpetual fear, not knowing what would happen next. Somehow she and her mother weren't discovered and deported; most of their relatives died in Auschwitz.

Ligocka's father survived the camp and found his wife and child again, only to be arrested by the new communist regime in Poland a year later and placed in another prison camp, where he died.

A day after the 'Schindler's List' premiére, Ligocka decided to write her story. She says she felt like an archaeologist going into her own mind and finding the painful memories still there.

As well as being anxious to tell her story, Ligocka is ready to defend her book against attacks from people such as Norman Finkelstein. In his recent book, *The Holocaust Industry,* Finkelstein condemns what he sees as the exploitation for profit of the Holocaust by the Jewish community.

Ligocka, today a painter in Munich, defends herself simply. 'I just wanted to tell my story,' she says. 'I am a painter, not a professional Holocaust victim.'

Picking Through the Wreckage of a Life

Kathy Sheridan

It's like passing the scene of a car crash. The brazen ghoul slows to crawling speed and does all but park and pick over the remains. The rest of us tut-tut at the ghoul, while having a good gawp for ourselves. We know we shouldn't, but we do it anyway.

The life and death of Paula Yates was like that. We stared and forgave ourselves for staring because, well, hadn't she accepted that Faustian deal invariably trotted out to explain away even the grossest media violations? — that once she had 'used' them to make her name or get across her side of the story, every particle of her life was fair game?

Muriel Gray described this week being in a room with her in the early 1980s when Paula, then heavily pregnant with Fifi, read a piece in *New Musical Express* that suggested it would be best for the world if she aborted Bob Geldof's child: 'I haven't the stomach to relate the effect.'

This week the tabloid columnists were out in force, the ones who are paid to chronicle every 'incoherent', 'dishevelled', 'red-eyed', 'stumbling', sighting of every minor soap star with cocaine-rotted noses and television 'personality' whose child is having a nervous breakdown.

If you had the stomach you could have read, say, Dominic Mohan, the *Sun*'s Showbiz editor: 'I urged her: "Retreat somewhere quiet, relax and gather your thoughts. I don't want to be writing another story about … a suicide attempt …",' — all written as if some supernatural forces beyond his control compelled him to log, for public edification, the disintegration of a grievously ill, middle-aged mother of four and file it under 'showbiz'.

Much of the coverage focused on her desperate need for fame, on her facility for reinventing herself, the conviction that hers was a tragedy waiting to happen.

Some peddled the tiresome old chestnut of the free-thinking, ladette-before-her-time — whereby she 'subliminally' instructed all women that 'basically you could do what the bloody hell you liked' — only to be punished by a misogynistic media for daring to be her own master. Memorable examples of this free-thinking behaviour included asking Mick Jagger on *The Tube* (the early 1980s pop programme that made her name): 'What have you got down the front of your pants?'

Sure, she made her own choices. But to what extent were those 'choices' real, once shaped by a childhood starved of love or any semblance of security? Her cringingly intimate 1995 autobiography and an *Observer* interview with her batty mother a couple of months ago, alone were enough to confirm that Paula's notorious craving for 'celebrity' was not the impulse of an airhead, but the lifelong yearning of a tiny, love-starved child.

She was unquestionably a clever, determined woman. Soon after her autobiography appeared and was being generally trashed, the very cultured director of a serious London publishing house who had just met her, told me that he had liked her enormously: 'I found her to be an extremely witty and original thinker.'

But why would such a woman parlay those gifts into packaging herself as that male fantasy, the rock chick who loved it? 'In truth,' wrote Yvonne Roberts in the *Guardian*, 'what she cultivated was a peculiarly British dated chauvinist image; the blonde bimbo with breasts who acts dead saucy; a junior Barbara Windsor.'

When her death was announced, snippets of her autobiography about her early life suddenly took on new meaning: 'I had a boyfriend, some cash, a bag of drugs … I felt careless, organic and sexy. I was 12.'

About the man she believed to be her father (Jess Yates, the 'Stars on Sunday' presenter who was caught on holiday with a 16-year-old and had to be smuggled out of the BBC in the boot of a

Paula Yates, former television presenter, who died 17 October 2000. Photograph: Neil Munns.

car): a manic depressive who used to lock her in a box and spend all night playing his Wurlitzer organ for her, stopping now and then to tend his septic leg wound, incurred after he (purposely) sliced it with the lid of a cat-food tin.

About her mother (author of the recent book *Cat Chat*, about cats): 'I used to pine like a dog for my mother … When she finally came home, I would lie prone outside the toilet door in case she tried to escape through the window.'

Over the top? To this day, her mother, the 62-year-old Helene Thornton (née Elaine Smith, Blackpool beauty queen, aka Heller Toren, bit-part actress and author of torrid novels), comes across like a creature from a parallel universe.

Helene's father was a Blackpool policeman; her mother took Mandrax 'and slept seven-eighths of the day'. Not nearly interesting enough, however, for her. So she claims to have discovered at 36 that her real father was a Frenchman, with 'the presence of an emperor, you know'. Approached many years later by this 'very stylish gentleman' to have lunch with her, she agreed. But it was not to be. Because he died two weeks later.

And could she explain at all how it happened that Paula's real father turned out, upon DNA testing, to be Hughie 'Opportunity Knocks' Green? Some sinister meddling with the DNA test, she suggests … or maybe it was Hughie Green that night touching her right shoulder, when she woke up to find Jess snoring on her left. The important thing in any event, is that she was the innocent party: 'I'm supposed to take the blame for absolutely everything.'

When this interview took place, Paula had not been in touch for five years: 'I can't make her want to see me again. I always hope that she'll stop this need to play Orphan Annie.'

And her analysis of Paula's aching neediness, her chronic lack of self-esteem? 'Famous people want to be, very often, somebody else. Paula, from a tiny child, always wanted to be famous. Jess always wanted to be famous. Jess Yates, BBC.

Paula Yates, Famous Person. I wanted to be me … There are rocklike personalities who are sure of their own beliefs and their own selves, and there are those who need the accolade of celebrity. I see celebrity as something terrible.'

So, absolutely nothing to do with her, then, even if Paula herself acknowledged her exhibitionism was part of a desperate strategy to overcome childhood rejection.

But her mother is right about the celebrity. We know far more about Paula Yates than is decent. We disdain the details and the media that carry them but lap them up none the less, however insignificant, vulnerable and fragile the 'personality' or their extended family. So much the better if it features a slow-motion ride to disintegration and death, and the script includes a small child who finds the body.

Perhaps the one truism highlighted by this entire tragedy is that no, you basically can't do whatever the hell you like. For every action there is a consequence — in this case, one little orphaned girl and three more children left without a mother.

What further grief is being stored for succeeding generations?

Letters to the Editor September 2000

The Poison of Racism

Sir, — I have just read a full page article in the very prominent Portuguese newspaper Diario de Noticias *about the racist behaviour of my countrymen. I left Ireland 35 years ago and have returned only for short holidays, so maybe my views on Ireland and the Irish were those of a romantic idealist. What a shock! I feel such disappointment and disgust.*

The article begins thus: 'Céad míle fáilte — this is what one can read in the colourful brochures of the Irish Tourist Board, céad míle fáilte — not for everyone, judging by the increase in racist crimes happening in Ireland today.'

The Irish must have very short memories. It was only yesterday that our forefathers, fathers, sons and daughters had to flee the country in search of food. Is there any Irish family today who does not have a family member living abroad?

The Land of Saints and Scholars. What has happened to Catholicism, Christianity, love and humanity? Are the Irish no longer interested in learning? These people have so much to share. Like all human beings they need love, understanding and respect. Open your insular hearts and minds!

I am lucky to teach in an international school in Lisbon (owned by the Irish Dominican Sisters) where we have children of more than 40 different nationalities. These children are so fortunate to be able to experience this multiracial and multicultural environment. They are citizens of the world, and go into the world unprejudiced, enlightened and with open minds. Can no one see how our Irish children could benefit from this experience too?

Ireland, the world is looking at you and my shame is profound. — Yours, etc., Geraldine Watson, Rua Dom Jos D'Avilez, 2750 Cascais, Portugal. 7 September 2000.

Mo Mowlam

Sir, — In appreciation of her immense contribution to the Belfast Agreement, Mo Mowlam must be offered honorary citizenship. — Yours, etc., Adrian Carroll, Gladstone Street, Clonmel, Co. Tipperary. 7 September 2000.

Sir, — I agree with Adrian Carroll (7 September). Mo Mowlam played a major and quite beneficial part in Northern Irish politics, despite her illness and her disownment by her own Government, which she served so well. She worked constantly for the good of the people, in contrast to many politicians we are so familiar with at present. Ms Mowlam is a wonderful person and a first-rate politician. She has done us all a service in her dedication to the peace process. One can only hope we find a suitable manner in which to show our appreciation. — Yours, etc., Cormac Molloy, Portmarnock, Co. Dublin. 8 September 2000.

Sir, — The suggestion that Mo Mowlam be given honorary Irish citizenship is ridiculous. Mo was working for Britain while she was a member of that government, and her contribution to anything happening in Ireland was at best minimal, and sometimes counterproductive. — Yours, etc., Robert O'Sullivan, Bantry, Co. Cork. 8 September 2000.

EIRCOM

Sir, — Eircon. — Yours, etc., Brendan Treacy, Drumree, Co. Meath. 15 September 2000.

2 OCTOBER 2000

Access to Healthcare Based on Ability to Pay

Maev-Ann Wren

It is evident that the State has a health system in crisis. The symptoms are everywhere: staff shortages, waiting lists, patient care which too often fails to reach the standards expected in one of Europe's wealthier states.

What is less readily apparent is that the State has a health system which almost defies rational analysis. The OECD has diplomatically described it as 'unique'. Others might term it 'bizarre'.

And it is a health system which is changing rapidly. Private medicine is booming, as a result of inadequacies in the public system, which is suffering from lack of resources, poor management and the vested interests of some medical professionals taking precedence over patients' needs.

Never having offered equitable access to healthcare for everybody in the manner of Britain's National Health Service, the State is now moving rapidly towards an American-style system where people's ability to pay delivers access to care. Some doctors employed in the public service are also earning very large incomes from private practice — far more than they receive from the State.

The strangest element of the Irish health system is the manner in which it combines private and public patient care. There is in Ireland 'an extraordinary symbiosis of public and private medicine', the consequence of decades of conflict between State, church and the medical profession, the chief executive officer of the Health Research Board, Dr Ruth Barrington, concluded in her doctoral thesis.

Built on such political foundations rather than on any rational analysis of the health needs of the population, the health system then suffered the large cutbacks of the 1980s. Although spending rose again during the 1990s, the health system will remain in crisis unless there is reform of the deep-seated inequities and irrationalities of the present system — and this will have to include confronting vested interests. Today, it is an open secret that to be a public patient is a status best avoided.

'I know people who would scrub floors, just to get the money for VHI cover, out of fear of having to depend on the public health service,' says the chairman of the Irish Patients Association, Mr Stephen McMahon.

It is in public healthcare that the long waiting lists for treatment occur — nearly 32,000 people this summer. Public patients wait years for treatments which are available within weeks for private patients.

It is small wonder that membership of the VHI, seen as the way to jump queues, has soared from 22 per cent of the population in 1979 — before the 1980s health cutbacks — to 41 per cent today. When other private insurance schemes are included, some 45 per cent of the population is thought to be in the private sector. If private insurance cover continues to grow, the fate of public patients — who will then account for a minority of the population — may cease to be an issue which exercises most politicians. As in America, Ireland's system will be essentially dominated by private insurance companies.

The VHI disputes the view that membership growth is driven by fear of waiting lists.

'It is wrong to say that there is a direct relationship between the growth in membership and the health cutbacks of the late 1980s,' according to the VHI's medical director, Dr Bernadette Carr. 'It is a cultural thing. Here, if people can afford something, they will pay for it. We are culturally different from the UK. People seem to want to be self-sufficient in education, housing and health.'

However, an ESRI study by Prof Brian Nolan, published in 1991 just after the decade of cutbacks, found 'constrained public provision playing a major role in the demand for private care and therefore health insurance'.

A consumer survey conducted by the ESRI for the EU in 1990 discovered that among respondents who had VHI cover, 62 per cent cited 'being sure of getting into hospital quickly when you need treatment' as the most important reason for having it. Having a private room, choosing your consultant and getting into a private hospital were not regarded as nearly so important.

Dr Carr confirms that waiting times 'do not seem to be an issue' for VHI members. 'In excess of 80 per cent are admitted for treatment within four weeks of seeing a specialist,' she says.

When the VHI was founded in 1957 the motivation was to provide private income for doctors who had successfully, and with the help of the Catholic Church, fought off decades of politicians' efforts at establishing a comprehensive public health system. The VHI and private medicine were heavily subsidised by the State.

Today, VHI members still receive tax relief on their subscriptions and, like other insurance companies, the VHI does not pay the economic cost of the use of public hospital beds.

Private insurance contributes a mere 9 per cent of health spending; most of the remainder is funded by the State from general taxation.

Irish private patients, as a result, get cut price, preferential access to healthcare. Health insurance premiums are low compared to the US. The Minister for Health, Mr Martin, has recently refused the VHI permission to put up its fees.

'There is huge dishonesty about how we organise the health services,' comments one health

Members of the Legionary of Christ, based in Dublin, after the solemn requiem mass for the Most Reverend Luciano Storero, Apostolic Nuncio to Ireland, at the Pro-Cathedral. Photograph: Dara Mac Dónaill.

service administrator. 'We are giving one set of tax-payers more rapid access to better treatment for the payment of very little extra money.'

At least when the VHI was founded as a semi-state organisation it was not expected to be motivated by the need to make profits. Now, however, with the opening up of the health insurance market to foreign companies such as BUPA and the probable privatisation of the VHI, a new element has entered the Irish health system. It is to be milked for profit by private sector companies. This is a major change.

People without private health insurance — still the majority of the population — are covered by the General Medical Scheme (GMS) or have no cover. The GMS gives free hospital and general practitioner care to holders of medical cards — 31 per cent of the population today. The proportion of the population covered by the GMS has been falling as the threshold for eligibility has failed to keep pace with changing incomes. Membership of the scheme has been as high as 39 per cent of the population. The Irish Medical Organisation has called for 250,000 more medical cards to be provided.

There remains approximately 25 per cent of the population who have neither medical cards nor private insurance. They may be on very low incomes. A couple with two children on just £9,000 a year after payment of PRSI will not qualify for medical cards, according to the eligibility guidelines issued to health boards. The system is designed for the elderly and social welfare recipients — not for the working poor. People without medical cards must pay for every GP visit. They will receive free medical care in hospital, apart from a charge of £26 a night for a hospital bed up to a maximum of £260 a year. Since 1991, the entire population has been entitled to free medical care in hospital apart from the nightly charge, but fear of public patient treatment has continued to drive the growth of private health insurance.

It is particularly unusual, by comparison with other countries, that apart from medical card holders, all other patients — including children — must pay for GP visits here. The OECD commented: 'There appears to be a general social consensus in Ireland that, apart from the most economically disfavoured parts of society, first-level medical care, such as general practitioners, should not be a publicly provided service.'

Is this a general social consensus? The history of the evolution of our healthcare system in the 1940s and 1950s when this was a hotly contested political issue would suggest otherwise.

Prof Nolan comments: 'It is very surprising that the notion of free GP care for children has not emerged as an issue.'

Consequently, parents on very low incomes must weigh up the cost every time they suspect their child needs to see a doctor.

This has not been seen as a health issue. A Government-appointed expert working group recently considered whether free child GP care might be introduced to provide an incentive for social welfare recipients to take up work without fear of the consequences of losing their medical card. It says something for the current Irish view of health that children's access to healthcare should emerge as an issue only when labour shortages are being considered.

Irish governments 50 years ago tenaciously pursued the goal of a publicly funded system where everybody would be treated equally according to their need. The present Government's position was stated last year in the White Paper on private health insurance. It rejected changing the current two-tier system, commenting that concerns about equity for public patients could be dealt with by 'targeted initiatives and general improvements in the public health system'.

4 OCTOBER 2000

Settlement Shows PAC Inquiry's Effectiveness

Siobhán Creaton

After all the talk of amnesties and High Court challenges, AIB has made the biggest tax settlement in the history of the State, writing a cheque for £90.04 million (€114.33 million) to the Revenue Commissioners in full payment of its DIRT liabilities.

It is £90.04 million more than it should have paid if it had secured the tax amnesty it continues to claim it had. But the figure is considerably less than most observers had expected the bank to pay in the light of evidence given to the DIRT inquiry.

It is in fact the amount of money that AIB believes will make the entire DIRT fiasco go away. In AIB chairman Mr Lochlann Quinn's words, it was the 'sensible' thing to do. 'We still believe we had an amnesty, but it was not in anyone's interest, either the bank's, customers' or taxpayers', to spend another three or four years fighting it in court.'

AIB made it clear that it was prepared to fight its claims of an amnesty in the courts. This was important both to uphold the reputation of the bank's senior staff who negotiated the amnesty with Revenue officials and to contain its potential financial liabilities, it claimed.

Its resolve was probably most severely tested by the findings contained in the report of the Public Accounts Committee (PAC) which investigated the DIRT affair and which was scathing in its criticism of AIB.

The PAC dismissed the bank's claims of a tax amnesty on pre-1991 tax liabilities, questioned the reliability of one of its key internal documents submitted as evidence and directed the Revenue to start trawling through its accounts and collect what was owed on bogus non-resident accounts.

The £90 million figure falls short of the £100 million DIRT liability estimated by AIB's head of internal audit, Mr Tony Spollen, which was the basis for the PAC's inquiry. And as the bank was viewed as being the main offender when it came to opening bogus non-resident accounts, the expectation was that its eventual tax bill could be as high as £200 million.

AIB consistently rubbished the £100 million figure as wholly without foundation and initially was slow to make any stab at what it could theoretically owe in unpaid tax. The PAC committee sent it away to come up with a figure and Mr Quinn subsequently furnished an estimate of £35 million as its maximum liability. As it turned out, after 15 months of audits, the Revenue Commissioners calculated that AIB had an underlying DIRT liability of £32.9 million and levied a further £54.23 million in interest and penalties.

The bank is keen to emphasise that its misdemeanours relate back to a different era and have long since been rectified. It will now be hoping the settlement brings an end to the sorry saga and that it is seen to have apologised for its sins.

And while Mr Quinn insists that the affair did not have any commercial impact on the bank's business, it undoubtedly dealt a severe blow to its reputation both at home and overseas.

With the DIRT issue out of the way, it is now free to focus on repairing this damage.

Mr Dan Tierney (left) chairman, NSAI, with Ms Darina Allen, Ballymaloe Cookery School and Senator Fergal Quinn, chief executive, Superquinn, during the morning coffee break of 'Food Safety — From Farm to Fork', the NSAI annual conference in Dublin. Photograph: Peter Thursfield.

The result is a further vindication of the work of the Dáil Public Accounts Committee, which has so far resulted in the recovery of £157 million in unpaid DIRT, with the eventual tax take expected to be substantially greater.

Following the PAC's DIRT inquiry, the Revenue undertook audits in 37 financial institutions which have resulted in five settlements so far. Its chairman, Mr Dermot Quigley, is due to outline the various settlements to the PAC next month and is likely to be closely questioned on individual institutions.

So far the Revenue has been consistent in levying hefty penalties and interest on the underlying tax liability, which in each case have amounted to around 60 per cent of the total settlement.

After AIB, the biggest payment has been by Bank of Ireland. It made a settlement of £30.5 million, of which £17.75 million was interest and penalties. The State-owned ACCBank paid £17.5 million, including £10.4 million in interest and penalties.

The PAC chairman, Mr Jim Mitchell, pointed out yesterday that its inquiry, which cost £1.8 million, has more than paid for itself.

6 OCTOBER 2000

Everything Is Broken But That's OK, We Can Build

Gillian Sandford in Belgrade

Youths with flags and iron poles charged up the steps of Yugoslavia's parliament. 'Let's go forward, let's attack,' they cried. 'Save Serbia and kill yourself, Slobodan.'

They pushed forward. Police fired tear gas but could not hold. Belgrade was in revolt.

A million people came to the capital yesterday and so did the police — with armoured vehicles, batons and guns. By 6 p.m., many police were kissing protesters. Youngsters sported blue helmets and riot shields. But as night closed in, the capital was out of control.

First, protesters moved against the federal parliament. There was supposed to be an opposition rally there, addressed by political leaders, but chaos broke out before the 3 p.m. start.

'More than a hundred people are trying to get in,' said Aleksandar, aged 18. 'Police are in there,' said another man, Zoran. 'We came to hear the opposition speak, but they couldn't because of the tear gas.'

As youngsters repeatedly charged the parliament building, special police units fought them back and fired tear gas.

But the swarming youths moved forward again and again. Finally, many police officers retreated by a back door and others left on the front steps. Some even embraced protesters.

By 4 p.m. the parliament building was in the hands of the crowd. Heady with victory, the teenagers who had entered smashed windows, swarming over the stone ledges. Then from the balcony, to cheers from the crowd, they shovelled out ballot papers.

The papers swirled down like crazy confetti. The demonstrators moved on, heady with defiance and excitement. They were claiming the capital — and destroying the symbols and instruments of the Milosevic regime.

Police continued to fire tear gas in front of the parliament for more than two hours. But the youngsters, wearing sunglasses and with homemade turbans tied around their heads and mouths, kept pushing to get in. 'Slobo down,' cried one 15-year-old.

Many protesters went in to claim their booty. They emerged clutching typewriters, office equipment, documents, even lampshades and chairs.

'There's nothing inside there any more. Everything is broken. The chairs, pictures, they have all gone,' said Marija, aged 22, a student from Batacina, south of Belgrade. 'But that's OK.

Opposition supporters enter the Yugoslav parliament building during clashes between riot police and opposition supporters in Belgrade. Photograph: Reuters/Goran Tomasevic.

But we can build it again. Gotov Je (he is finished),' she said.

At about 4.30 p.m. the activists moved to claim Milosevic's main propaganda machine — Radio Television Serbia.

A bar worker in a café nearby said youngsters began attacking from two sides, from the park behind and from the road. They threw Molotov cocktails and police responded with tear gas.

Mr Branko Pavlovic, a vice-president of an opposition party, the Social Democratic Union, said: 'I was there. It was pretty nasty. I was in the street that links the parliament with television, Takovska Street. The protesters made several assaults on the television.

'Police responded with tear gas. Then rubber bullets, then real bullets. Then a bulldozer driven by the demonstrators started to smash the building. The demonstrators then set alight a corner of the building and then they stormed in.'

Another participant, Mr Vladko Sekulovic, said: 'For a moment it seemed as if police would push people back. Five or six people with flags, including me, entered the building. There were a lot of shots with real and rubber bullets.

'The crucial thing was the bulldozer that broke the doors. After that, police stepped back and the building was set on fire. Lower down the street a huge group of people began approaching the building — and then the police withdrew.

'I saw three demonstrators who appeared to be dead.'

On a street nearby, Ilija Garasanina, police anti-terrorist units arrived. But they never clashed with demonstrators.

'The commander came out and asked what was happening. People began running. There was a lot of tear gas,' said Veljko Popovic (28). He fled and when he returned, the demonstrators and police were embracing each other.

9 OCTOBER 2000

Kerry Thrive With A More Even Tempo

Seán Moran

Kerry 0–16 Galway 1–10

The finely-balanced scales of this year's All-Ireland tipped decisively against Galway and in favour of Kerry on Saturday afternoon at Croke Park. The Bank of Ireland football final replay was a fast, exciting match kept alive (somewhat against the odds) by Kerry's poor shooting and Galway's resilience. But in the end the verdict was clear and the Munster champions deservedly clocked up the county's 32nd title.

Unlike the drawn match, or indeed virtually any of Kerry's previous outings, this was a steadily played 70 minutes. There were none of the extremes of performance so evident two weeks ago.

Probably the most impressive aspect of the victory was the manner in which Kerry sustained their pressure despite a number of demoralising setbacks. There was never a period in which they weren't creating chances of some sort, but at times, and particularly in the third quarter, the finishing was abysmal. Yet they fought on.

Aodán MacGearailt deserves mention in this regard. All afternoon he worked hard and gobbled up a stack of possession but the fates were unkind.

He either used the possession poorly or lost it. Still, he worked hard and continued to contest the breaks very effectively. His luck deservedly changed and he ended with two points.

The first was significant because it brought Kerry level going into the final quarter. Galway were never again in front and chased the remainder of the match as Kerry moved steadily away from them.

After the plaudits of the drawn match, Galway manager John O'Mahony had no answer for his year's most implacable foe — misfortune. It struck again in the 18th minute when Kevin Walsh, one of the key influences in the drawn match, had to retire with a twisted knee. There was a mocking symmetry to his departure which came at almost exactly the same time as his influential entry into the first match.

His injury turned out to be less serious than feared, but by the time he was re-introduced, the tide had turned in Kerry's favour. In Walsh's absence, Joe Bergin was given a shot at redemption which the talented 19-year-old largely took. But the Kerry pair of Darragh Sé and Donal Daly appeared less intimidated with the big Galwayman hors de combat.

Galway's other big successes from a fortnight ago didn't fire. Pádraig Joyce started at full forward, but never got a grip on the game and when he was moved to the 40, he was unable to rediscover the rhythms which had made him so influential there in the drawn match. To be fair to the Galway captain, none of his attacking colleagues were fully on their game either and despite excellent approach work, they struggled to carve out the clear-cut chances of the drawn match and certainly lacked the finishing sharpness of the earlier encounter.

This problem was reflected in the statistics. Five wides indicate that the Connacht champions weren't even creating good opportunities and as a further commentary on the extent of their eclipse, the most inventive forward play came from wing back Declan Meehan. Yet only once did his verve get its just reward.

In the seventh minute, he scored the goal of the season. It started in Galway's goalmouth. Dara Cinnide's 45 was blocked down by Walsh. John Divilly snapped up the ball and raced out to initiate an eight-pass movement down the left flank.

As the ambition of the play increased, Pádraig Joyce moved the ball into the centre where Paul Clancy gathered and fired a brilliant pass over the cover and into the arms of the advancing Meehan. It couldn't have been more elegantly served up had the ball come wrapped in a ribbon.

The finish was a cherry. Meehan motored through before letting go a right-foot shot across Declan O'Keeffe and into the corner of the net. Galway maintained their challenge until near the end, but their attack wasn't again to conjure up anything approaching the deadly effect of that goal.

The difference between the teams was defined by the forwards. None of Galway's played particularly well. Half of Kerry's did. Liam Hassett worked tirelessly and kicked three points to mark another fine display in what has been a great year for him. John Crowley's lively display and three points stood as further rebuke to the decision to substitute him two weeks ago.

Maurice Fitzgerald entered the fray early. With the match delicately poised, it was as if Páid Sé decided he wasn't going to be hanged for leaving the Cahirciveen virtuoso on the bench any longer. Again, though, the wrong option was persisted with and Fitzgerald laboured fruitlessly at full forward until the overdue decision to move him out was taken in the second half.

At the controls of the team, Fitzgerald had a significant impact. He won ball, used it well and in the space of two minutes pushed Kerry decisively in front. Niall Finnegan had just wasted a good scoring opportunity set up by the tireless Meehan when Fitzgerald won the restart and supplied Hassett for his third point. The match entered its final 10 minutes and with the margin again down to one, thanks to a Finnegan free, Fitzgerald once more caught the kick-out and soloed through for a point.

Kerry were well served throughout the field, but the full-back line was exceptional. Mike Hassett expunged the memories of three years ago with a tight and controlled display on Finnegan. Mike McCarthy learned enough from the drawn match to curtail Derek Savage and made a fabulous block on the Galway corner forward in the 48th minute.

And then there was Seamus Moynihan. All year he has given amazing displays in the alien environs of the full back position. Again on Saturday he was immense in his attention to defensive detail. The team has lost out on his presence further out, but it was significant that just after Galway's goal, the Kerry captain made a galvanising burst from the back to set up a point in reply.

All season his performances have been touched by that ability to respond when the team's need is greatest; his influence has been the single biggest determinant in the success of this memorable campaign.

13 OCTOBER 2000

Conclusions of Inquest Fail to Satisfy Abbeylara Locals

Sean MacConnell

In the middle of last month Abbeylara's footballers won the Longford Senior Football Championship, giving the small community a chance to celebrate.

Yesterday evening in the red-and-white bedecked village, it was clear the celebrations were at an end and that the spectre of the Holy Thursday killing of one of its native sons was uppermost in the minds of locals.

The bunting seemed out of kilter with the mood of locals, who were very unhappy with the outcome of the inquest, which took place in the county town about 20 miles away.

A man wheeling a bicycle near the huge hand-ball alley where John Carthy spent many hours playing his favourite game made no bones about what he thought of the inquest.

'There will have to be a public inquiry into what went on there. We didn't get all the information,' he said.

Like other locals, the man did not want to be named but he wanted to make his point nevertheless.

In the privacy of their homes away from the windswept street, the people were even more bitter, especially about the treatment meted out to the Carthy family.

'It was a terrible thing to say that his sister had drink taken and that was why they would not let her talk to him,' said one local woman who had kept all the daily papers to read the reports.

'I see a whole lot of things here that I am not satisfied about at all. There is a lot of contradiction in the evidence about a whole lot of things,' she said.

A neighbour, who had dropped in after hearing the outcome of the verdict on the RTÉ television news, was highly critical of the jury's failure to add riders to their verdict.

'Sure we all know John Carthy was killed by the guards, but we thought we would find out why. We still don't know,' he said.

The local people are even more fully convinced now of the need for a public inquiry.

A man in a bar in nearby Granard said that

The scene on Inch Strand in West County Kerry where 180 fishermen participated in the Dingle Peninsula Daiwa Pairs organised by the Surf Angling Match Federation. Photograph: Bryan O'Brien.

people in the area will remain suspicious of what had happened until a public inquiry is held.

Mr Eugene McGee, the editor of the *Longford Leader,* who had posed 10 questions on the circumstances surrounding the killing in his paper for which he sought answers, said he felt the majority of the questions had been answered.

'We now know the basic things, like how many shots were fired and by whom, but there are crucial questions which came up during the inquest which still remain hanging,' he said.

'There was quite a conflict of evidence in relation to a number of things and the newspaper will be supporting the call by the family for a public inquiry into the incident,' he said.

14 OCTOBER 2000

Using Faith to Feel at Home

Tom McCann

A church in Dublin attracts hundreds of mostly Nigerian born-again Christians with booming voices and raucous rhythms.

Walk by too fast and you could easily miss the Redeemed Christian Church of God. Housed in a former antique store down a quiet lane off Capel Street, Dublin, a space it shares with the neighbourhood laundromat, the only evidence of the church's existence during the week is a faded sign that hangs above the door.

But Sunday never fails to attract attention as hundreds of mostly Nigerian born-again Christians fill the street with booming voices and the sound of raucous African rhythms pounded out on snare drums, cymbals, bongos and tambourines.

Two years old, the makeshift church serves as a place where Dublin's newly-arrived Africans can baptise their young, mourn their dead, worship God, and begin to develop some sense of community in a strange and sometimes hostile land.

'When I first got here, I tried to get used to the Catholic Mass you practise, but it's just not the way we do things,' said Ola Iginla (32), a former trainer in the Nigerian military who was forced to leave in 1998 after being accused of plotting a coup. 'We praise God by letting him hear us — by dancing, playing music, singing at the top of our lungs. Without this place to come to, we would all be very depressed here.'

Theirs is a percussive religion. The congregation gathered on Sunday afternoon around newborn Tunde Odediran, held in his mother's arms for a musical baptismal ceremony. As they danced, clapped and waved their hands, Kunle Daniel, half pastor-half performer, doused the baby's head in water while leading them in song. 'Let us welcome the newest member of our community,' he said to loud cheers.

Longing for a more permanent home, the church's 500 adult members are each trying to contribute £1,000 to build a more elaborate church in the city.

'When you come to a new place, with no relatives or people your own colour in sight, you feel very much alone,' said Niyi Ogundare (39), a former Nigerian union leader who now works for the church. 'But with this church, with a place to come to, you have a new family, and it doesn't feel so bad.'

The immigration experience is still new to Ireland. But already the same phenomenon of furious church building that marked new ethnic groups arriving in the US in the last century is beginning to take place. The Redeemed Christian Church also has branches for Nigerians in Ennis, Naas and Mullingar.

Dublin's Romanian community is getting actively involved in the Greek Orthodox Church. But Romanians in Monaghan have set up their own Orthodox church while the Dundalk's Romanian community is busily searching for land on which to build.

'The church is the most recognisable symbol of community and nationality. So once a group

Prayer meeting attracting asylum seekers at The Redeemed Christain Church of God Worship Centre, Mary's Abbey, Dublin. Photograph: Matt Kavanagh.

resettles in a new land, they won't feel truly settled until they have that place of their own,' said Pierce Mac Einír of the Irish Centre for Migration Studies. Ireland's new immigrant groups haven't had enough time to settle down yet, he said, especially those outside Dublin.

'But soon we're going to hear a lot more clamour for new mosques and churches of all denominations.'

Though its congregation includes a small number of Kenyans, Sudanese, Zimbabweans, even Irish, the Redeemed Christian Church of God mainly serves as a Nigerian Community Centre where members can find everything from apartments to steady jobs.

Ruth Ogundare is one who appreciated its help. Her first few months in Ireland two years ago were 'beyond terrible', she recalls. 'All of a sudden, I had no one. People would stare at me, they wouldn't sit next to me on the bus, they'd make crude remarks.

'Then I found out about this church,' Ms Ogundare said, 'and it helped me get back a little bit of my country. Things are much better now, but I don't think I could have adjusted without this place.'

23 OCTOBER 2000

12 Reasons Why Charlie Should Be Forgiven

John Waters

I am taken aback by the cynicism concerning Charles Haughey's state of health and the obvious unwillingness to forgive him 'just' because he might die soon. It's not that I truly believed we were 'still' a Christian people, but rather that I am surprised at our willingness to hold out for so long before stopping in our tracks, turning around and neurotically charging in the opposite moral direction. So as to be of assistance to the national conscience, I would therefore like to offer the following dozen reasons why we should forgive Mr Haughey.

1. We created him. I don't mean we elected him, but that we imagined him into what he became. Everything he did was in his role as Fat Chieftain, a role imposed on him by us. Being poor and hungry, we desperately needed to believe that this man, with his aura of riches and mystery, could make us plump and happy. More than anything else, he did not want to disappoint us.

2. The main reason we are mad at him is that we have discovered there was no magic, that he accumulated riches not by wizardry but by supplicancy. This rendered us disappointed by him, but more fundamentally disappointed by the illusion he had helped us create concerning the possibility of material acquisition. This, however, was a necessary lesson, and in a sense Charles Haughey has spared us having to learn it in a more difficult way.

3. There is considerable circumstantial evidence that Mr Haughey delivered on the contract he made with us. When he walked into Government Buildings 13 years ago, this State was on the verge of bankruptcy. Today our economy is, as we keep being told, the envy of Europe. This turnaround in the national fortunes has much more in common with the manner of Charles Haughey's own enrichment than with the careful, muddling husbandry of his political rivals.

4. Most of the reasons we advance for seeking vengeance on Charles Haughey do not stand up. There is no evidence, for example, that any of his benefactors received anything tangible, or indeed that they sought favours from him. Like many of us, the merchant princes who supported him seem to have been simply infatuated by his aura of majesty and power.

5. More than any other leader or public figure since de Valera, Charles Haughey defined his time, his country and his people. This is not necessarily a compliment to Mr Haughey or his people, but it is true none the less. The imagination of a nation cannot survive without epic characters, and Charles Haughey was, for more than 30 years, the central character in the national drama. He was our Hamlet, our King Lear, our J.R. and our Mike Baldwin.

6. He was a star, and we have decided stars in other spheres of endeavour deserve to be paid vast sums. Pop singers, TV presenters, footballers and actors 'earn' much more than Charlie managed to stroke over the years, and we do not think this odd. Haughey made them all look like extras, and yet we expected him to be star, chieftain, hero and villain, while surviving on a TD's salary. And he was running the country as well.

7. Although it is true that he did not serve his people as well as he might have — more in the sense of failing to do things which were necessary and possible than of stroking left, right and centre — Mr Haughey still did more good than most of his peers. It is remarkable that, in my lifetime, only Mr Haughey's great friend, Donogh O'Malley, and his arch-enemy Noel Browne, were comparable when it came to implementing changes in the public good.

8. Charles Haughey had occasional flashes of fierce principle, as in his response to the murderous sinking of the Belgrano in 1982.

9. He gave us lots of laughs. Any Taoiseach who presents a British prime minister with a teapot has got to be a national treasure.

10. Even at the worst construction, Charles Haughey was infinitely preferable to some of the loathsome creeps who have spent their lives attacking him. Consider the fact that several of those who have done little except snipe at the Fat Chieftain have themselves made strenuous efforts to avail of his provision of tax-free status for creative artists — not for books, plays, symphonies

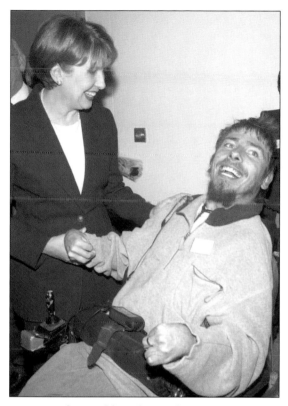

Artist Stephen Walsh with President McAleese at the official name change of Cerebral Palsy Ireland to Enable Ireland and official opening of the new £8.5 million school and clinic at Sandymount. Photograph: Alan Betson.

or paintings, but for the articles they wrote attacking Charles Haughey.

Get this: these beauties, who could see no good in Mr Haughey otherwise, were prepared to acknowledge that this provision was actually admirable, provided, of course, that they were given the benefit of it in a manner for which it had never been intended. I know of one journalist who approached leading artists requesting them to write references asserting that his venomous attacks on Mr Haughey were pure poetry. To their credit, most declined. And to the credit of the Revenue Commissioners, let it be noted that none of these applications was successful: these creeps still pay tax.

11. Anyone who can face into the storm of hatred Charles Haughey has evoked and still walk like Napoleon has something we need to pause and look at. Mr Haughey, for all his faults, has grace and dignity, as he showed at Jack Lynch's funeral last year.

12. If he dies without forgiveness, our initial pangs of regret will rapidly turn to guilt and ferment into a profound self-loathing. The emotions we have about 'Charlie', unlike those we feel towards other public figures — with the possible exception of Gay Byrne — are comparable to the emotions existing in a family situation. Hate is fused with love, scorn with compassion, and frustration with admiration. The bitterness that is felt now will soon pass, to be replaced by nostalgia, sadness and regret.

Forgiveness would therefore also be a selfish act, albeit a graceful one. If we don't forgive Charlie, we can never forgive ourselves.

28 OCTOBER 2000

Synon Rant Has Roots in New Right Culture

Fintan O'Toole

It would be comforting to imagine that Mary Ellen Synon's decision to describe the Paralympics as 'perverse' and its athletes as 'cripples' who 'wobble around a track in a wheelchair' was a momentary misjudgment or even a ham-fisted attempt at humour.

But the *Sunday Independent* columnist has seldom made any secret of her contempt for those who do not meet her standards of normality.

In 1996 she launched an attack on the entire Travelling community using rhetoric which would not, in its portrayal of an entire ethnic group as essentially sub-human, have been out of place in Nazi diatribes against Jews.

Travellers, she wrote in the *Sunday Independent*, lead 'a life of appetite ungoverned by intellect … a life worse than the life of beasts … This tinker culture is without achievement, discipline, reason or intellectual ambition.'

The only surprise, she added, was that 'some individuals among the tinkers find the will not to become evil'. It was clear from the context that she wanted her readers to feel that the majority of Travellers were evil.

In 1998 Miss Synon argued that if the source of intolerance and hatred felt by some Irish people towards Ireland's 'exotic newcomers' (immigrants and asylum-seekers) had 'a logical basis', then it should be acted on. She went on to say that 'Ireland, already split by religion, is about to be tinted by colour'.

With such form behind her, it seems clear that the *Sunday Independent* knew its columnist had a penchant for targeting entire groups with hate-filled rhetoric and that it was happy for her to continue to do so.

Last Sunday's outburst, moreover, had deep roots in the New Right political culture to which Miss Synon emphatically belongs.

Milton Friedman, the intellectual guru of Thatcherism and Reaganism, pointed to the natural physical differences between people as evidence that we were not, after all, meant to be equal.

'Life is not fair,' he wrote in his hugely influential *Free To Choose*. 'It is tempting to believe that government can rectify what nature has spawned.' But this temptation must be resisted because 'there's nothing fair about Marlene Dietrich's having been born with beautiful legs that we all want to look at; or with Muhammad Ali having been born with the skill that made him a great fighter'.

Conversely, of course, people who are born with cerebral palsy or a visual impairment should not expect government to interfere with 'what nature has spawned'. In a similar vein, Margaret Thatcher talked contemptuously of people 'dribbling and drooling about compassion'.

Miss Synon's article last Sunday, therefore, merely made explicit what is implicit in much of the New Right ideology. What she objected to in the Paralympics is that they suggest (as they undoubtedly do) that 'all lives are equal in value'.

If many of her colleagues on the radical Right would probably prefer that she had not put it so bluntly, few of them have any great difficulty acting on the belief that all lives are not of equal value and that those of the disabled, the poor or members of ethnic minorities are clearly of lesser importance than those of, for example, *Sunday Independent* columnists.

Yet, like it or not, the New Right is one of the most influential strands in current political thinking. How far, then, should a newspaper editor go in censoring the expression of that ideology? And should the general outrage at Miss Synon's attack be backed up with legal sanctions or, if necessary, tougher laws? Where is the line between the robust expression of controversial views and incitement to hatred?

Part of the problem is that the people who should answer that question in the first instance — the editors of the newspaper in question — seemed all at sea this week. Aengus Fanning and the *Sunday Independent* at first stood over the decision to publish Miss Synon's rant, citing a liberal policy of encouraging the expression of different views.

Then as official and unofficial expressions of disgust continued to rain down on him, Mr Fanning issued an abject apology for the offence caused. The two statements were hardly compatible.

Nor, however, has the law been notably more effective. Though Travellers' groups tried to have Miss Synon prosecuted under the Incitement to Hatred Act for her sweeping attack on their community, the director of public prosecutions at the time did not feel there was a strong enough case.

Yet it is hard to see why, when a bus driver who racially abuses a black passenger is prosecuted and sentenced, the mass dissemination of such insults through a national newspaper should not result in legal sanctions.

Freedom of expression is a vital aspect of democracy. However, most democracies accept

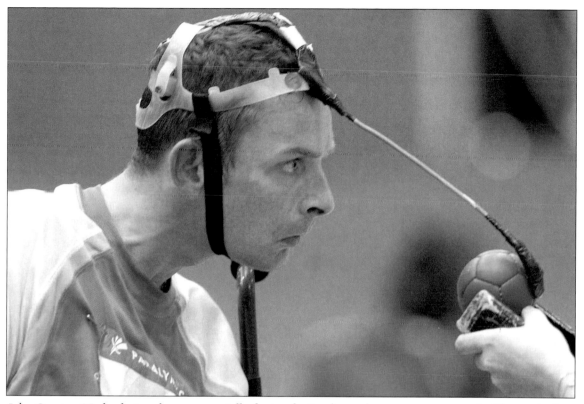

John Cronin of Ireland aims the course carefully during the Paralympic boccia competition at the Olympic Park in Sydney. AP Photograph: Katsumi Kasahara.

that it is limited in particular by two considerations.

In the first place, free expression should not incite violence against others. In the second, it should not result, through the use of dehumanising stereotypes against entire groups, in a denial of the ability of members of those groups to exercise their rights to free expression.

Miss Synon's characterisation of the lives of people with disabilities as being of lesser value than those of others arguably breaches the first rule. Her contemptuous belittlement of them certainly breaches the second.

Journalists and editors have long argued that they are responsible enough to understand and apply those distinctions without the intervention of the law. After Miss Synon's rant, and her editors' confused response to it, that case has been damaged, perhaps irreparably.

30 OCTOBER 2000

New Height from Distance

Noel O'Reilly in Sydney

The metal detectors at Dublin Airport will be busy on Wednesday afternoon when the Irish Paralympic team arrive home bearing five gold medals, three silver and one bronze after 11 days of outstanding success.

As the curtain came down on the Paralympics, bringing to an end the 60-day festival of sport, the squad will have time to reflect upon an event that produced so many medals, their 31st place on the medal table giving all involved great pride in the most competitive Games to date.

Catherine Walsh got the ball rolling last Saturday, her bronze in the visually-impaired pentathlon opening the floodgates with Ireland securing eight more medals over the course of the week.

The golds came in athletics, boccia and swimming courtesy of Tom Leahy, Johnny Cronin and Margaret Grant, Gabriel Shelley, Mairéad Berry and David Malone.

Berry added two silver to her gold to earn a hat-trick of medals.

The last medal for the Irish came on Saturday night when Mary Rice was awarded silver in the 800 metres final.

Rice had actually finished third in the race, but was upgraded to second when the winner, Deborah Brennan of Great Britain, was disqualified for coming out of her lane.

That left Australia's Rebecca Felman in the gold medal spot, allowing Rice to go one better than the bronze she earned in Atlanta four years ago and keep her record of having won a medal in every major championship entered since 1995.

'I went into it pretty confident going into the race. I was aiming for bronze … It's wonderful,' she said immediately afterwards.

Her sister Sharon, who was well beaten into fifth in the same race, was quick to congratulate one of her greatest rivals.

'I'm thrilled for her,' was the response. 'There's been a lot of hard work put in out there so she deserves it all.'

Earlier in the day, Patrice Dockery ended her Paralympic campaign without the medal she so desperately wanted, but with much credit. Dockery took seconds off her own Irish record whilst finishing sixth in the 5,000-metres final and could well have had a top-three finish.

The race was won by Louise Sauvage, her second gold winning performance of the Games, but Dockery's tactics were spot on throughout and, but for a bump with two laps to go, seemed assured of a medal.

The 29-year-old dug deep within herself to make up the ground she lost in the collision and only just lost out in the sprint for the line. Afterwards, she preferred not to concentrate on the 'what ifs', instead believing that the time of 12 minutes, 48.10 seconds felt like a medal in itself.

'I don't think you can fault my performance,' she said. 'I can't believe I reeled them back in. I just said this is it, I have to get back up there, I have to get back in there.'

The Games themselves finished the way they started, with another spectacular party. Fears the public wouldn't embrace the Paralympics after the highs of the Olympics fell by the wayside very quickly in Sydney with people turning up in their droves.

The cliché of 'the most successful Games ever' had a new resonance last night and Athens will have a tough job coming close to matching this event.

In a week and a half of competition, over 1,100,000 sports-mad Aussies, the largest crowd ever and double the expectations, came through the turn-styles at Sydney Olympic Park.

Last night Stadium Australia was again full to the brim as the athletes received a send-off to remember.

The reception the Australians received was breathtaking, the host nation sitting proudly on top of the medal table after emphatically beating the British, who just pipped Spain for second spot.

And the efforts of the Irish team were not unnoticed, Micheal Cunningham, an eight-time Paralympian, receiving a generous ovation as he carried the flag into the Stadium.

The only blemish on a near-perfect Games for the organisers were the positive drug tests, 10 in all, a phenomenon not exclusive to able-bodied sport.

The biggest culprits were in power-lifting where nine competitors were caught. But the highest profile cheat was American 100-metres silver medallist Brian Frasure who tested positive to the banned substance nandrolone.

In the lead-up to the Paralympics, much had been made of the fact that Frasure is a training partner of Olympic 100m and 200m gold medallist Marion Jones, with a mass of column inches dedicated to the sprinter.

The International Paralympic Committee (IPC) announced over the weekend that his A and B samples tested positive to the steroid during competition testing.

Officials have vowed to introduce even more stringent testing and punishment to combat the cheats.

'We've got to make sure our rules and regulations and sanctions are so strict that it will deter athletes from wanting to take drugs in the future,' said Bob Steadward, chairman of the IPC.

Letters to the Editor October 2000

Saving Spiders

Sir, — Kevin Myers' excellent article on spiders interests me. For years I have talked of the distress of spiders who get into a bath looking for water and are trapped. I always leave a rough towel draped over the edge, and have saved many lives. — Yours etc., Joan Johnstone, Johar, Co. Kilkenny. 5 October 2000.

An Unhealthy State

Sir, — We, the undersigned consultant obstetricians/gynaecologists, reject the unsubstantiated claims made by Ms Maev-Ann Wren regarding consultants' work commitment in her series of articles on our health services. In particular we reject her claims that we do not fulfil our contractual and ethical obligations to our patients. Ms Wren should know that the Medical Council obliges doctors to 'practice without consideration of religion, nationality, gender, race, politics or social standing'. And, dare we say it, whether the patient is public or private.

There are 88 obstetricians attached to our public hospitals. We carry ultimate medical responsibility for the delivery of about 51,000 infants each year. While we would never claim that the service provided is perfect, readers — and in particular expectant mothers — might like to note that, according to figures published by the World Health Organisation, the maternal mortality rate in Ireland is the lowest in the world.

The three Dublin maternity hospitals are responsible for 21,000 deliveries annually. The ultimate responsibility for these deliveries rests with the equivalent of just over 26 full-time obstetricians. The 18 obstetric units attached to hospitals outside of Dublin are responsible for 30,000 deliveries annually. There are five obstetricians in each of the units in Cork, Limerick and Galway. The remaining 15 units are each staffed by three consultants or fewer, with two units staffed by single handed obstetricians. How can two or three obstetricians provide an on-site service for 168 hours a week?

The morbidity rate among obstetricians is far higher than that of their patients. More than any other group in the health services, we have campaigned for the appointment of extra consultants. Indeed the very reason for the meeting on 7 October, at which this letter was written, was to highlight the shortcomings in the State's obstetric services.

We reject the unproven claims that we delegate all or virtually all of our public work to junior doctors. We equally reject claims that our work, either in terms of quantity or quality, is not or cannot be monitored. Some of us have had outpatient and theatre sessions fixed for the same time and the same day for between 10 and 20 years. Unsubstantiated claims by nameless health officials that we cannot be monitored places a question mark over their competence and dedication rather than ours.

Health policy is decided by the government of the day. If we have a shortage of nurses and an over-dependence on non-EU NCHDs, or if we have the lowest acute bed ratio to population in the EU, or if the 850 admitting consultants cannot personally manage the 2 million outpatient attendances per annum, or if the national quota of 16 A & E consultants cannot provide a personal service to the 1.25 million attendees at A & E units, that is the fault of successive governments and not consultants.

It is not the profession that decides to keep some small, underfunded hospitals open; or to close beds without regard for the medical consequences; or to cancel theatre sessions at a moment's notice. Had the number of consultants in the public system grown at the same rate as the number of administrators over the past 20 years, and had our spending on health been more in line with our European neighbours, then patients would certainly have a better service delivered within a medically acceptable time-frame.

The standard of hospital medicine in Ireland is on a par with anywhere in the developed world. The problem of access to hospitals can and must be resolved by the Government. We do not decide government policy, but we do have to work with the consequences of government in action. Rather than resisting change, as Ms Wren claims, we are to the forefront in seeking such change both for our own sakes and that of our patients.
— Yours, etc., Dr Paul Bowman, Coombe Hospital, Dr George Henry, Rotunda Hospital, Dr Christopher Fitzpatrick, Dr Diarmuid Mooney, Dr Carol Barrykinsella, Rotunda Hospital, Wexford General Hospital, Dr Brendan Gill, Sligo General Hospital, Dr Peter Boylan, National Maternity Hospital, Dr Ray Howard, Dr Brendan Powell, St Joseph's Hospital, Clonmel, Dr Malachy Coughlan, Rotunda Hospital, Dr Mary McCaffrey, Tralee General Hospital, Mr Al Kennedy, Monaghan General Hospital, Dr David Mortell, Mullingar General Hospital, Dr J.J. Fallon, Louth County Hospital, Dr John Monaghan, Portiuncula Hospital.
11 October 2000.

Forgiving Charles Haughey

Sir, — The tendency of many of your columnists to use the words 'we', 'us' and 'our' when discussing Irish life, as if the nation were one homogeneous mass with no conflict of viewpoint or interest, can be a source of irritation. Normally this irritation remains just that, but John Waters's indulgence in this form of intellectual laziness sends it right through the pain threshold ('12 Reasons Why Charlie Should Be Forgiven', Opinion, 23 October).

Will John Waters object if I, along with possibly half or more of the population, dissociate myself from the 'we' who, he claims, 'created' Charles Haughey, were 'defined' by him, got 'lots of laughs' from him and now seek 'vengeance' on him? The only aspect of Haughey's persona on which there was a national consensus was his ability, and in the case of a goodly fraction of 'us', this translated into a fear of how that ability might be abused, to the ultimate detriment of democratic institutions. The people who felt like this belonged to every section of Irish society, including a sizeable portion of Mr Haughey's own party.

This was why he was never granted an overall majority, and why his leadership excited so much dissension within Fianna Fáil. The facts revealed at the tribunals have shown how well grounded was that fear. Saying, as Mr Waters does, that there is no evidence that any of his benefactors sought or received favours from him misses the point. The notion that one can use political life to enrich oneself personally is deeply corrosive of any democracy, and it is one whose origin, overwhelmingly, is identified with the career of Mr Haughey. Still, for Mr Waters there is always the consolation of the 'aura of majesty and power' of the 'epic character' — concepts which sit very uneasily with the idea of political life as public service in a democratic republic.

Forgiveness tendered when it has not been sought is unusual enough; when it is offered in the face of an insistence that there is no case to answer and of contempt shown to efforts to get at the truth, it begins to look like something else — maybe self-abasement? But then, isn't that what people do in front of majesty? — Yours, etc., Dermot Meleady, Dublin 3.
26 October 2000.

Sir, — In the event that one were to give credence to John Waters's rationale, are there not some vital elements missing? Surely forgiveness is preceded by confession, restitution (say Kinsealy donated to the State to provide accommodation and therapy for runaway and

deprived children) and penance (perhaps the ignominy of revelation and the ensuing fall from national grace could, in the foregoing circumstances, be sufficent).
Come on Charlie, while there's still time. Redemption is yours for the asking. — Yours, etc., Joe Geoghegan, Balliol Street, Toronto, Canada. 26 October 2000.

Sir, — I know John Waters is not known for his humorous writing, but please tell me he was joking in his piece in Monday's paper on forgiving Charlie Haughey. — Yours, etc., Frances Walsh, Ryevale Lawns, Leixlip, Co. Kildare. 27 October 2000.

Teachers' Pay Claim

Sir, — Give the teachers a rise — maybe even 30 per cent. We don't want the profession to be debased in the way it has been in the UK. But there has to be a quid pro quo. They want to share in the fruits of the current boom, just as our IT folk do. So they should not object to accepting the work practices enjoyed by IT professionals. I have worked in both areas, so here are some suggestions based on my experience.

1. Ditch the unions — the IT industry does not enjoy union protection. 2. Reduce the holiday entitlement — the IT industry averages 23 days a year. 3. Sack incompetent staff — the IT industry is a meritocracy; only the strong survive. 4. Reward achievement not longevity. Most IT companies do quarterly assessments and reward only their high achievers. 5. Lay off teachers when class sizes diminish. IT companies wax and wane; employment is precarious.

And as for stress, IT shareholders and the unforgiving NASDAQ are far more severe judges than any Leaving Certificate examiner. — Yours, etc., John P. O'Sullivan, Saval Park Crescent, Dalkey, Co. Dublin.

Members of the 19th Air Corps Cadet Class saluting during the closing stages of the Aer Corps Commissioning Ceremony at Casement Aerodrome Baldonel. Photograph: Alan Betson.

6 NOVEMBER 2000

China Becoming an Economic Superpower

Asia Letter by Conor O'Clery

I am assured this story is true. A visitor to Co. Antrim went to a Chinese restaurant. He was served by a local waitress who wrote his order in Chinese characters. 'Do you speak Chinese?' he asked in astonishment. 'Oh no,' she replied. 'They just taught me how to write the orders, it's way easy.'

Next time he dined in the same restaurant he was served by a Chinese waitress. After she took his order she looked at him quizzically and remarked, 'You're no' from these parts, are you?'

Almost every town and village in Ireland has a Chinese restaurant. It is possibly true what John Taylor once said, that 'more people speak Chinese to each other in Northern Ireland than speak Irish'. The Chinese in Ireland are mostly Cantonese from southern China and Hong Kong who came to work in Chinese restaurants and cafés.

But a new generation is arriving today from all over China. They come to study and will work in Irish establishments, not just Chinese take-aways.

On a recent trip home I took a visiting American to Johnny Fox's pub in Glencullen for the ultimate Irish pub experience, and encountered two Chinese youths loading crates in the yard.

With the Chinese government currently conducting a 10-day census of its population, the focus is once again on the vast pool of energetic and talented people which makes up a fifth of the world's population and has provided a diaspora of 25 million people, scattered through almost every country.

For reporters like myself based in Beijing, and I suspect the leadership itself, the basic facts about China remain elusive. Even the size of the population and the acreage of arable land is hotly disputed.

The publication of Jasper Becker's book, *The Chinese*, is therefore especially timely.

By travelling to the far corners of China, as Becker has done for many years as correspondent of the *South China Morning Post*, and talking to people at every level, he has produced a meticulous study and drawn some realistic conclusions about the state of China today and its people.

It is a bleak picture. Becker finds a society 'in which everyone seems to be engaged in deceiving one another', from the distortion of news and history to the corruption in business.

China is nevertheless on the brink of becoming an economic superpower. It is the world's largest garment maker and manufacturer of sports shoes. Its cities are booming. In 20 years it could equal the US in world influence.

What is remarkable, Becker points out, is how little has changed for the people in 4,000 years. China's social pyramid has survived almost intact, as has the unique legalist tradition of governance inherited from Qin Shihuangdi, the country's founding emperor. Only in China can one interview a bureaucrat charged with civil service reforms who recalls how officials of the Han dynasty (206 BC–AD 220) dealt with the problems of nepotism.

The catastrophic failure by Mao to engineer the most egalitarian society in history has given way to acceptance of one of the most unequal. The peasantry who constitute a billion people — more than the combined population of the US and the EU — are still subject to authoritarian rule, and the imposition of crushing taxes.

Urban élites live as well as New Yorkers, but half the population cannot read or write and a third exists below the poverty line. His conclusion is that China needs to urbanise quickly, and on a massive scale.

Becker brings to bear the same understated outrage at the cruel burdens imposed on the poor and helpless by the system and its officials, as in *Hungry Ghosts*, the highly-acclaimed exposé of China's secret famine under Mao Zedong.

The book concludes on a hopeful note. The switch from military rule to democracy in Taiwan in the 1980s and 1990s means that for the first time 'one of the two parties that have controlled China's destiny as a modern state has irrefutably abandoned the common heritage of dictatorship'.

China, too, may haltingly move to reform itself politically, though genuine reform may have to wait until there is a change in status of the ruling party.

The key factor will be education. In the Han dynasty a small part of the population had access to higher education, and went on to form the core of the bureaucracy. Now urban Chinese families can send their sons and daughters abroad to become the core of a new, educated, high-tech society.

Today, there are regular queues outside the Irish embassy and other missions in Beijing of people seeking visas to go abroad, not to work in a Chinese restaurant, but to study at a foreign university. Education, along with the Internet, could yet bring profound change to China.

The Chinese, by Jasper Becker. Published by John Murray. St£25.

9 NOVEMBER 2000

Election Will be Marvelled at in Years to Come

Joe Carroll

This is the incredible election that will be marvelled at and dissected by the historians and the political scientists for the next 100 years and longer. That it took place in the most powerful country in the world which is also the cradle of modern democracy makes it only weirder.

Millions of Americans dutifully went to the polls and cast their ballots for the next president. As they sat in front of their TV sets later that night, they saw amazing scenes.

Vice-President Al Gore, who earlier in the night seemed to have the election won with victories in the big states on each coast and in the Midwest, was by 2.30 a.m. on his way to tell supporters in downtown Nashville that he had conceded victory in a call to his Republican opponent, Governor George Bush.

Florida, which the TV networks had declared early in the count as a win for Mr Gore, was now switched to Bush and so delivering him the election and the White House for the next four years.

But just before Mr Gore stepped out to give his concession speech to his stunned supporters, he got a message that there would have to be a recount in Florida where a 50,000-vote margin for Mr Bush had suddenly dwindled to a few hundred and Mr Gore could still win.

Mr Gore called Mr Bush a second time to say he was withdrawing his concession. All bets were off until Florida's voters were recounted. Mr Bush's reply has not been revealed.

Foreign ambassadors who had rushed to congratulate Mr Bush had to withdraw their good wishes. Viewers who had gone to bed with Bush safely elected woke up with still no new president. Newspaper headlines changed hourly. It was chaos.

But out of chaos some stability must emerge or we are all in trouble. The US, and the world for that matter, cannot stand much more of this bungling over the election of the man who must lead for the next four years.

The media, meaning the TV networks, bear much responsibility for the theatrical bouleversements which marked election night. But it is the archaic 18th century electoral system which could mean that Vice-President Al Gore wins more votes while Mr Bush wins the Electoral College and thus the Presidency.

The networks were irresponsible to call Florida for Mr Gore within minutes of the polls closing there on the basis of exit polls which did not reflect the closeness of the voting.

As dawn broke yesterday we learned that after a full count Mr Bush led Mr Gore by several hundred votes out of nearly six million cast. How

Texas Governor and Republican presidential candidate George W. Bush signs an autograph for a supporter at a rally at Drew University in Madison, New Jersey on 4 November. Photograph: Reuters, Rick Wilking.

could the crude methods of an exit poll correctly reflect that razor-edge situation?

The networks blundered on, putting Florida back into the 'too close to call' column, then into the Bush column and then back to 'too close to call'.

As fate would have it, Florida was the crucial state to decide the election because of the electoral college system. Florida had the 25 votes which Mr Bush and Mr Gore needed to reach the magic number of 270 after all the other states had declared.

So even if the media had not miscalled throughout the night, there would still have had to be the recount. Steps will presumably be taken to ensure that the exit polls fiasco never happens again and there may even be a ban on them in future elections.

What happens the electoral college is a different matter. Even before this election there were frequent calls to abolish the electoral college and allow presidents to be elected directly by popular vote.

This would avoid the danger that the vote of the people could be nullified by the state-by-state count of the college. This happened in the 1888 election, but presidents then were nothing like as high-profile as today.

A change now would mean a constitutional amendment which is a cumbersome business involving Congress and all the states and it could backfire.

When the Florida recount is ended later today it may well be that the popular vote winner and the electoral college winner will be the same person. That would be a relief.

The last thing the country needs after the trauma of this election is a constitutional crisis. With a Congress virtually tied between Republicans and Democrats, the idea of a president without a popular mandate could be a recipe for political instability. No president in that situation would be comfortable in taking hard decisions involving, say, military action abroad.

The next president, in any case, is certain to have problems with a Congress balanced on the thinnest of margins between the two parties. Republicans seem to have kept control of the House of Representatives and the Senate but there will be little scope for either Mr Bush or Mr Gore pushing through the ambitious reforms in social security, health insurance and education which figure largely in their policy documents.

Mr Bush's huge tax cut may also wither on the vine as the notional budget surplus of trillions of dollars over the next decade is mainly spent by a jealous Congress.

Appointments by the next president to the Supreme Court and to federal posts, including ambassadorships, will be scrutinised even more sharply than before and may lead to ill-will on both sides.

The election also reveals a country of sharp divisions, with support for the Democrats and Republicans splitting geographically, racially and ethnically, between the genders and between city and countryside.

The electoral map is a striking graphic of how the Democratic majority is concentrated on opposite coasts and around the Great Lakes while the Republicans occupy vast tracts in the centre, the Rocky Mountains and the south.

But the country's motto is 'Out of Many, One'. Elections down the years are putting this federal ideal under increasing strain, but so far good sense and loyalty to their country have ensured that Americans can take the anomalies of the oldest constitution in the world in their stride.

Their patience with the politicians who run the system should not be taken for granted.

9 NOVEMBER 2000

Sunshine State Plunges Poll Outcome into Darkness

Elaine Lafferty

It is somehow fitting that the resolution of the most extraordinary election in US history should now rest in Florida, a state of uniquely American contradiction.

This sun-drenched land at the southernmost tip of the US displays some of the gaudiest and most traditional of sensibilities: there is Disneyworld in Orlando, a living commercial for Americana; but also Little Havana, a poor and crime-ridden part of immigrant Miami that is only minutes away from the glitz and riches and white sand shores of South Beach.

There is Daytona Beach, where car racers and the 'spring break' kids come for sleepless days and nights of beer drinking and wildness. And all over the state are the retirees, the elderly people who come from all over the US to live out their lives in tranquil paradise. That is, of course, until the hurricanes hit. Every decade or so brutal storms wipe out hundreds of homes and take lives, leaving the state in tatters.

At this moment it is the state's political landscape that has left the election of the 43rd US president in tatters. Some 1,800 votes appear to separate Vice-President Al Gore and Texas Governor George W. Bush. The recount is unlikely to decide the election conclusively. That is because, in part, some 3,000 voters in Palm Beach, a traditional Democratic stronghold, are claiming their votes were not counted as intended.

In a confusing ballot used only in this single one of Florida's 67 counties, many voters contend that their votes for Mr Gore were counted as votes for Mr Pat Buchanan, a right-wing minor party candidate. And in fact, results showed Mr Buchanan winning 3,407 votes in Palm Beach, or 7.9 per cent of the vote, an unlikely and extraordinary feat in a liberal district.

'It bothered me all day long,' said Ms Sue Blum, an elderly Palm Beach voter. She said she worried that her vote had not been counted correctly because the ballot was so confusing. 'And then when I heard that the ballots were bad and Buchanan got those votes I knew something was wrong.'

The switchboard at the election board's headquarters in Tallahassee was lit up yesterday afternoon with complaints from people like Mrs Blum.

Mr Gore dispatched a legal team headed by former secretary of state Mr Warren Christopher to oversee the recount and contemplate a possible legal challenge. Mr Bush was reportedly also sending a team to Florida, headed by the former secretary of state, Mr James Baker.

There were also reports that a locked box filled with uncounted ballots was discovered in a church in Miami. Between investigation into voting irregularities, recounting of votes, and the arrival of some 2,300 posted votes cast by Americans living overseas, the resolution of this election could take several days — or longer.

15 NOVEMBER 2000

Maasai Effort to Save Cattle from Drought

Declan Walsh

KENYA: A century ago the fierce Maasai warriors were expelled from Nairobi to make way for British colonists. Now the spear-wielding tribesmen are back on the streets of the Kenyan capital, not to make war but to find food for their starving cattle.

Kenya is struggling through its worst drought in living memory. Meadows and grassy plains all over the country have been turned into barren dustbowls by the catastrophic failure of seasonal rains for the third successive year.

The Maasai homelands south of Nairobi have been among the worst affected. Up to 40 per cent of cattle have died, according to a recent survey by a Dutch aid agency, although Maasai elders claim that twice that many have perished.

Faced with the destruction of their only source of income, desperate herders have been driving thousands of animals on to the last available green zone, central Nairobi.

The sight of Maasai warriors, decorated in colourful beads and bearing spears, has become commonplace in one of Africa's largest cities. Their search for grazing sometimes brings herders and their cattle down narrow streets bordered by skyscrapers.

'I suppose there are no traffic lights in the bush,' one motorist wryly remarked while stuck in a cattle jam.

City dwellers relaxing in the central Uhuru Park find themselves sharing the grass with hundreds of cattle.

'This is not a good place for us to be,' admitted one Maasai herder, Mr Simon Lemel, on a recent Sunday afternoon in the park. 'But it's all that's left because of this drought.'

Some people have clashed with the country visitors, particularly those who find their neat flowerbeds turned into fodder. But most Kenyans, themselves suffering from stringent water and electricity rationing, are tolerant of the mini-invasion.

'It's tough for everyone these days. Cattle are everything to these people. It's like their life savings,' said Mr Peter Muya Mging, a vegetable-stall owner, as he guarded his produce from a passing herd.

Kenya is more usually associated with safaris than starvation, but many of its people are feeling the pinch of hunger.

Nairobi citizens surrounded by cattle owned by drought-stricken Maasai herders in the city centre Uhuru Park. Photograph: Declan Walsh.

Some four million are receiving emergency food rations, and as many as one child in four goes hungry in certain villages. One in 10 is severely malnourished, according to the United Nations.

'These communities are on the edge of disaster. Some farmers have planted seeds in recent weeks but they are withering already,' said Ms Anne Holmes of Trócaire, which has made a £1 million appeal for Kenya and its drought-stricken neighbours in the Horn of Africa: Somalia, Ethiopia and Eritrea.

Maikona, a small town near the northern border with Ethiopia, is in the heart of one of the worst affected areas. The earth is as hard as rock from the oven-like heat, and 'dust devils' — mini tornadoes of hot air — spin through the main street.

Up to two-thirds of cattle have died, and herders have driven the remainder into Ethiopia, where there are greener pastures. Man and animal are fighting for survival.

One schoolboy was badly mauled when he tried to defend his donkey from marauding lions with only a spear.

'We're expecting the rains in December. If they don't come, even the little livestock we have will die. We fear the people will be next,' said Mr Boru Dalacha of a local Catholic relief agency.

But the likelihood of a full-blown famine is receding. Western aid has been flowing in and the United Nations World Food Programme (WFP) has received pledges for 80 per cent of its $88.5 million relief programme, which runs until the end of December.

However, aid workers say it was a close-run thing. Some countries were slow to respond to appeals from a land with a notorious reputation for corruption.

Pilferage of foreign aid by provincial officials is 'arguably the largest scandal of recent years', said one business commentator, Mr Robert Shaw.

Donor concerns about corruption were eventually allayed when a new system, which took responsibility for food distribution away from the government, was introduced.

The hard times are far from over, however. Some areas, particularly Nairobi, are starting to receive regular rain, but others are not.

Next year's maize crop will be down 36 per cent on 1999, itself a bad year, according to government estimates.

And regardless of the weather the food crisis is expected to deepen in the pastoral communities which have seen their herds decimated by drought.

17 NOVEMBER 2000

Here's to Absinthe Friends

Times Square by Brendan Glacken

It is very decent of the Musée d'Orsay in Paris to lend us Edgar Degas's 'L'Absinthe', the Impressionist painting valued at about 33 million. In return, the Hugh Lane Gallery, where 'L'Absinthe' will be on view for the next few weeks, has lent Manet's portrait of Eva Gonzales for the same period.

Fair enough. Manet and Degas were good pals and both had the good sense to stand well back from the main Impressionist crowd and not get carried away, paying more heed to draughtsmanship and the structural principles of formal composition than the likes of Pissarro, Cezanne, Sisley and the rest of the crew.

As was reported in this paper recently, the Degas painting caused a huge row when first shown in Brighton.

Absinthe, now regarded as poisonous, was a very popular drink among the Parisian working classes at the turn of the century, and 'L'Absinthe', featuring a depressed-looking couple staring at a glass of the stuff in a cafe, was seen as a commentary on the evils of alcohol.

The pair shown in the picture were not actually Parisian alcoholics but pals of Degas, Ellen Andree and Marcellin Desboutin.

Being an artist, Desboutin didn't care a hoot about his less than flattering depiction, but Ellen, an actress and leading beauty of the day, wasn't too happy about her glum and down-at-heel appearance. Nor did she like having the single glass of absinthe placed in front of her rather than Desboutin.

'L'Absinthe' is a fine picture, but, of course, it isn't a patch on the lost masterpiece 'L'Guinness' by the Irish Impressionist Pius Kelly.

This great work, also featuring a depressed couple in a bar, caused similar outrage to that occasioned by 'L'Absinthe' when it was first exhibited in Kelly's local parish hall in Toomevara, Co. Tipperary, back in the 1880s.

'L'Guinness' was seen as an outrageously negative commentary on drink, and since Pius was known to be fond of a jar himself it didn't go down too well with the local public (or publicans).

The whole affair caused great scandal at the time, though Kelly himself regarded it as a cause célèbre. Barred from local inns for two weeks, he spent the fortnight drinking his way around New Inn, Cashel and Cahir, taking perverse delight in the bad publicity.

Kelly was friendly with another artist, Tommy Maher, a Mullinahone man who for reasons known only to himself specialised in vaguely elegiac paintings of letters and parcels. He was one of the early Post Impressionists.

It was Maher who sat for 'L'Guinness' along with Gearoidin O'Rahilly, a powerfully-built Toomevara girl who had just got the call to training in St Pat's in Drumcondra.

Alexander Abbott (3) from Blackrock, Co. Dublin, watches Madagascar cockroaches which formed part of a waste-eating experiment by Carlow Institute of Technology students at the Best of Irish Science Show in Leopardstown, Dublin. Photograph: Joe St Leger.

A moderately intelligent girl, Gearoidin had gone to the Ursuline Convent in Thurles, where she got an impressive five honours in the Leaving Cert.

The good nuns were of course delighted that Gearoidin had got the call, and managed to hide their disappointment that she wasn't going into the novitiate. But they got an awful shock on seeing her, large as life, lowering a pint of porter with evident relish in 'L'Guinness'.

As it turned out, Gearoidin developed a taste for the stuff after that, and over the next three years of training in St Patrick's she could be found most nights of the week in the Cat and Cage, and sometimes in the Brian Boru or even up in Beneavin House.

When she got the NT after her name she went on to teach for many years in a small national school near Knockmore in Co. Mayo, Currabaggan I think it was, and all her life she was pleased to be pointed out as Pius Kelly's model for 'L'Guinness'.

Tommy Maher, however, was absolutely outraged at his depiction in the portrait, sipping a modest half-pint as if he were not a man at all. He never got over the shame of the powerful-looking Gearoidin sinking the full pint beside him and wiping her lips with obvious enjoyment.

Maher and Kelly fell out shortly after that, and the picture itself disappeared around the same time that Monet's 'Impression: Sunrise' (which of course gave the movement its name) was stolen in Paris. It would be worth a fair few bob now.

The Taoiseach Bertie Ahern congratulating Mr James Coughlan, retired Garda Sergeant (1931–71), on his 93rd birthday and the graduation of his grandson Garda Aidan Coughlan (right) at the graduation ceremony in the Garda Training College in Templemore. Also photographed is Aidan's father Dr Michael Coughlan (background) all from Galway. Photograph: Alan Betson.

As for the oblique angle from which the 'L'Absinthe' couple were observed by Degas, many people who saw 'L'Guinness' years ago also commented on the peculiar angle at which Gearoidin and Tommy are observed. In fact they look like they are about to pitch forward on their faces.

This arose from the fact that Pius Kelly was known to paint 'in a reclining position' as the renowned art historian Ernst Gombrich tells us.

In other words he would lie sprawled on his back on the floor while the wife (Margaret Mary Alacoque) would hold the canvas above him hour after hour. It was a peculiar way of working, and no doubt restful for the artist, if not for poor Margaret, but sure someone has to suffer for art's sake.

17 NOVEMBER 2000

Acute Bed Shortages Still the Problem

Pádraig O'Morain

The Estimates published yesterday include the biggest-ever annual increase in health spending, which makes it all the more strange that much of the exercise has about it a feeling of things standing still.

This is not altogether a bad thing. The feeling of standing still comes from the fact that a lot of money is being spent to bring aspects of the health service up to a reasonable standard.

Much of the money will go to paying for costs arising out of the settlement of the nurses' and hospital doctors' disputes. Money will also go to such projects as providing a much-needed new casualty department at Cork University Hospital, upgrading the infrastructure at Holles Street Hospital, Dublin, and upgrading medical wards at Portlaoise General Hospital.

The extra money for home helps is an especially welcome move in bringing things up to a reasonable level. The £6.50 an hour they will get from January contrasts dramatically with the £2.50 an hour some of them were earning a couple of years ago.

It is, in many respects, good that the Minister is choosing to make investments to bring facilities and conditions into the 21st century, instead of engaging in flashy political gestures, though he might be saving one or two of these for Budget day.

It must be acknowledged that 3,000 extra posts in the health services are being funded next year on top of the 3,000 this year. It is a great pity many of these will have to be funded by agency staff or overtime because of staff shortages. Nevertheless, the move represents an intent to substantially improve health services.

The great leap forward which we are not getting, however, is an increase in acute beds. One of the most gruelling experiences faced by people engaging with the hospital system is the business of waiting for a bed. A lengthy wait in the casualty department is bad enough: it is compounded mercilessly by the many hours spent on a trolley in a casualty department waiting for a bed to be free.

Behind the trolley experience is the uncomfortable fact that 3,000 acute beds were lost out of the system in the 1980s and 1990s. Fewer beds and a bigger population add up to excruciating queues in casualty departments and lengthier waiting lists.

It isn't hard to see why there hasn't been a dramatic rise in acute bed numbers. The capital cost of adding a new acute bed to a hospital is around £100,000. After all, you don't just buy a new bed and shove it in a corner. The bed has to be housed, the housing (an extra wing, say) has to be designed and the equipment has to be provided to treat the patient in the new bed. So to get back 3,000 beds would carry a capital cost of £300 million. That's a lot of money.

Then there's the running cost including staff, drugs, surgery and so on for the patient in the new bed. This varies a good deal from city hospitals

Kate Doorley (3) from Ballybrack, Dublin, holds the Concern Star at the launch of the Concern Christmas Campaign 2000. Photograph: Bryan O'Brien.

such as Cork University Hospital (£292 a day), Beaumont, Dublin (£273 a day), University College Hospital, Galway (£247 a day) to hospitals outside the main cities such as Tullamore General, Co. Offaly (£187 a day) and St Luke's, Kilkenny (£180 a day).

Taking a cost of £250 a day (because the biggest demand is in the big cities) the cost of running those 3,000 beds, if we got them, would be about £274 million a year.

That's an impossible aspiration — or is it? We spend about half as much of our national income on health as the French who, in a World Health Organisation survey, came out as having the best health service in the world.

We can have the beds if we are prepared to pay substantially more for our health service.

That reforming the health service will be a costly business is, it has to be said, recognised by the Minister, Mr Martin. Speaking yesterday evening at the announcement of guidelines for the care of children with special needs in hospital, by Children in Hospital Ireland, he referred to the increase in health spending projected for next year.

'We are going to have to spend more on health now and in the future if we are to have the kind of standards of care we expect in this day and age,' he said.

What is under way, and what these Estimates are, is a long-term and laudable project. But where are the extra beds we need?

18 NOVEMBER 2000

Smashing the Taxi Cartel

Editorial

The bully-boy tactics traditionally employed by the powerful taximen's lobby should not dissuade the Government, and especially the Progressive Democrats, from vindicating the rights of citizens to an efficient and cost-effective transport service. This cartel, whose growth has been facilitated over the years by restrictive State rules and regulations, should be broken up and open competition introduced into the system. New licences should be awarded for a small fee and on the basis of quality transport and standards of competence set for the driver.

A report in this newspaper that Minister of State, Mr Bobby Molloy, intends to sign orders next week that may put an extra 700 taxis on the streets of Dublin before Christmas caused an immediate withdrawal of taxi services at Dublin airport yesterday. After some hours, service was resumed. But a spokesman for the Taxi Federation threatened to seek a court injunction to prevent deregulation of the service and, if that failed, to seek compensation for the inevitable fall in value of existing licences. At the same time, SIPTU, which represents some taxi drivers, asked that the issues be discussed under the Programme for Prosperity and Fairness.

A compassionate case might be made for State compensation where an individual had purchased a taxi plate for as much as £90,000 within the past few years. But most plates have been in circulation for a very long time and have gained an artificial value because of their scarcity, rather than through any particular contribution by their owners. In fact, they have become a tradeable commodity and have been treated as such by wealthy individuals.

Just as shares on the stock exchange and other investments can increase or decrease in value over time, there is no compelling reason why the State should compensate such individuals and effectively carry the risk element of their investments. The

Blockading taximen try to stop another taxi driver leaving Dublin Airport. Photograph: Joe St Leger.

chairman of the Competition Authority, Dr John Fingleton, has been particularly critical of the taxi cartel. And he has identified the most serious curbs on competition in this economy as Government regulations.

In that regard, he mentioned taxis, pubs, pharmacies, banking, airports, broadcasting, health insurance and milk production as areas requiring deregulation so that consumers can benefit from greater competition and falling prices. The Progressive Democrats are willing to listen. But Fianna Fáil appears to be reluctant to confront powerful vested interests.

Last month's decision by the High Court vindicated the views of Dr Fingleton when it found the Government had no right to restrict the number of taxi licences. Such an approach, it ruled, prevented citizens from working in an industry for which they might be qualified; affected the right of the public to a reliable taxi service and restricted the development of the industry. Taxi drivers are at present appealing that ruling to the Supreme Court. But the prospect of overturning the judgment is said to be poor and the Government has withdrawn from the case.

The Attorney General is scheduled to approve the wording for new orders affecting taxi licences next Monday. And Mr Molloy has indicated he will sign them into law during the week. The taxi lobby will almost certainly attempt to prevent that happening through a disruption of services, legal challenges and intensive political lobbying. Such a campaign should not be allowed to succeed.

The Government is already committed to spending hundreds of millions of pounds in upgrading bus and rail services and is determined to encourage competition in that sector. It makes no political or economic sense in that context to retain a grossly inefficient and inadequate taxi service. Deregulation of taxis would be a start. After that, the interests of consumers would be served by liberalising the drinks trade.

25 NOVEMBER 2000

Possessed by Greatness

Tom Humphries

He stares across the concourse at the milling journalists. Everyone pretends not to have been watching him. Ain't nobody here, but us chickens, Roy, ain't nobody here at all. He knows, though. He's got those dark serial killer eyes and that gaunt look. Black sheep in lone wolf's clothing. He's happy that way. Frightening in his self-containment. Frightening. Full stop.

That's right. Ain't nobody here at all.

It's Lisbon in October. Time to dawdle. The Irish soccer squad stand gossiping and laughing at the trundling airport carousel. When the time comes each player fishes his kitbag up into his fist and moves off towards the bus. Except one.

Roy Keane stands apart. Silent and serene. With a cartoon villain's swathe of dark stubble running from his chin right up his bony cheeks and over the crown of his scalp, he could be anyone's bad guy. In the shadows it's hard to tell whether he is scowling to himself or smiling to himself. Whatever. He is in a world that is entirely his own. From under the crook of his arm peeps a book. *Hard Cases*, by Gene Kerrigan. One good photo-opportunity missed. 'How's the book, Roy?'

He looks startled at the trespass. Glances at his book guiltily. 'Don't know yet,' he says. 'I just started it. Then somebody sat beside me on the plane.'

Pause. 'I had to talk to them.'

And he gives a rueful, razor-thin smile. More fodder perhaps. KEANE'S SMALL TALK NIGHTMARE! — NEVER AGAIN, SAYS UNITED STAR. He's in the thick of the large-point headlines again this morning and he doesn't need it. His mother is sick in Cork and his leg is troubling him slightly, and his decision to stay in Manchester an extra day at the start of the week opened in the heavens above a hole in the team's ozone layer. There's a new downpour of rumours about a feud to the death between himself and Mick McCarthy.

It all seemed so reasonable. He stayed in Manchester because they have more equipment there, machines, a pool, and the physio he always works with. He knows that the physios will want to speak to each other, so he mentioned that if the

footballer, evidence which will be used to adjudicate in the great feud. Of course, he rooms alone at Manchester United as well, but nobody asks him about this and he's not going out of his way to tell them about how he just likes to read, likes to lie there and read a book and not have a mindless foreign TV programme blasting away in the background. He likes being able to ring Theresa and the kids and speak privately. He likes not having to talk

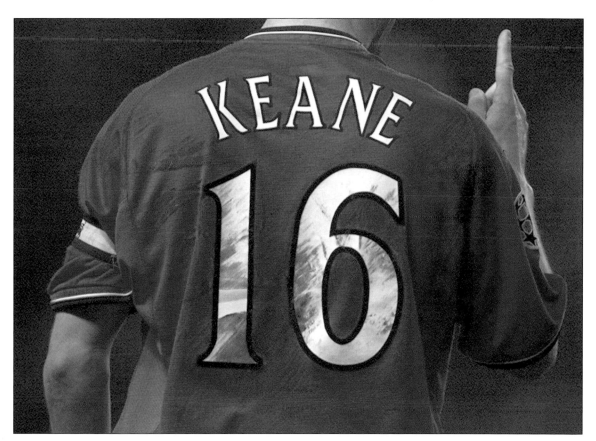

Roy Keane, number 16!

physio is ringing anyway, well, do us a favour and tell the FAI what's up.

But the message has vanished and it's silly time. The papers have gotten hold of the fact that since Denis Irwin retired, Roy has been rooming by himself on Irish trips. This is a big deal, evidence of the brooding disaffection of Ireland's greatest

just for the sake of it. He likes knowing that all he has to do for company is walk out the door and all he has to do for privacy is walk back in. He likes privacy. If that's a crime, so shoot him.

So at the airport in Lisbon, even though it's a bad time, you tell him that you want to ask him about what's it like being Roy Keane, captain of

Ireland and Manchester United, maybe the most influential footballer on the planet, the man whose wage packet has become the standard by which all other wage packets are judged? What's it like always being in the centre when every cell of your genetic programming makes you an outsider?

And he agrees happily. Maybe it needs explaining.

What's it like? Well, this morning perhaps he half feels as if he should be in the midst of things with his team-mates, joshing and gossiping and putting on a show for the press who are watching just in case.

KEANE SLAYS McCARTHY in CAROUSEL BLOODBATH! — Onlookers heard Big Nose taunt.

But something inside him resists. He can't stand the raging idiocy of fame, so he sticks with his own thoughts and his own company regardless. You can think what you like of that. He enjoys being here, but Irish trips have always been different for him. He began in Jack Charlton's old and settled team and plays now with Mick McCarthy's babies. He never had a three amigos period or a Brian Kerr apprenticeship.

'That's typical. I'm always the oddball in between. I'm not complaining about that. It's other people who go on about it.'

Other people approach him when he's with his wife and kids on a family day out. They want photos taken with their hammy arms hanging around Roy's neck. When he says 'sorry, look I'm with my family', other people get snippy, then stroppy and abuse him about his wage packet. Other people think that will make him change his mind.

He never gets to explain that he wants his two daughters and his little son to see him just as Dad. He's noticed it recently, he's noticed that they notice. He's putting the girls to bed and they start asking him questions about football.

'Tactics, Roy?'

'No,' he breaks into his grin, 'they're settled on 4-4-2 really, but they ask questions about other players. They have their little favourites already. They know there's something different going on. I try to protect them from all that, from other people, and from the whole Manchester United thing. In fairness, they go to the local Catholic school and the nuns there are good about it, too. It's other people that make the trouble.'

All this fame stuff. His problem is he can't bring himself to fake sincerity. The other week he was talking to Jesper Blomqvist. Jesper has done his cruciate.

'I said to him, "Jesper, how is it?",' and he said, "It's fine, thanks," and I could see in his face he was annoyed because everyone asks the same thing, and I said, "Jesper, when I had it and somebody asked, I said it was bloody agony, I was in trouble, that I was icing it every day and exercising and it was a slow process and the mental stress was just as bad and I didn't know if I'd get through it all. Other people stop asking you pretty soon if you tell them the truth".'

Other people. They live in Ireland, too. Once, at the behest of a Sunday newspaper hack, he was booed for the course of a game playing for Ireland. He shrugs and shakes his head at the memory.

'In Ireland I think that's a way of life to be honest, people knocking you. I've found that hard at home. There's always somebody having a go. That's worse at home than it is here.' Home. Here. Quick scene change. Here is this afternoon, a few weeks after Lisbon, the captain of Manchester United has just walked into a hotel on the outskirts of Manchester. It's a couple of days after the infamous prawn sandwich remark which turned the humble crustacean between two buttery slices into a term of abuse in football. Fair to say that a number of people in the lobby today must have been wondering if Roy was abusing them. Nevertheless, his presence freezes every face. If the Queen thinks the world smells of fresh paint, Roy Keane must reckon that it looks like Pompeii, people frozen with their mouths open.

He says it himself, without vanity, that he has

Roy Keane at the opening of the Manchester United Store in Dublin City Centre. Photograph: Bryan O'Brien.

to go pretty far to find a place these days where he might not be recognised. In the next week or so, he's taking the kids to Lapland for a pre-Christmas treat. He tells you this and his eyes cloud a little, worrying about …

£52,000-A-WEEK KEANE IN SANTA CLAUS BUST-UP — Rudolph Shaken By Venison jibe.

Quickly he shifts away from the details and into the sort of general talk that the tabloids can't pilfer ammunition from. Don't get me wrong, he says, and patiently elucidates yet another point lest a damaging inference be drawn from it. Dwight Yorke had a party for players' families and Roy didn't go — don't get him wrong, he couldn't go. Being captain brings responsibilities, but don't get

him wrong, the other lads are great. Etc, etc. He has been taken up wrong again and again. The back-page caricature of Keane as psychotic thicko with hair-trigger temper misses the point entirely. There's scarcely a more interesting footballer in the game today. Lots to say and humour as sharp as a fish hook. Still you goad him a bit.

'What newspaper do you read?'

'This will look stupid, but I read *The Times* mainly.' He rolls his eyes.

UNITED'S KEANE IN BROADSHEET ORGY! PLAYER CONSUMED BIG WORDS.

'Perhaps you should just put the *People*.' 'No, *The Times* is interesting. Who does the soccer there?'

Withering look.

'Ah now, to be honest I don't buy papers to find out about soccer.'

Keane 1 Journalism 0 This is his prime. Twenty-nine-years old and indispensable. He'll never be at this altitude again. The bookshops are currently flogging two Roy Keane biographies while Michael Kennedy, his solicitor and agent, is conducting the auction among five other publishers for the rights to the official version. That's just the quieter part of his life.

Then there's that certain madness attached to Manchester United which has woven itself into his daily life. With two years left at Old Trafford he feels he's just mastered that. Slow was the lesson …

'I don't go anywhere unusual now. I don't go out much. I don't meet with people I don't know. I don't allow myself to be taken by surprise. I don't do anything I have any doubts about.'

Another grin.

'So, you're very fortunate!'

Of course life tackles from behind. It's not 18 months since a rising sun found Roy Keane sitting in a cell in Bootle Police Station. On Sunday he'd lifted the league trophy as captain of Manchester United. On Monday night, happy and bulletproof, he'd been lifted himself. His path intersected with the paths of Leanne Carey and Maxine Rourke and a male friend of theirs in Henry's cafe bar in Manchester. Words were exchanged. Keane exited later than he should have. By 10 o'clock, he was in Quo Vadis in King Street, but so was the *Sun* newspaper, so was the Old Bill. Describe that morning.

'Well, I was tired. I hadn't slept. I was just going over and over it. How could I let this happen? Then they said Alex Ferguson was on his way.'

How did the police treat you?

'Fine. They were fine.'

Any autograph requests?

'No. They must have been City fans. They were still fine, though. Most people saw it for what it was, but I'm lucky I get on with Alex Ferguson. I'm not silly enough to think that he won't get fed up if it happens again. The same with Diadora, my boot people. They were great, but if they pick up the paper and see that again, some executive is going to think: no smoke without fire. It was a set-up, but Theresa, the kids, and all these other people deserve more. It was a blip. Nothing came of it.'

What did you learn?

'Well. I've been naïve maybe. I'm 29 now with three kids and I don't want them to wake up again and hear that I'm in a prison cell. I don't want it to be morning in a prison cell and Alex Ferguson to be walking in. I wasn't expecting to see his face that time to be honest. That's what they call learning the hard way. The whole thing hurt me. It was the final nail. What are you doing, Roy? It was daft. They had an agenda, but I never saw it coming. People say ignore it, but it hurts.'

More recently, the latest serious assault on his character was an allegation of drink dependency which arose after he visited a friend with that problem. He won't discuss the subject for fear of lending the story legs. Anyway, he's suing. 'There will be action taken on that and I hope it will come to a head quite soon.' He's cool about it all, though. It's not a moan or a rant when he talks about these things. He thinks a lot about fate, about things happening for a reason.

He did his cruciate ligament one September day, stretching to trip Alfie Inge Haaland at Elland Road. The next year was wiped off his career. The world kept turning, though.

Mentally he switched himself off from the team and realised that Old Trafford functioned just fine anyway. They still made jokes in the dressing-room. They still trained and played. They still celebrated goals. Nobody painted the swans black. Nothing stops when you are gone. 'So, I put on my selfish head and I thought about Roy Keane.'

KEANE IN TWO HEADS REVELATION — Star's Grotesque Secret!! He remembers being out with the family one day for a pub lunch and the woman behind the counter slapped the plates up and said 'your lot won two-nothing'.

'I just looked at her and she might as well have been talking about Rockmount or Cobh Ramblers because for a minute I didn't know what she was talking about.' Finally, he came back and the loneliness of isolation and recovery wore off. He asked that the lads not tippy-toe around him in training and, out of regard for all the onpitch bollockings he has administered down the years, they obliged.

'Believe me they didn't go gentle. I suppose that was how I wanted it. I knew when I got to Leeds or Liverpool they weren't going to hold a meeting and say, "go easy on Keane, he's just back from his cruciate".' He kept his selfish head handy. He admires Alex Ferguson, for instance, but he's not going to risk deep-vein thrombosis from sitting on his bench for long periods.

'Manchester United will go on. In the end, you have to look after yourself. We have the squad rotation thing at United and I always say that it's good, we need that, but if you're not in the team, well, fuck the squad rotation. You want the best contract you can get, you want to play the most you can. You have to think of these things.'

So when it came contract time and Michael Kennedy set about negotiating to make Roy the highest-paid player in Britain, the experience of the year out injured shielded him emotionally. Italy beckoned, but he preferred the option of maintaining excellence with United if they rewarded him accordingly. It was a point he had to make. He was willing to walk.

At that level of income, surely the point is lost anyway, you say. What's the practical difference between, say, £44,000-a-week and £52,000-a-week?

'£8,000?' he says swiftly. 'Nah. The challenge was to maintain (the standard). To win things. I missed out on the European Cup, I was there, but I wasn't part of it, it was a bit false for me. But if I'd played I'd be just as hungry. Every year I want to win the league and the European Cup. I want to tot them all up when I finish. As well, I felt maybe

I owed something to the club. I've let them down once or twice.'

So here it is. The view from the summit. He's thinking about the descent already. In two years' time, after 10 years at Old Trafford, he'll be crowding 32, Alex Ferguson will be gone, and he suspects United won't be offering an equivalent contract. He has said before he'd like to go to Celtic and he reiterates that now. By then, though, he hopes to be immersed in a World Cup final. That's the other running soap opera of his life, his dastardly plans to assassinate Mick McCarthy. Road Runner and Wile E Coyote.

'Mick McCarthy and me? That'll run and run. People will never be happy until we go away on holidays together. Look. It's fine with Mick and it's always been fine. I don't go on holidays with Alex Ferguson either, that doesn't mean I don't like the bloke. It'll stay with me and Mick because they can use it to put him under pressure and to make me look as if I think I'm something special because I'm with United.'

He appreciates where McCarthy was coming from in terms of pressure when Ireland drew in Amsterdam earlier this year, but he reiterates his view that it's time to start thinking more positively. 'It's not a criticism, but I'm not into all the hugging on the pitch if we get a draw. We should be expecting more from ourselves. This stuff about the good old Irish, they'll have a sing-song anyway. Sod that. We should be qualifying for World Cups. Let's win games. Two-nil up with 15 minutes left, let's go and win it. We should be kicking each other, kicking ourselves when we throw away points like that.

'Let's think higher. Mick has us playing good football now. The lads could tell by my body language that night that I wasn't pleased. I didn't have to say it. Sometimes silence is golden. I'm good at that sometimes.' That's all. More lines from the top of the world. Like the prawn sandwiches stuff, it had to be said, but it was a small thing blown out of proportion. The usual turbulence.

He doesn't care too much. He's on good terms with himself these days. A crazy night out is bringing his girls to Britney Spears. His biggest worry is whether The Grinch will be too scary for them to see in the cinema.

A man in his prime. He loves this time. He's busy and full of perspective and, well, mischief too. It's Manchester Derby week and his old nemesis, Alfie Inge Haaland, is winding him up in the papers, little digs about the £52,000 and the prawn sandwiches! So, on Saturday morning at Maine Road, Roy shakes hands with the Man City mascot instead of Alfie. Then he plays Alfie off the field.

Tuesday arrives and so do Panathinaikos. The prawn sandwich question is still nibbling at journalistic minds. Afterwards Roy Keane peeps out of the dressing-room and sees a hundred prawn sandwich questions waiting to be coyly launched in the mixed zone. He turns left instead. Towards the players' car park and the sanctuary of his grey Mercedes. Don't get him wrong, but, well, life is too short.

Letters to the Editor November 2000

EU Rapid Reaction Force

Sir, — The Peace and Neutrality Alliance would like to congratulate The Irish Times *for drawing attention to the decision of the Government to allocate between 800 and 1,000 soldiers to the European Union's army, the Rapid Reaction Force, through your Editorial of 1 November and articles by Edward Horgan and Laura Marlowe. However, since* The Irish Times *is one of the few media to cover this issue in a balanced way, we doubt if many people are aware that the new European Army will be made up of between 200,000 and 250,000 soldiers and will be capable of placing 80,000 of them into a area of conflict within a radius of 2,500 miles from the borders of the European Union.*

While your Editorial says the decision of the Irish Government to provide a regiment of the army of the European Union does not affect our 'neutrality', we do not agree. They will be no more 'neutral' than Irish Regiments were when they were part of the army of the British Union.

This new army of the European Union is to play the same role as that of the British Union and Empire, that is, to defend the 'interests' of the élite of the Union. When the mostly European NATO states went to war against Yugoslavia they did so without a United Nations mandate. You are fooling itself and your readers to suggest that the élite of the newly forming European empire would feel itself constrained by the charter of the United Nations.

The new army is being established as a consequence of the provisions of the Amsterdam Treaty. At the time of the treaty referendum, PANA called for a protocol similar to that achieved by the Danes to exclude them from militarisation of the EU and 38 per cent of the people agreed with us. We now demand a referendum on the Treaty of Nice and again call for a protocol to exclude Irish participation in the new imperial army.

PANA believes that the future of Ireland is that of an independent, democratic state supporting collective security through the UN. The Irish élite wants Ireland to be gradually integrated into an empire. The Irish people should have the right to decide. If given the chance, PANA is confident that, like the Danes, next time we win. — Yours, etc., Roger Cole, Chair, Peace & Neutrality Alliance, Blackrock, Co. Dublin. 6 November 2000.

Sir, — Roger Cole, Chair of the Peace and Neutrality Alliance (6 November) describes the EU Rapid Reaction Force as 'the European Union's Army'. He goes on to say that 'the new European Army will be made up of between 200,000 and 250,000 soldiers and will be capable of placing 80,000 of them into an area of conflict within a radius of 2,500 miles from the borders of the European Union'.

In each of these assertions, Mr Cole is factually incorrect.

US President Bill Clinton in Dundalk when he visited the County Louth town before going on to Belfast. Photograph: Bryan O'Brien.

The Rapid Reaction Force is intended to be composed of some 60,000 troops, capable of being mobilised within six months and of being maintained in the field for one year.

They would be used to carrying out the 'Petersberg Tasks', which are essentially peace-keeping and peace-making, and humanitarian tasks.

It is reckoned that the armies providing contingents for the Rapid Reaction Force would have to train and prepare a pool of between 200,000 and 250,000 personnel to ensure that 60,000 would be operationally available at any given time. That is clearly not the same as saying that the 'European Army' would consist of that large total number.

It is patently absurd of Mr Cole to state that Irish troops participating in this Rapid Reaction Force 'will be no more neutral than Irish Regiments were when they were part of the Army of the British Union'. They would, in fact, be participating in missions with the agreement of the Irish Government, on terms agreed by the Irish Government with its partners in the European Union, on terms not dictated by any imperial power. The only purpose of that reference in Mr Cole's letter is clearly to make a jingoistic appeal to old emotions which have no relevance in today's world.

The facts of the situation give the lie to Mr Cole's contention that 'this new Army of the European Union is to play the same role as that of the British Union and Empire'. This is simply more jingoism on Mr Cole's part.

Mr Cole is quite entitled to point out, as he did, that 'when the mostly European NATO states went to war against Yugoslavia they did so without a United Nations mandate'. That statement, however, has no relevance in the context of his letter. The decision to go to war against Yugoslavia was not made by the

European Union. The confusions and inconsistencies that characterised the planning and implementation of the military intervention of Yugoslavia are a fascinating study in themselves, but they have nothing whatever to do with the EU's Rapid Reaction Force.

Mr Cole and PANA have no monopoly on the wish that collective security be guaranteed through the UN. Curiously enough, he supports reforms in the UN of a kind which he opposes in the EU. Perhaps it is because he is convinced that there is very little possibility of securing these reforms in the UN, while those in the EU seem to be coming closer.

Finally, he should perhaps take account of the views of hundreds of thousands of Kosovar refugees, hundreds of thousands of Serbs who have finally succeeded in restoring democracy to their country, and hundreds of thousands of Montenegrins, all of whom are looking for guarantees for their security. Most of these people, and millions of others in Central and Eastern Europe, would like the EU to be able to guarantee their security. In default of that, they opt massively for NATO.

Mr Cole and his comrades in PANA seem to be quite happy to let the best be the enemy of the good and, in the meantime, to tell people who need security now that they must wait. I do not believe that Ireland, or the Irish people, are 'neutral' on this issue. — Yours, etc., Alan M. Dukes TD, Dáil Éireann, Dublin 2. 10 November 2000.

The Dart to Greystones

Sir, — I am the owner of a great work of fiction, which cost me only 50p: the 1999–2000 DART timetable. This fantastic publication listed a regular DART service to Greystones, with an asterisk noting: 'Due to open late 1999.' A couple of months into 2000 there was still no sign of these ghost trains, proudly included in the (then) current timetable.

DART drivers demanded £8,000 each for them to permit their company to hire six new staff to operate the extended service to Greystones and Malahide.

Earlier this year they got the money, but they still will not permit Irish Rail to run the full DART service to Greystones and Malahide.

Currently an extremely limited service operates to Greystones, and if you miss the 7.39 a.m. from Greystones into Dublin, you'll be waiting almost 11 hours for the next one! I also note with dismay a sign in Bray station advising of the Sunday DART service to Greystones — approximately one every hour throughout the day — a vastly superior service to that operating on weekdays. Whoever formulated this demented scheme is evidently of the opinion that the purpose of extending the DART was to facilitate those based in the city who would like to take their family to the seaside on a Sunday. Who would ever need to get a train during the week?

I don't know whether to laugh or cry when I see the posters plastered around the DART network proudly advising of the new service to Malahide. There is no peak-hour service, the first train leaves at 11.10 a.m. and there is a lack of services between 3.45 p.m. and 8.10 p.m. And this limited service was made possible only by cancelling the equivalent DARTS from Howth.

I wanted to buy the new DART timetable this week, having not read a good piece of fiction in a while. I gave up, disappointed, when I read the tattered piece of paper stuck up in the ticket office in Pearse Station. On it was scribbled in marker: 'No DART timetables available until further notice.'

And they won't give me my 50p back. — Is mise, Tadgh O'Brien, Hawkins Lane, Greystones, Co. Wicklow. 11 November 2000.

Deregulating Taxis

Sir, — To all the taxi drivers who in the past have either refused or proposed extortionate charges to take me home to Bray from Dublin city centre: my day has come. Welcome to the free market, a market in which you will welcome my custom, no longer be able to cherry-pick, and be forced to offer a better and more competitive service. — Yours, etc., Darragh Butler, Bray, Co. Wicklow. 24 November 2000.

1 DECEMBER 2000

In Time's Eye

Have you ever tried eating for, let's say a week, without the usual implements — knife, fork, spoon? When Thomas Mason, author of *The Islands of Ireland*, brought his wife and four sons to the Saltee Island some time in the 1930s, they were landed by a boatman who was told to come back in a week. No mobile phones, of course, not much radio about, even. Nor was there any certainty that attention could be attracted by signalling with a torch, or flares, that could bring the boatman plying his oars back in a hurry. They had had to wait three days at Kilmore Quay before a landing could be attempted, and two rabbit trappers, who had been weatherbound for over a week, were just arriving back on the mainland.

At mealtime Mrs Mason asked him where he had put the cutlery. 'Imagine the consternation when I confessed that I had put them in one of the pockets of the car after an *al fresco* lunch on the way down and had forgotten all about it. No knives, forks or spoons for a week.

'We managed by using Boy Scout knives and penknives, metal tent-pegs for forks, and — necessity is the mother of invention — we fabricated useful spoons by binding limpet shells into the split ends of pieces of wood which we got from the box from the grocer to hold our food. The boys really enjoyed using these weapons at their meals — it was more like Robinson Crusoe than civilised spoons and forks.'

Síle de Valera TD, Minister for Arts, Heritage, Gaeltacht and the Islands, examining one of the 27 pages of James Joyce's Ulysses *'Circle' manuscript, acquired for the National Library by Mr Edward Maggs, MD of Maggs Brothers Ltd, agents for the Library, at a cost of US$1.4 million at a Christies Auction in New York. Photograph: Alan Betson.*

Fantastic bird life and 37 different species on the island, mostly nesting there. But the book is not about birds. Its about islands and people. And he has many friends among the people of the islands he covers. He was a modest man, and this book, while not covering all the islands of Ireland, nevertheless gives us a picture of how we were. The photographs, mostly taken by himself, are magnificent — and particularly so of the people, many of whom wore clothing which is today considered out-of-date.

He admires the people on Aran who, he writes, are 'intensely religious'. And, 'it is this all-pervading sense of a Divine Providence that enables them to lead happy and contented lives in circumstances that, under a materialistic philosophy, would lead to a loosening of all moral standards of comfort'.

Above all, Mason was a brilliant photographer, and this book displays his expertise to the full. Published by Batsford of London in 1936, it may have gone into other editions, but is hard to get today. Not a 'period piece'. But a monument to a life well lived, which brightened that of many others.

2 DECEMBER 2000

A Right Royal Scam

Frank McDonald

Among the rich and bitchy expatriate community in Tangier, they would like to be revered as the Irish Royals. But Terence McCarthy, self-styled MacCarthy MSr, Prince of Desmond, and his 'Hereditary Chamberlain', Andrew Davison, *soi disant* Count of Clandermond, are more commonly known as 'the royal blimps'. This pair may be seen almost daily making a regal progress through the Grand Socco, Tangier's bustling marketplace. Protocol requires that Davison walks a deferential three paces behind the man who ennobled him, usually carrying their 'royal cat' in a wicket basket.

More likely than not, they are on their way to Madame Porte's, a delightful 1930s 'salon de thé', done in restrained art deco style, which the original owner's son is said to have lost in a game of cards. To the delight of Tangier's expats, it re-opened last year after being closed for a decade when it was used only occasionally as a film set.

In Porte's, where they serve petit dejeuner for just 16.50 dirhams (about £1.40), McCarthy and Davison would take a table by one of the open windows with billowing white curtains. The purring cat would be parked on the window sill, attached by a long pink ribbon to one of its masters while they dined out on croissants and toast.

In the five-star El Minzah Hotel, Tangier's finest, staff were instructed to address McCarthy as 'Your Highness'. The pair even arranged to have their framed photographic portraits, each surmounted by a coronet, hung in positions of honour in the hotel's wine bar alongside such luminaries as Rita Hayworth and Rock Hudson.

What's more, they used 'the Minzah', as every expat in town calls it, as an accommodation address for their quite lucrative business of selling 'titles' for up to $20,000 apiece to gullible north Americans, who would never have suspected that McCarthy grew up in the Twinbrook estate in west Belfast.

Their elaborate genealogical construct began to fall apart in June of last year when the *Sunday Times* ran a story saying that McCarthy was likely to be 'stripped of his title' following a two-year investigation by the Chief Herald, Brendan O'Donoghue. Four weeks later, it reported that McCarthy's claim to be the chief of his clan was bogus.

O'Donoghue concluded that the 'pedigree' he had supplied to the Chief Herald's office, which was registered in 1980, was 'without genealogical integrity'. Accordingly, his courtesy recognition as MacCarthy MSr, granted in 1992, 'must be regarded as null and void' and an earlier decision to ratify and confirm his arms was 'invalid'.

He's behind you ... Seamus Brennan TD, Chairman of the National Millennium Committee, is set upon by the drag-on from the Aladdin pantomime at yesterday's unveiling of the completed restoration of the façade of the Gaiety Theatre to its former Victorian splendour. Photograph: Bryan O'Brien.

Once the Chief Herald had made that decision, he was subjected to a torrent of abuse from McCarthy's supporters. He even had to call in the Garda to investigate veiled threats against him, posted on the Internet by the 'G2' security branch of the Royal Galloglass, which claimed to be the 'duly sworn bodyguard' of the MacCarthy MSr.

As a former Secretary of the Department of the Environment and one-time member of An Bord Pleanála, O'Donoghue was astonished to find himself drawn into such a venomous circle.

'There were hundreds of messages flying around on genealogical websites (rec.heraldry and alt.talk.royalty), and many of them were highly critical and abusive,' he says.

But the facts could not be gainsaid. Terence McCarthy's father was a dance teacher, his mother a typist and his paternal grandfather a labourer and sometime soldier, who was born in a tenement in Tomb Street, Belfast. There was no evidence of any links to the landed gentry. In fact, many of his ancestors were illiterate labourers. McCarthy's elder brother, Anthony — known as 'Boot' McCarthy — was a member of the INLA. He was shot dead by Dominic McGlinchey in 1987.

'The extraordinary thing is that he gained so much acceptance for so long,' said the Chief Herald. 'But once the letter issued by me became available, even some of his strongest supporters deserted him. Davison's grants of arms have been annulled and we are also reviewing other cases of clan chiefs about whom questions have been raised.'

Tangier is, perhaps, the only place they could have concealed the truth for so long. It is the closest city to Europe that seems really foreign and, probably for that reason, it has long been a mecca for pretenders of every hue. And there are so many snobs among the city's expats that even a self-styled Irish clan chief was more than welcome.

Founded by the Phoenicians around 1100 BC, Tangier has always been a bridgehead between Africa and Europe. Facing north, it lies diagonally across the mouth of the Mediterranean from Gibraltar, to the east of Ceuta, one of that curious pair of Spanish enclaves on the Moroccan coast (the other being more distant Melilla).

In 711 AD, Tangier was the staging post for the Moorish conquest of Spain itself. Much later, it fell into the hands of the Portuguese and, briefly, the British, who blew up its fortifications when they withdrew in 1684. Diarist Samuel Pepys, who enriched himself as the city's treasurer, observed that it was full of 'vice of all sorts'.

SOUTH-EAST : WAIST HIGH

KILDARE, DUBLIN : KNEE DEEP

LIAM LAWLOR : UP TO HIS NECK IN IT......

From 1923 to 1956, when it became part of an independent Morocco, Tangier was run by a consortium of eight European countries, including France. The French made a lasting cultural impression: *Le Monde* still sells out faster than any other foreign newspaper, and French is much more useful than Spanish or English.

The French consulate flies the flag over an elegant villa in its own grounds opposite the busy, chattering Café de Paris on the Place de France. There are even some royalist French cannon on the esplanade of Boulevard Pasteur overlooking the port, and the most reliable — and readily available — transport in town is by Petit Taxi.

It is not uncommon for native Tangerines to speak French almost as fluently as their own version of Arabic and to have a smattering of several other European languages. No doubt this explains why so few of the city's 2,000 expats seem to have bothered learning Arabic, other than some handy phrases with which to address the servants.

The city is bursting at the seams. Officially, its population is one million, but it could be more. The sewerage is dubious, giving off quite an unpleasant whiff even along the beach-front promenade, but the sea still looks invitingly blue. Ferries ply their way to and from the Spanish port of Algeciras, mainly carrying Moroccans lucky enough to have European visas.

The first view of Tangier, in silhouette against the sun, shows a jagged line of modern buildings strung along a crescent-shaped bay. In the immediate foreground is the Casbah, the oldest part of the city, with houses seemingly on top of each other, clinging to the hillside and so dense that it couldn't possibly contain streets. And yet it does.

The ferry terminal is crawling with ecrivains and other hustlers, who pester arriving foreigners — but not so much now as in the past. 'Don't worry, I'm with the tourist office,' one surly-looking man said to me as he offered to do various things, such as find a taxi. When I told him I could fend for myself, he was annoyed.

There is surprisingly little social contact between the expatriate community and indigenous Tangier society. At a glittering party hosted by socialite Anna McHugh, whose present husband is Moroccan, few of the guests ambling about their enchanting multi-layered garden were local people — though, inevitably, all the servants were.

What the expats do know about are things such as Moroccan art, antiques, carpets and the prices of houses in the better parts of Tangier. Living in a ghetto of privilege, under preternaturally blue skies, these blow-ins — many of them unattached, middle-aged men — thrive on gossip about each other and who's doing what and to whom.

'They look at Moroccans to serve them or to f★★★ them,' according to Hisham, a 29-year-old gay Tangerine. Money changes hands.

How could it be otherwise in a city where unemployment is close to 30 per cent, with many young men idling their time in cafés playing draughts, and those seeking to be 'serviced' are wealthy male expats?

It has been going on like this for years. If it wasn't for 'the boys', why would Francis Bacon, Truman Capote or EM Foster have become so attached to Tangier? The ready availability of sex, for a modest outlay of around £10, remains at least as powerful a draw for many expats as the sunny climate and the relatively affordable price of housing.

All of this makes Tangier ripe for a treatment along the lines of *Midnight in the Garden of Good and Evil*, John Berendt's scandalous exposé of high and low life in Savannah, Georgia.

Indeed, Berendt has already been there and is said to be quite intrigued by the prospect — but he is up to his eyes fulfilling a commission to 'do' Venice first.

There was a frisson of excitement earlier this year when it was revealed that Morocco's young king, Mohammed VI — known as 'M6' — had bought the Forbes mansion in Tangier as a guest-house for foreign VIPs while his court is in town.

Cedric the seal with ice on his whiskers at the Irish Seal Sanctuary in Garristown, Co. Dublin. Cedric is one of several three-month-old seals awaiting release following rehabilitation at the centre. Photograph: Frank Miller.

This move by the king, who is single and in his 30s, set a lot of expat tongues wagging.

The white mansion had been the home of Malcolm Forbes, the mega-rich US publishing magnate. His 70th birthday party there was so sensational that Lawrence Mynott, an English-born society columnist-turned-artist, who had been sent to cover it by *Vogue*, couldn't bring himself to go home. Years later, he is still in Tangier.

It was the likes of Forbes and Barbara Hutton, the multiply-married Woolworth's heiress, who put it on the map. Sidi Hosni, Hutton's fabulous house in the Casbah, was the venue for jet-set parties in the 1960s, though there is apparently no truth in the old story that she had the gates of the citadel widened to accommodate her Rolls Royce.

The king's purchase of the Forbes mansion in the leafy Marchan quarter of the city appears to herald a new golden age for Tangier.

Yves St Laurent recently bought a house nearby, as did fellow fashion designer Kenzo. Mick Jagger and Naomi Campbell were also seen in town during last summer, staying in Jagger's favourite house in the Casbah.

Not that the expat community lacks colour. Its current doyenne, Lady Baird, a diminutive Nancy Mitford lookalike, buried her baronet husband in England and then drove all the way to Tangier, at the age of 80, accompanied only by her Norfolk terrier. 'There's terrible poverty here, you know, but what can you do about it?' she says.

On the dusty road to Cape Spartel, site of the

Caves of Hercules, you can see shoeless boys herding sheep and goats outside the white walls of a Saudi palace, with its own mosque just inside the gates. Everyone entering the labyrinthine Casbah is joined by a Pied Piper-like retinue of children offering to act as guides for a dirham or two.

Another remarkable old bird, Doogie Harbach, who has been living in one of the oldest houses outside the Casbah for 30 years, exercises by hanging upside down like a bat in her red leotards from a steel bar suspended across the door of her kitchen. This onerous regime has clearly achieved results; aged 87, she looks 20 years younger.

Also in her 80s is Mercedes Guitta, an Argentinian-Moroccan Jew, who has been living in Tangier since the 1930s. She still runs her own restaurant, Madame Guitta's, a small building in an overgrown garden opposite the Grand Mosque, attended by a faithful old retainer in a red fez. When they go, it's bound to be replaced by an apartment block.

Meanwhile, Madame Guitta satiates Tangier's expats with her Sunday roasts and the best zabaglione this side of Naples. Some of them dine out there every day, exchanging the latest gossip over French onion soup and chicken croquettes. But even they know that this throwback to the 1950s is on its last legs, just like its vieille patronne.

The great sport among expats is to put one over on everyone else by acquiring relics associated with previous expat residents, particularly if they were famous, even if it's just a stick of furniture.

Paintings by Sir John Lavery, who had a house here for many years, are the most sought-after.

It was into this milieu that Terence McCarthy and his boyfriend, Andrew Davison, the son of a deceased RUC constable, inserted themselves in the late-1980s. They were welcomed with open arms. 'We hadn't had proper twisters here for years!' says one excited British expat. Among those taken in by them were Barry Stern, a canny Australian art dealer, and Kathy Jelen, a tempestuous Hungarian countess, both of whom were rewarded with investiture in McCarthy's Order of the Niadh Nask (Golden Chain). Also 'knighted' was a former Portuguese honorary consul, now in jail awaiting trial on drug smuggling charges.

When McCarthy and his boyfriend first arrived in Tangier in 1987, they befriended Stern and even stayed in his renovated house on one of the narrow streets of the Casbah. 'I was their friend for over a decade, but now I feel betrayed,' he says sadly. 'They were never true friends because, effectively, they lied to me from day one.'

Gloria Kirby, a wealthy and charming US resident of Tangier, has known the pair for many years. She is related through marriage to the Grand Duchess Marie of Russia, a frequent visitor, whose claim to the Romanov throne was disputed by McCarthy. It wasn't enough for him to falsify his own family tree; he had to denigrate others.

McCarthy's great coup was that, having had himself recognised (however briefly) as an Irish clan chief, he was able to accumulate a succession of impressive honours and decorations such as the Imperial Ethiopian Order of the Seal of Solomon and Knight Commander of the Royal Italian Order of St Maurice and St Lazarus.

He also bagged other titles: Grand Officer of the Royal Albanian Order of Skanderberg from ex-King Leka I; Knight of Justice of the Sacred Military Constantinian Order of St George of Naples, bestowed by Prince Don Carlos of Bourbon; and Knight of the Royal Portuguese Order of St Michael of the Wing, courtesy of the Duke of Braganza.

In return, he conferred Niadh Nask orders of merit on his benefactors. Among the many who accepted these 'honours' in good faith were Charles Haughey, Albert Reynolds and General William Westmoreland. Such was McCarthy's success in reinventing himself that even Mary Robinson and her husband Nicholas posed for a photograph with him in 1993.

By then, he had ennobled Davison as the Count of Clandermond and conferred the title

Countess of Clandermond on Davison's mother, the RUC constable's widow. She lists herself as a lady-in-waiting to Queen Susan of Albania and as a Dame of Merit of the Military and Hospitaller Order of St Lazarus of Jerusalem, among other baubles.

Davison, who describes himself as 'an author of numerous historical works', has similar foreign decorations as well as fellowships of the Royal Society of Antiquaries of Ireland, the Royal Commonwealth Society and the Winston Churchill Memorial Trust.

Like McCarthy, he is an honorary colonel in the US state of Alabama. In one of his historical works, *Tangier Bookplates*, published by the Co. Antrim-based Black Eagle Press in 1998, he lovingly and sometimes scathingly documents a variety of ex-libris plates commissioned by past and present expatriate residents — such as the Honourable David Herbert, second son of the 16th Earl of Pembroke, who died in 1995.

The news that McCarthy had been 'stripped of his title' spread like wildfire through the expatriate community in Tangier. Some expats were appalled at the exposure of their own gullibility, while others laughed out loud, recalling pompous letters received in the past from the bogus clan chief upbraiding them for not addressing him properly.

They had always been deeply sceptical about McCarthy's and Davison's credentials. Philip Ramey, a US-born composer, had nicknamed them the 'royal blimps', while Johnny Whitworth, another distinguished old boy, is reported to have sniffed: 'I knew they were frauds. I've seen those peasant faces in every village in Ireland.'

There was something deeply unpleasant about discovering that Davison had been sentenced in 1986 at Downpatrick Court to two years in jail after being convicted on six counts of blackmailing gay men in Belfast. It was after he got out of prison that he and McCarthy decided to make a new life for themselves in Tangier.

He hasn't lost everything, however. Though the website has been closed down and the heirlooms he gave to the Cashel Heritage Centre returned, he still has a house in Ann Street, Clonmel, a rented apartment in Tangier, with his coat of arms still on the door, and another house in the hills where he indulges his passion for painting.

When McCarthy sought to deny membership of the Association of Irish Clan Chiefs to one Randal MacDonnell, McDonnell retaliated by carrying out much of the meticulous genealogical research which was to prove conclusively that McCarthy was an outright impostor.

Last September, MacDonnell travelled to Tangier to apprise its most influential expatriates of the full weight of evidence against McCarthy. And though a few snorted that he may have over-played his hand, nobody could deny that the MacCarthy MSr's inquisitor had done his research thoroughly.

The Genealogical Office is now investigating a claim that the true clan chief is a retired accountant in Wiltshire called Barry Trant MacCarthy. However, given its previous mistake in dealing with the incessant pleadings of Terence McCarthy, the Chief Herald said this required considerable further investigation before a decision could be made.

Back in Tangier, young men gather to play draughts and drink cold, milky coffee in the Hafa Café. The Hafa is a dingy place off one of the narrow streets of the Casbah, but what makes it different is that its terrace is perched above the sea, with a tantalising view of the dark coastal mountains of Spain. That's where most of them want to be.

A few of the more colonially-minded expats still refer to the local people in conversation as the Moors, Los Moros. Terence McCarthy would have more sensitivity. Hundreds were duped by his regal charms, including David Wooton, who has since described him as one of the greatest conmen of the century — MacCarthy No MSr.

What drove McCarthy to perpetuate such an elaborate hoax, even to the extent of having his own website on the Internet? In the view of Dublin-based genealogist Seán Murphy, who helped establish the fraud, perhaps McCarthy thought — like Patricia Highsmith's Talented Mr Ripley — that it was better to be a fake somebody than a real nobody.

Filling a Hole Without a Shovel

LockerRoom by Tom Humphries

Think. Think. Think. Sunday afternoon. Take head. Beat head off desk until bleeding occurs. Go to bathroom. Bathe head in cool water. Return to laptop. Still no column on screen.

Sunday afternoon. Have been thinking of subject for a column for best part of a week now. Have decided it will be a fine column. Many ideas have been held up to the light. Many ideas have been rejected.

Sunday afternoon: Meant to drive to Portlaoise to see Na Fianna play today. This involved shifting column out of way early. This week's column is as easy to shift as a grand piano with an elephant in a red cocktail dress disporting herself on its top. Have dispensed with requirement for column to be 'fine'. 'Barely adequate' and 'just the right length' are the qualities I will settle for.

It's almost five o'clock. Haven't even seen the Na Fianna result on the teletext. Am now thinking of writing column about Na Fianna. Should have thought of this on Wednesday, made a phone call, that sort of thing. Bah. Column about teletext?

Realise that all the regular columns have been done to death recently. Davo. Drugs. Michelle. No Income Park. Me. Pledge that in year I will start writing occasional column involving fictional character. Spend hour fantasising about how this fictional character's exploits will fill the fallow weeks. Consider it likely that film rights for this series of fillers will make me very rich. Consider life with a tan. Glance back at screen. Words Fictional Character are all that is written there.

Go to shops and buy Sunday papers. Every journalist with a corner of newspaper space to call his or her own has a fresh and tingly sporty topic to be dealing with. Columns everywhere. Hate and resent them all. Consider lifting somebody else's column and paraphrasing it but haven't the energy even for that. Consider lifting somebody else's column and running it as is. Claim it was a colossal coincidence like that monkey which will eventually type Hamlet if left for eternity banging the keys.

Think. Think. Think. God why can those other columnists all get their danders up at the drop of a hat? My dander is dead.

— Isn't there something which you feel outraged about?
— No.
— Not even the slightest stirring of curmudgeonliness?
— I'm sorry. I don't know what's wrong. This doesn't happen often. I'm not usually like this.
— Don't worry. It happens sometimes.

Think. Think. Think.
Met some drug-testing people on Saturday. Interesting. Interesting. Too soon though. Needs to be tied into something else. Need to round up a few anecdotes. Write a column with a point to it. Resolution: in near future will write a column with a point to it.

Meanwhile back at the ranch.
The All Stars! Yes! Justice for Paddy Christie! What about Mossie McGrane? Write several paragraphs, beginning even to sputter with indignation when Achilles heel starts playing up. Was living in America. Didn't actually see any championship matches, did I? Struck cold by fear that some cold-hearted reader may point this out.

Leaf through Jimmy Magee's autobiography. He has scarcely anything to say on the drugs issue. Just playing to the gallery. Doesn't seem to have

'Love at First Bite' — Mrs Jane Hutchinson reunited with Sambo her singing parrot. Photograph: Niall Marshall/Pacemaker Press.

noticed that Michelle had androstenodione in her sample for instance. Feel like beating him up but recall that not long ago I beat Marian Finucane up over the same thing and then last week I had to stop the car to listen teary-eyed to her interviewing a man whose wife suffered a slow and heartbreaking death in Holles Street and I thought it was the best interview I'd heard on radio in years. And I felt sorry for beating Marian up. Jimmy gets to walk.

Begin writing a few lame pars about Pat Hickey and Jim McDaid. Realise that heart isn't in it. It's December. Nobody cares about the Grinches Who Stole the Olympics.

There's an idea that I like. It's not my own of course. Jimmy Cannon, the great American sports writer of the 1950s used to write occasional columns which began with the line Nobody Asked Me But

… and thereafter there would be a collection of completely unconnected thoughts. Bizarre stuff.

For example: I don't like Boston because all the men look like me. England produces the best fat actors. Never met a meek guy who carries a lucky coin.

Men who eat a lot of candy don't do much boasting.

Decide to try a few lines worth of this myself. Cramped by own lack of originality. Hours later just two lines on screen.

Is a bird in the hand worth two in the bush if you are a vegetarian? Meek guys don't do much boasting. Resolution: will write down witty lines I hear people say and use them all up in column just like Jimmy Cannon's sometime later. Opt late in day for clumsy contrast piece depicting Padraig Harrington as the patron saint of sportingness having been so good about The Belfry people chucking him out and all and then having called that shot on himself at Pebble Beach. Use Tiger Woods' demands for TV revenue as counterpoint. Tiger is the Devil. Write this. Send it off. Read it again. Hate it. Afraid of Tiger Woods' lawyers. Recall all copies of said column due to faulty wiring.

Sunday evening. Five o' clock. It's dark outside. Not a line written. Take head. Bang off table till bleeding profusely. Type cloying apology to readers before passing out. The author is suffering from columnar dysfunction, scribblers droop, dander failure.

So sorry about today's …

8 DECEMBER 2000

Parrot Who Lashes Out The Sash Up Before the Beaks

Frank McNally

Everyone knows why the chicken crossed Garvaghy Road: because his feathers and forefeathers had been crossing it for generations.

But the question of who legally owns a parrot that can sing and whistle The Sash is proving harder to answer, and has now been referred to the beaks in the Belfast Magistrates' Court.

Events came to a head in October 1998 when Sambo, an African grey parrot (with Orange tendencies), escaped from his new home in Belfast. Tensions were running high then after the Belfast Agreement — the Rev Ian Paisley had even called Queen Elizabeth 'a parrot' — but it appears the bird had simply been frightened by fireworks.

When he was found he was given to a vet who had looked after him since. But Sambo is now at the centre of a Drumcree-style impasse involving his original owner and a man who believes he bought him legally. And the RUC is again caught

in the middle.

The court heard yesterday that the trouble began when Sambo's owner at the time, Elizabeth Jamison, moved to Scotland. Once settled, she instructed her solicitor to write to her estranged husband asking for the £800 parrot and his cage, only to be told Sambo was lost. But evidence was given that the bird had instead been sold by Mrs Jamison's husband, Sam, to a Belfast neighbour.

Mr Bret Hutchinson said he bought the parrot for his wife Jane, paying £400, and it was from Mr Hutchinson's home that Sambo fled. Now both Mrs Jamison and the Hutchinsons are applying for the bird's return.

The RUC initially laughed when Mrs Hutchinson reported that the missing parrot could whistle The Sash, but its wildlife liaison officer confirmed in evidence that Sambo was 'quite vocal' and could sing a number of songs, including the Orange standard.

The Resident Magistrate, Ms Sarah Creanor, reserved her decision. 'This is something that does not arise every day, and I would like to check up on the legal position,' she said.

(In January 2001, Ms Creanor ruled that Sambo should be returned to Mrs Hutchinson, subject to her paying £2,300 sterling for board and lodging with the vet who had cared for the bird for two years.)

9 DECEMBER 2000

In Terms of Kindness, Rich Ireland's Budget Is Poor

Fintan O'Toole

The morning after the Budget, the Taoiseach reminded listeners to 'Morning Ireland' that it was the first to be based on the fact that Ireland, in terms of wealth, was now an average European Union society.

With a projected surplus of over £6 billion to play with, it seems reasonable to expect that Ireland can attain European levels of social equity. When all the hoopla has died down, the simple fact will be that Charlie McCreevy made a deliberate decision not to attain such levels.

A few days before the Budget, the EU's statistics service, Eurostat, issued a report comparing expenditure across the EU on what it calls 'social protection' (welfare and anti-poverty measures).

Right at the bottom is Ireland. Sweden spends twice as much on creating a just society as we do. While countries like Sweden, Denmark and Germany spend around 30 per cent of Gross Domestic Product on social protection, and the EU average is 28 per cent, Ireland spends just 16 per cent. The next-worst performer, Spain, is still far above us at 22 per cent.

Even taking into account demographic factors and the inflated nature of our GDP, the picture is stark. We may have reached average EU levels of wealth, but we are far above average in terms of meanness, injustice and the ability to turn away from misery. The basic message of the Budget, in spite of a few gestures of social solidarity, is that this situation is just fine.

Ireland is more unequal and has higher poverty rates than comparable EU countries. The poorest fifth of Irish households gets just 5 per cent of national income. The richest fifth gets 44 per cent. The haves earn five times as much as the have-nots.

On a broader canvas, the bottom 60 per cent of households gets just a third of national disposable income, while the top 40 per cent gets the other two-thirds. This year's UN Human Development Report ranks Ireland 17th of 18 industrialised countries on its poverty index. Every other major European country does better.

A quarter of children and a fifth of adults live below the poverty line. And the gap between those in poverty and the rest of society has been growing ever wider, not least because social welfare rates have fallen from 48 per cent of average income in 1991 to 38 per cent in 1999. Yet again this week, in spite of having the resources to lift everyone out of poverty, the Government has chosen to spend the money in other ways.

The generally accepted poverty line for a single person (50 per cent of average income) is £92 a week this year and, for 2001, around £100 a week. Yet many of the key social welfare payments, even after April 2001, will be much less than £100. Payments like disability benefit, unemployment assistance, invalidity pensions, carers' allowance and the blind person's pension will all remain around £15 short of the poverty line.

So while, in percentage terms, the increases in social welfare may seem generous, they need to be put in perspective. The increase of £8 a week for most social welfare recipients is about what a TD (or a journalist) would expect to leave as a tip in a restaurant after a nice dinner. And that's essentially what it is, a nice little tip.

In the overall scheme of things, the £384 million extra that the Exchequer will spend on social welfare in 2001 is perhaps a third of what the State will save multinational telecom companies by not auctioning off third-generation mobile-phone licences, and over £200 million less than the National Roads Authority is getting.

Even the most socially progressive measure in the Budget, the increases in child benefit which go beyond what was sought by the Child Poverty Initiative, has to be seen in context. The basic cost of rearing a child in Ireland is at least £36.50 a week. The new, vastly improved rate provides about £17 of this.

Even with the child dependant allowance that is added to social welfare payments, this still leaves a situation in which the State is consciously and deliberately leaving children with less than the basic income they need to grow up with dignity.

The top level of child benefit, besides, is still £14 short of the £100-a-month level to which the Government committed itself in the PPF. In his Budget speech, Charlie McCreevy got over this problem by announcing that this year's increase is part of a 'three-year programme'. Given the likelihood that the current Government will not introduce another Budget, and the certainty that it will introduce no more than one more, this is almost meaningless.

The sense of priorities that underlies all of this emerges from a few simple comparisons. The Government is spending £30 million on abolishing probate tax; £140 million on capital allowances for cars used in business; and £350 million on reductions in VAT and excise duty on diesel. These three benefits to well-off people cost £520 million.

By contrast, £28 million extra for services to people with intellectual disabilities; £15 million extra to tackle the drugs problem in deprived communities and £13.5 million extra for hospital cancer services amount to £56.5 million — not much more than a tenth of what is being spent on reliefs for the well-to-do.

In the past, it might have been possible to argue that poverty was a sad inevitability which the Government would end if it could. Now we know the truth. The Government could have done it but chose not to.

9 DECEMBER 2000

A Babe Whose Name Will Be Linked Forever With Pigs

The Saturday Profile by Rosita Boland

Ned O'Keeffe landed himself rightly in the muck this week, or would that be in the muc? The Minister of State in the Department of Agriculture, Food and Rural Development, with special responsibility for Food, was reminded all week of that special responsibility for food.

In May 1998, O'Keeffe stated: 'The farmer is more and more aware every day of safety and quality. There is no one more conscious of that now than the farming community.' Two years on, it could be argued that the public is now very well-informed, and just as aware of potential dangers within the food chain, and as conscious of the need for food safety as those people who produce food.

On Tuesday's 'Morning Ireland', Richard Downes conducted a Myles na gCopaleen-type interview with O'Keeffe, finally asking him the question, 'So, as Junior Minster, you don't have a problem with pigs eating pigs?' At that point, the breakfasting nation probably abandoned what remained of their rashers and sausages.

Ned O'Keeffe, the Fianna Fáil TD for Cork East, like many TDs, has concerns beyond the Dáil. O'Keeffe has a farm in the Golden Vale, near Mitchelstown, aproximately 200 acres in size. As the jolly children's song about venerable farmer Old MacDonald goes, 'And on that farm he had … some pigs!'

These particular pigs have been the source of much discussion this week. This is because the O'Keeffe porkies have been, ahem, pigging-out on feed featuring meat-and-bone-meal — meal which has been linked to the cause of BSE (Bovine Spongiform Encephalopathy). The O'Keeffe piggery is one of the largest in the State, capable of producing some 50,000 animals a year. It is also one of 17 piggeries with a special licence to use this meal.

So, unappetising as it may sound to those of us who used to enjoy the odd fried breakfast, it's not illegal for pigs to be fattening themselves up on their fellow trottered ones. These little piggies will still be going to market. However, once the news broke of the porcine menu down Mitchelstown way, there were calls for O'Keeffe's resignation.

There were two issues in particular which exercised his Dáil colleagues. One was the fact that the Department of Agriculture, for which Ned O'Keeffe works, lists the promotion of food safety as one of its objectives. Since 1997, the use of this meat and bone meal in animal feed has been effectively

Babe … 'I believe that there is a case to be made whereby Irish people should boycott this ridiculous and harmful film and enjoy their ham at Christmas.'

banned for all creatures — except pigs. Some creatures, as George Orwell famously reminded us in *Animal Farm*, are more equal than others.

The other issue was the fact that O'Keeffe was accused of breaching the Ethics in Public Office Act by not declaring his interest in the family pig farm. Only last week, before the pig-droppings hit the fan, he had voted against a total ban on the feeding of this meat and bone meal to all animals.

When repeatedly pressed this week on 'Morning Ireland' about whether his family pig farm and his stance in the Dáil represented a conflict of interest, O'Keeffe admitted to no such thing. One has to wonder if the words 'pig-headed' were going through interviewer Richard Downes's mind at the time.

This was not the first time that Ned O'Keeffe and the curly-tailed ones have been in the news. In 1995, he got terribly het up about a hugely popular movie called 'Babe', which featured a cute little talking pig. (We're not sure what Babe's diet at the time included to produce this special verbal characteristic.)

There were reports that pork consumption in the US had dropped since the movie's release. The Americans, you see, didn't want to have their movie and eat it. Incidentally, the many pigs who acted in 'Babe' were butchered not long after the cameras stopped rolling.

Without having seen the film, Ned issued a press release that caused almost as much merriment among punters as the film itself. The news of the drop in pork products in the US was, he stated, 'very worrying and of considerable concern to the pork industry and pig farmers of Ireland ... I believe that there is a case to be made whereby Irish people should boycott this ridiculous and harmful film and enjoy their ham at Christmas.'

For quite some time afterwards, Ned O'Keeffe was known to his colleagues as 'Babe'. Many punters will know that the word babe also translates into something roughly meaning 'grand young lassie'. The other thing which the public will recall in the babe line of things is the Twink incident, which enlivened the Fine Gael Ardfheis in 1991.

In May of that year, O'Keeffe apologised to Una Claffey, then political correspondent with RTÉ. He was reported to have had an altercation with her in the Dáil bar. Unsurprisingly, this caused considerable embarrassment both for O'Keeffe and his party colleagues.

The opposition did as oppositions do — they made whoppee with the story. The FG Ardfheis later that year featured Twink in a sketch which included several decidedly coarse references to the incident. The whole thing was televised, and uproar ensued, bringing Ned's name before us once more. Twink, as we know, is particularly at home in pantomime. Many think it was her finest performance.

It is the fate of some politicians to be eternally welded to particular events. Years might pass, and yet the same stories get trotted out on their little hooves to remind the public of the past events that once entertained us so richly. With Ned 'Babe' O'Keeffe, it seems he will be forever linked to pigs.

RTÉ has just announced the details of its Christmas schedule. The big Christmas Day movie? Yes, it's 'Babe'. Will the television be on in the O'Keeffe household that afternoon? Having eaten his Christmas ham, will Ned then eat his words?

You never know. As the saying goes, pigs might fly.

14 DECEMBER 2000

Bush's Transition Honeymoon May Be Cut

Joe Carroll

'Bringing America Together' and 'I'm a uniter, not a divider' were the slogans George Bush campaigned on, but putting them into practice is going to be his biggest challenge.

The five weeks since election night when Vice-President Al Gore first conceded victory in a phone call, and withdrew it 30 minutes later to wait for a recount in Florida, have revealed strains in the body politic.

Now that Mr Bush appears certain to become president thanks to an extraordinary set of opinions from the US Supreme Court which have brought out its own partisan make-up, the Democrats inevitably believe Vice-President Al Gore 'wuz robbed'.

Mr Bush will be the first US President since 1888 to be elected without winning the popular vote. And Mr Bush is poised to win the electoral college by the narrowest margin of one vote.

It is customary for new presidents to be given a honeymoon period to allow them propose their budget and to enact executive orders setting the tone of the new administration.

If George Bush is seen as getting to the White House only by preventing a full count of the votes in Florida it will be difficult for the Democrats to afford him the traditional honeymoon. Already, Rev Jesse Jackson is denouncing the Supreme

Soloists Charlie Bowder and Darragh Ware during rehearsals in St Patrick's Cathedral. Photograph: David Sleator.

Court as a 'willing tool of the Bush campaign' that has 'orchestrated a questionable velvet coup'.

The 'legitimacy' of a Bush presidency will be challenged by some and already efforts are being made by the media and public interest bodies to have access to the uncounted ballots in Florida. The Supreme Court majority in effect said there should be a recount but that it was too late to do it properly. That will be seen as a challenge by those who are convinced Mr Gore was the real winner in Florida and thus of the presidency.

The first reaction for most Americans will be one of relief that this bruising period has ended. Whether they will be satisfied with the way the Supreme Court has ended this wait is not so certain. Three of the judges have said: 'Although we may never know with complete certainty the identity of the winner of this year's presidential election, the identity of the loser is perfectly clear. It is the nation's confidence in the judge as an impartial guardian of the rule of law.'

There will be a widespread feeling now that the winner should be given time to catch up on his transition arrangements. There will also be fervent hopes that nothing else can go wrong between now and inauguration day on 20 January. Next Monday, the electoral college votes for president as laid down in the constitution.

Mr Bush, with Florida under his belt, should get 271 votes, one more than the required majority. But if just two of the 538 members of the college turns out to be a 'faithless elector' and switches to Gore, what then?

No one wants to think about it. But this would

throw the mess into the new Congress which meets on 6 January to count the electoral votes and declare the winner. The electoral votes can be challenged in the Senate and the House of Representatives.

If the electoral wrangles have been smoothed out by 20 January and President Bush and Vice-President Dick Cheney are sworn in, what can America and the world expect from the first Republican administration since George Bush Snr left the White House eight years before?

It will be the first time since the Eisenhower years of the 1950s that the Republicans will control the White House and the two Houses of Congress, although in the Senate they will depend on the tie-breaker vote of Mr Cheney as presiding officer. It will take Americans and especially Democrats some time to come to terms with that situation.

By inauguration day the new president will have selected his cabinet and senior White House staff and be hoping that the Senate will approve his choices. Mr Bush will try to win over Democrats by appointing some of them to senior posts even if it annoys his own conservative wing. Feelers have already been put out to Democratic Senator John Breaux of Louisiana who would be a key figure in any future reform of social security.

At this stage the only name sure of a cabinet post is former Gen Colin Powell for Secretary of State. He had long been touted as a senior member of the Bush cabinet but his African-American credentials did nothing to help Bush with this constituency, which turned out in huge numbers to try to ensure his defeat.

Other names from his father's presidency who will serve the son include Cheney, of course, and Condoleeza Rice, the foreign affairs expert who will be Bush's National Security Adviser.

Bush will not have the personal involvement in Northern Ireland of Bill Clinton and he knows far less about it than Al Gore. Sinn Féin, the UUP and other Northern Ireland politicians will have to come to terms with a White House where the door will not be as open to appeals for help.

The so-called 'Texas Gang', the kitchen cabinet of advisers who have been running the Bush campaign from Austin for almost three years, are all assured of jobs. These include his close friend, Don Evans, the oil-man who served as campaign chairman; Karl Rove, the chief strategist; Joe Allbaugh, the campaign manager; Karen Hughes, the head of communications.

On the legislative front, Bush would like to have the first phase of his ambitious tax cut proposal taken on board by Congress but because of his shaky victory, he will have to scale it back and seek accommodation with the Democrats. He should be able to find a compromise with Democrats on education reforms which he and Gore campaigned on.

In foreign and security policy, Bush will be anxious to show that he will be more decisive than Bill Clinton. Bush will probably decide fairly soon to go ahead with a missile defence system which breaches the ABM treaty with Russia but which he claims he can renegotiate successfully.

On the Middle East, Bush will want to show he has good standing in the Arab world where his father built a coalition to oppose Saddam Hussein. How he deals with the shifting political scene in Israel could be his first big test on the world scene.

28 DECEMBER 2000

Gardaí Step Up Searches For Missing Persons

Clare Murphy

Searches are continuing for a number of people missing from their homes.

The family of Trevor Deely (22) plan to continue their poster campaign around Dublin city following his disappearance in the early hours of 8 December from the Baggot Street area.

Garda have also appealed for assistance in tracing Ms Dolores Doyle who went missing from

Family and friends distributing posters calling for information as to the whereabouts of Trevor Deely, missing since 7 December. Photograph: Eric Luke.

Dublin city centre on 23 December. The 20-year-old from Sallynoggin was last seen on Harcourt Street at 3 a.m. Ms Doyle is described as five feet, three inches, with shoulder-length black hair and brown eyes. She was wearing a white top, a black-and-gold skirt and black knee-high boots. Anyone with information is asked to contact gardaí at Kill of the Grange on (01) 666 5500. Searches will also continue for Mr Declan Mooney (31) missing from Kilcormac, Co. Offaly, and Mr Padraig Crudden (23), last seen on Christmas Eve in Cork city.

Mr Mooney is five feet, 10 inches, of thin build with short brown hair and a sallow complexion. The search is being coordinated by gardaí at Birr on 0509-20016. Mr Crudden is five feet, 10 inches, 12 stone, medium build, with shoulder-length brown hair. He was wearing a brown duffel coat.

Gardaí in Ballina, Co. Mayo, are still seeking assistance in tracing Ms Sandra Collins (28), who has been missing since 4 December. She is five feet, of slim build with short brown hair with red highlights. She was wearing black trousers and a maroon polo-neck jumper under a beige sleeveless fleece. Anyone with information should contact gardaí in Ballina on 096-21422.

Letters to the Editor December 2000

Deregulation of Taxi Service

Sir, — I write as the wife of a Dublin taxi driver, until now an unheard voice. I wish to present the human side of the man behind the wheel, a view which has been lost amid the mêlée.

My husband has worked as a taxi driver, serving the needs of the public, for the past 12 years and for six of those we have been married. Our life has been almost entirely based on our commitments, financial, physical and emotional, to my husband's taxi-driving business.

It is true we have enjoyed a relatively good material lifestyle, with a few luxuries here and there, but the benefits have not justified the price. We are ships passing in the night. My husband works an average of 14 hours a day over a nine-night fortnight, and as I work nine to five daily, there are times when I do not see him for several days. When he does take time off, he is too exhausted, both mentally and physically, to do much except try to recover from the previous 98-hour week.

I dread the telephone call which might come in the night to say that he has been attacked or involved in an accident with a drunken driver or a stolen car. I cannot count the number of times when he has come home and regaled me with accounts of terrifying situations after he stopped for the 'wrong' people. He has been threatened with syringes and physically and verbally abused. His car has been kicked and banged, not to mention the numerous 'results' of too much drink, all of this from some of those members of the public who are so bitterly complaining about the guy who just wants to take them home and earn his living.

My husband is a hard-working, courteous, intelligent gentleman who is trying to go about his work in the best manner possible in order to pay back the money he borrowed to buy into his job. He is prepared to put up with the hassle of the traffic, the seamier side of Dublin at night and the abuse he gets, with the associated threat of violence, in order to get on and meet his commitments. There are also, of course, upsides to his job, when he gets the nice guy in his taxi who shares a joke, the child who prompts a smile with an innocent remark, or the person who just treats him as what he is, an intelligent human being.

So please remember, the next time you sit in a taxi, the driver is somebody's husband, father or son. Don't threaten him, refuse to pay, abuse him or generally treat him as just another 'scumbag' taxi driver. He just wants to do his job and get home in one piece at the end of his shift, as do all the other workers in this world whose jobs are considered dangerous and unsociable.

Friends often remark that, metaphorically speaking, I am a taxi widow; I just hope it remains a metaphor. — Yours etc., Wendy O'Brien, Blackrock, Co. Dublin. 5 December 2000.

Sir, — Those who paid dearly to buy their way into the taxi business, believing a licence represented some kind a secure capital asset, were mistaken. Those who assumed a regime of industry regulation would persist for the lifetime of their investment took a gamble. And those taxi drivers who expect compassion and support from the public after their actions over the past week merely demonstrate how irrelevant are customers' needs and perceptions to the taxi drivers' decision-making process.

There can be no question that the blockade was aimed at inflicting massive public disruption. At the airport, my wife, who is eight months pregnant, had to transport both herself and her luggage a considerable distance as a consequence of the taxi drivers' illegal action. The fact that this exercise was largely directed at their primary business channel — the general public — only makes their action more despicable. While Wendy O'Brien (5 December) presented a compelling argument for compassion for taxi drivers and their families, what can she expect after the taxi drivers' treatment of the public last week? What did their customers do to deserve such treatment?

Taxi drivers have the right to protest. They have the right to withdraw their services for as long they wish. However, they have no right to use physical obstruction and intimidation to prevent other law-abiding people going about their business. I hope gardaí do not hesitate to take whatever measures are necessary to foil any attempts to repeat last week's events. — Yours, etc., Loman Brophy, Dunshaughlin, Co. Meath. 7 December 2000.

Marriage In Mind ... recently engaged couple Joanne O'Donnell and Dermot Harold both from Ballybofey, Co. Donegal, express their feelings on the new Bachelors Walk, Liffey Boardwalk, officially opened by the Lord Mayor in Dublin. Photograph: Matt Kavanagh.

Celia Larkin

Sir, — It was with surprise and disappointment I watched Celia Larkin in a prominent position during the Clinton visit. I ask: what is her role or function? She is not the Taoiseach's wife so, to me, she has no role or function at such events.

I call on the Taoiseach to give us the lead in upholding the values that have always been an integral part of our Irish nation. — Yours, etc.,
Eilish Sheridan, Cabinteely, Dublin 18.
21 December 2000.

2 JANUARY 2001

Enniskillen Bomb Victim Is Laid To Rest After 13 Years

Suzanne Breen

Thirteen years after slipping into a coma following the Enniskillen bomb, Ronnie Hill was laid to rest on a cold afternoon in Kilkeel, Co. Down.

Mourners lined the streets last Saturday as his coffin was carried through the town for a service at Mourne Presbyterian Church where he had married his wife, Noreen.

Mr Hill (69), the principal of Enniskillen High School, fell into a coma two days after the Provisional IRA's Remembrance Day bombing in which 11 people died.

After her husband had been in the Erne Hospital for four years, Mrs Hill set up her own residential nursing home in Holywood, Co. Down, to take care of Ronnie and others. She was holding his hand when he died on Thursday.

Their children, Siobhan, Averill, Marilyn and Keith, were among the mourners. Also present was the South Belfast Ulster Unionist MP, the Rev Martin Smyth.

The service was conducted by the former Presbyterian moderator, Dr David McCaughey. The current Presbyterian Moderator, Dr Trevor Morrow, and the Church of Ireland Bishop of Clogher, the Rev Brian Hannon, also took part.

Dr Hannon, a former rector in Enniskillen, recalled that on the day of the bomb Mr Hill, a Presbyterian elder, had been taking a Bible class for teenagers. 'As usual on that Sunday, the class got out early and Ronnie joined them at the war memorial. The bomb went off and Ronnie was among those rescued from the rubble still with a chance of life.' However, Dr Hannon said, his condition deteriorated.

He paid tribute to all who had cared for Mr Hill. 'It is to these wonderful people's credit that in the 13 years of Ronnie's trauma he never once suffered from a bedsore. That to me is quite astonishing.'

Dr Hannon said Mr Hill had 'loved life and had an extraordinary will to live'. He praised Mrs Hill's response to the bomb. 'Noreen was convinced that at times Ronnie was aware of what was going on around him and over the years she sat with him for countless hours, talked to him, read the Bible and prayed with him.

'I found no evidence of bitterness but rather of prayer for the perpetrators and of the good that comes out of evil.'

He recalled Mr Hill's response when a pupil asked what three things he would take if marooned on an island. He had replied: 'I would take the Bible because it contains all the knowledge that you need to know; the book *Robinson Crusoe* because he has been there before, and my wife because I couldn't live without her.'

Dr McCaughey said the Hills must remain strong and the church had also to be courageous in condemning evil.

Mr Hill was buried in the cemetery adjoining the church.

2 JANUARY 2001

Enniskillen's Last Victim

Suzanne Breen

Ronnie Hill grew up in Bray, Co. Wicklow, and studied at St Andrew's College where he captained the cricket team. He moved to the North to teach at Mourne Grange in Kilkeel, Co. Down.

He met his wife, Noreen, at a Presbyterian Church social evening there in 1953. They married three years later and moved to Edinburgh to train as missionary teachers.

They worked at Calibar in eastern Nigeria and in Freetown in Sierra Leone. They returned to the North in the mid-1960s. Mr Hill taught at a variety of schools before becoming principal of Enniskillen High School.

Bishop Brian Hannon said of him: 'I saw a careful administrator, a sportsman and a family man who cared deeply about the boys and girls for whom he was responsible. He wanted every one of them to develop their full potential.

'He shared with them his love of books, of chess, of table tennis, of football and, of course, of people. He was competitive, forward-looking and courageous whether it was in launching into cross-community and cross-Border links or into information technology.'

Mr Hill's wife was not with her husband at the Remembrance Day service in November 1987 because she was recovering from chemotherapy treatment for cancer.

When the bomb exploded, a wall fell on top of him and rescuers spotted his gloved hand through the rubble. He suffered a fractured skull, jaw, pelvis and shoulder but his injuries did not appear critical.

When he lapsed into a coma two days later, his family thought it was temporary. When his wife set up her own nursing home, she filled his room with his favourite photographs and paintings. She would tell him about the progress of his six grandchildren whom he never saw.

Speaking three years ago on the 10th anniversary of the bomb, she said: 'People say he is in a vegetative state but to us he is a person. The girls talk to him as a father. I see him as my husband. His grandchildren see him as their grandfather.'

Mrs Hill has said she prays daily for Mr Gerry Adams and Mr Martin McGuinness. She has urged those bereaved in the Omagh bomb not to be bitter.

6 JANUARY 2001

Witnessing the Death of the Irish Mammy

Breda O'Brien

My much-loved mother-in law, Pat Conroy, died in her own bed on New Year's Eve. She was surrounded by her husband, six children and their spouses and boyfriends, and by her grandchildren, including two babies not yet a year old.

At her funeral, Father Ruairí Ó Domhnaill referred to her with affection and respect as a typical Irish mammy. The stories which he told about her evoked loving laughter and recognition, not just from her own family, but from many of the congregation who recognised elements of their own mothers' lives.

Just like my own mother, who is also dead, her family was the core of Pat's life. Both their lives rippled out to touch hundreds of people beyond the family circle. At her funeral a sombre thought crossed my mind. As that generation passes away, we may be witnessing not just their deaths, but the death of that style of mothering, the death of the Irish mammy.

No doubt such a change pleases some. I have no desire to sentimentalise or idealise the lives of earlier generations. In many ways, their roles were taxing of both body and soul. The far greater array of options open to younger women represents progress to a large degree.

Yet it is surely worthy of discussion that full-time child-rearing, which used to be the central and defining role of women, is now likely to become the exception rather than the norm. Such seismic changes cannot take place without repercussions for everyone.

The central thing about both my mother and my husband's mother was not that they did not work outside the home after marriage. Much more important was a set of expectations and beliefs which shaped all their actions.

They considered the ability to make sacrifices, particularly for their children, to be a badge of adulthood. They took the idea of passing on virtues and values to their children very seriously, and their greatest sorrows stemmed from the times when they felt they had failed in that task.

Some readers may already be seething at the implied suggestion that all mothers of that generation were like that, or mothers of this generation do not share those concerns. I am not suggesting for a moment that mothers today do not love their children just as much as their mothers loved them, or that everything which our mothers did was perfect. Some of the changes which have come about in child-rearing are extremely positive.

Fine Gael's Jim Mitchell TD speaking on his mobile phone, at Leinster House before the resumption of the Dáil. Photograph: Eric Luke.

No, the central point which I am trying to make is that an earlier generation of mothers had support from society for the idea that mothering was a vital role and that a huge amount of time was needed to do the job properly.

Whereas once working outside the home as a mother was frowned upon, which, of course, was very unfair to many women, nowadays there is an unspoken assumption that paid work outside the home is almost always more valuable.

Again it is important not to sentimentalise or idealise. Many elements of child-rearing are repetitive and boring. However, we almost never hear now about how rewarding it is to be the centre of a child's world and to fill a role no one else can.

Another group of readers may be enraged by the complete absence of fathers from what I am writing. It may reassure them that while I have never been a fulltime mother, my husband has been a stay-at-home father for years. I believe that fathers are central and vital to a child's happiness, and that the best situation for a child is to have a mother and father who are committed to each other and to the interests of their children.

Which means that I have also probably offended yet another group of readers, those whose lives do not match that description, but, of course, I accept that they love their children just as passionately.

If such readers could accept that I have no desire to offend or condescend, perhaps we could look at something on which almost everyone agrees. If roles within society are changing in fundamental ways, how do we ensure that the needs of children are given top priority?

Developmental psychology shows that children have huge needs for stability and time from key

Swimmers in fancy dress are engulfed by a large wave, while taking part in the Bray Charities Sea Swim, in aid of The Bray Cancer Support Group and the Carers in the Home Fund. Photograph: Eric Luke.

adults, preferably parents. This is particularly true of children under three, but parents will point out that in some ways the needs of teenagers are even more acute than those of toddlers. How then do we reconcile the fact of these needs with the reality that the one thing which parents have less and less of is time?

This is the key question. If being a mammy in the style of our mothers is becoming more and more rare, with what are we replacing all that time and dedication? With poorly paid temporary labour? With material things bought by guilt-ridden parents?

Charlie McCreevy attended my mother-in-law's funeral. She was a constituent of his, and they were long-time sparring partners who were on opposite sides on many issues. Through those battles, a respect for each other evolved, as well matched adversaries often do.

Pat's family appreciated some acts of kindness which Charlie did for her, including one particular conversation he may not even remember. Pat had told him that she was hanging up her sword, that she had the energy for no more battles. Charlie told her in robust terms to forget about hanging up her sword, that she had plenty still to give. That conversation meant a lot to her.

The sad reality was that as cancer sapped her more and more, campaigning became impossible or else she would have fought Charlie on individualisation with the same tenacity with which she fought on other issues which she saw as undermining family life.

We need a vision of family and of work which puts children first. Despite some shameful failures in Irish family life of the past, the majority of people still grew up in situations where parents did their best and usually succeeded well in child-rearing, not least because society supported the role of mothers. Today, neither mothers nor fathers have that support. In that context, the death of the Irish mammy is even more serious.

Fiery Figure at Centre of the Teachers' Dispute

Emmet Oliver

On 14 December about 300 slightly chilly exam students arrived outside the Dáil to protest at the continuing teachers' pay dispute. There were no politicans there to meet them, few reporters and no parents.

Apart from a few gardaí, the only person there to greet them was Ms Bernadine O'Sullivan.

Fitted out in ASTI placards, the teacher — originally from Rossnowlagh, Co. Donegal — warmly welcomed the somewhat bemused pupils and said she was glad to see them taking such a deep interest in the dispute.

She clapped them warmly on the back one by one, but the students appeared to be clueless about who she was. They eventually continued their march up Kildare Street. One remarked, 'Who's she?' and his friend replied, 'I haven't got a clue.'

The students were unaware they were talking to arguably the most crucial personality in the ASTI's pay campaign. The woman whose impassioned stance as ASTI president lit the touch-paper for the current dispute.

A week earlier she was on the same spot, this time wooing more than 10,000 ASTI members from the side of a lorry.

In a speech which even her opponents admitted was oratory at its finest, she castigated TDs and senators for looking for a generous pay rise for themselves and at the same time not backing the ASTI's 30 per cent claim.

'What's good for the goose is good for the gander,' she roared. The crowd screamed back their approval and another vintage Bernadine performance was chalked up. Some of the other ASTI leaders shifted uncomfortably in their seats. And well they might.

While she is no longer at the head of the union, Ms O'Sullivan remains a type of moral leader for the union's 16,000 members. Nominally, she occupies a middle ranking position as a member of the ASTI standing committee, but her real role is much more fundamental.

With her fiery speeches and unbending defence of the profession, she has become for many ASTI members an unsullied emblematic figure who stands firmly on the principle that teachers' pay has to be improved urgently or the profession will wither away.

Speaking at the weekend meeting, her almost evangelical belief in the teachers' cause was clear. Speaking to reporters, she said the ASTI dispute was not simply a pay campaign, but a 'crusade'. It was about the whole future of education and teaching.

Ms O'Sullivan, months after stepping down, remains the most crucial figure in the union. She inspires loyalty and dislike in equal measure. But at the moment large swathes of the ASTI regard her as a sort of moral compass guiding them through the various choices which have to be made in the dispute.

They admire her steadfast views and believe she will not lead them astray. Other leading figures in the union, because their job involves negotiating the nitty-gritty details of a resolution with the Government, tend to appear slightly more compromised figures in the eyes of some members.

Ms O'Sullivan did not support the weekend deal, whereas the general secretary, Mr Charlie Lennon, publicly backed it. Throughout this dispute Ms O'Sullivan's views have been crucial in the outcome of votes at the ASTI's standing committee.

Before Christmas she supported pulling out of the talks because the Government docked the pay of teachers for their work-to-rule.

As she has pointed out in this newspaper before, the ASTI's members are 'seasoned forty-somethings and fifty-somethings' who make their own decisions. This is true, but like everyone they make up their minds based on the information available and by listening to their peers and colleagues and Ms O'Sullivan's views carry serious weight in the organisation at the moment.

If this dispute is to be brought to an end, Government representatives are going to have to table something which will satisfy her and those who use her as a guiding light.

Ms O'Sullivan — to the dismay of senior civil servants — has poured scorn on their idea for fixing the ASTI dispute: benchmarking.

Ms Bernadine O'Sullivan, Past President of the ASTI, and Mr Vincent McCarvill, teacher at St Macartans College, Monaghan, speaking after an ASTI delegate meeting in Dublin. Photograph: Alan Betson.

As president of the union, she told its annual conference last April this concept (which involves comparing public and private sector pay) was too vague and would not be suitable for processing the 30 per cent claim.

At the union's rally in Kildare Street she warned that teachers would not be railroaded into a 'dressed up' form of benchmarking.

In the days preceding that civil servants and the ASTI appeared to be doing just that — setting up a negotiating forum for teachers allied in some way to the benchmarking body.

After her denouncement of this approach officials scurried off again and tried to tweak their plans for a teachers' forum so it was more (if not completely) independent of the benchmarking body.

Ms O'Sullivan does not see herself as blocking the way to a solution, but says a pay rise is the only real way to resolve the logjam or else teaching could become a second grade profession.

10 JANUARY 2001

Element of Blind Date in 1,000 km Elephant Ride

Gillian Ní Cheallaigh

Caroline Casey is about to embark on a 1,000 km trip across the south of India on the back of an elephant. But her biggest concern is how she's going to get on with her elephant, Bhadra.

Caroline Casey, the 29-year-old founder of the 'Aisling Project Indian Challenge' pictured at Dublin Airport as she prepared to depart her native Ireland for India and the journey of a lifetime. Photograph: Mac Innes.

'We'll be spending three months together. It's a bit like a blind date,' she said yesterday as she prepared to leave Dublin Airport.

Caroline, whose visual impairment means she is legally blind, will travel from 5 a.m. to 12 p.m. every day, then camp in tents with no shower, or toilet facilities. 'Showering is not really going to happen. I'll shower when the elephant bathes. I'm not even allowed to use toilet paper for environmental reasons.'

Bidding farewell to her family, friends and supporters at Dublin Airport yesterday, she said she was 'really excited'.

'It's hard to believe this day has finally arrived. This has been my dream for over a year now and to be an aeroplane journey away from it is incredible.'

After one and a half hour's sleep last night, she 'woke up this morning and thought: we did it. I'm really proud of everybody involved. I'm completely exhausted, this is the most challenging, draining thing I've ever done, but I've never got such a buzz from anything in my life.'

She admitted, though, to being 'nervous about being on my own' as no one is accompanying her to India. She will have two mahouts (elephant handlers) and two Indian guides with her, who she'll meet just two days before they set out.

Caroline, a management consultant with Accenture (formerly Andersen Consulting), founded the Aisling Project Indian Challenge six months ago to raise £250,000 for SightSavers International, the National Council for the Blind and the Protection of the Asian Elephant. Some £130,000 has been raised so far, and fundraising events will continue while she is away to raise the remaining £120,000.

The trip is also 'a way to capture public imagination to promote a positive image of disability, to stop telling people what they can't do. If I have a dream, I can achieve it, even if I have to do it back to front.'

Caroline and Bhadra will have a month in Delhi before the trek to develop a bond, which is crucial to success. She will learn to bathe, feed and ride the elephant to encourage trust and an understanding of her visual disability. She has opted to ride bareback, declining the generally-used howdah, because bareback is the tradition in the region.

Along the way Caroline and Bhadra will visit SightSavers Projects, hospitals and elephant care projects. A documentary of the odyssey is being made, for sale later, and a video featuring endorsements from patrons such as Andrea Corr and Christy Moore, will arrive in Irish schools later this month.

Day of the Untouchables Heads into Twilight

Paul Cullen

So who now will dare to follow in the steps of Mr Liam Lawlor and cock a snook at the Flood tribunal? What arrogant politician, secretive lawyer or large-pocketed builder will dare to defy, prevaricate, lie, flee or otherwise subvert the inquiry set up to get to the bottom of corruption in Irish society?

Yesterday's ruling was the answer for all those who legitimately asked: 'But will anyone go to jail for it?' Seven days in Mountjoy mightn't seem all that much, but it is a start, unprecedented and historic for all its brevity.

The decision to put a leading politician behind bars has breached a new frontier. 'No one is above the law … there are no untouchables,' said Mr Justice Smyth in a ringing declaration that served to remind us that Ireland has been full of untouchables up to now.

In Leinster House, in county council chambers, in solicitors' and accountants' offices, the realisation must be sinking in that defying the tribunal is no longer an option. The long arm of the law has found new ways of punishment, and a failure to co-operate can prove just as costly as outright proof of corruption.

There was more than a touch of righteous indignation about Mr Justice Smyth's description of the TD's behaviour as a 'scandal' and his liberal quotation from Shakespeare. All that was missing was for a bony finger to point to the accused at the back of the crowded courtroom and to call for fire and brimstone to rain down upon Mr Lawlor's head.

Mr Lawlor is now on the second-last stop of his three-year campaign of resistance to the tribunal. He is certain to end up in Mountjoy tomorrow unless he appeals to the Supreme Court before then.

Up to now, he has never balked at the expense and effort involved in launching appeals. However, this time the odds are stacked against him more than ever. Mr Justice Flood has found against him. A High Court judge has just torn strips off him. On his last visit, the Supreme Court didn't even need to hear the tribunal's arguments before deciding against the politician. True, on his first visit the court did find partially in Mr Lawlor's favour, but this turned out to be a pyrrhic victory.

Mr Justice Smyth's finely crafted ruling offers Mr Lawlor the option of a bearably short period behind bars. It might be that a self-defined martyrdom will prove preferable to a Supreme Court challenge, which may only be postponing the inevitable.

If he does go to the superior court, it could be to challenge the decision, the sentence or even the right of Mr Justice Smyth to rule in the case. Doubtless, veteran senior counsel Mr Paddy MacEntee, for Mr Lawlor, will examine all the possibilities for keeping his client out of jail over the next 36 hours.

Right from the start, things went badly for Mr Lawlor yesterday. Mr MacEntee appeared to have a sense of what was coming even before the judge read his verdict. He repeated his client's grovelling apologies. Then Mr Lawlor had to sit impassively through a 90-minute pummelling by Mr Justice Smyth.

The judge asked why Mr Lawlor went to his banks for information, but not to lawyers, accountants and others he had dealt with. He suggested Mr Lawlor tried to 'fob off' the tribunal by acting as a conduit between the banks and the tribunal.

He criticised the 'bare, minimalist approach' taken by the TD in his affidavits. He also attacked the standard of the affidavits, saying even the most recently-qualified solicitor would not have put together such sub-standard documents. Mr Lawlor's youthful solicitor must have been reduced to the role of a 'functionary clerk', the judge concluded.

Mr Lawlor knew 'full well' what he was doing, he said. He decided 'what the tribunal should receive and when' and provided information on a need-to-know basis that he determined.

Yesterday's defeat left Mr Lawlor with the bill for three senior counsel and other lawyers for the four days of last week's hearing. Most estimates put the bill at about £100,000. At least, the taxpayer won't be footing the bill.

But it doesn't end there. As the judge reminded us in his verdict, Mr Justice Flood has already complained to the Director of Public Prosecution about Mr Lawlor's alleged obstruction of the tribunal. This is separate from yesterday's case, in which he was found to be in contempt of the court's order.

None the less, Mr Justice Smyth freely delivered his view in the criminal contempt case, which is that Mr Lawlor is guilty of this offence too. The penalty here is a fine of £10,000 and up to two years in jail, although Mr George Redmond got off with just a fine on the same charge last year.

Finally, Mr Justice Smyth raised the issue of perjury, and pointed to a number of instances where he felt Mr Lawlor did not tell the truth. And all this before the West Dublin TD even begins his evidence proper.

18 JANUARY 2001

The Evasive TD Escapes Media in Break for Jail

Kitty Holland

Liam Lawlor slipped unnoticed into Mountjoy Prison yesterday. Travelling in a Wexford-registered Toyota Carina, he entered by the St Patrick's Institution gate, in good time for his 2 p.m. appointment.

Deputy Liam Lawlor leaving the High Court in Dublin after he was sentenced to a jail term and a fine for his failure to comply fully with the Tribunal. Photograph: Courtpix.

The 20 or so journalists, photographers and cameramen waiting for him around the corner at the main prison entrance were disappointed at 12.25 p.m. when they got the news that the beginning of Mr Lawlor's week-long prison sentence had happened without them.

Just one photographer had the St Patrick's entrance staked out and he managed to get a picture of the TD's suitcases.

With media crews assembled early yesterday morning at the Four Courts, at Mr Lawlor's home in Lucan, at his legal team's offices in Church Street, at Lucan Garda station as well as at Mountjoy Prison, word went around at about 10.30 a.m. that he would be arriving at Mountjoy at 11 a.m. 'to avoid the media'.

The 11th hour came and went, calls were made to the crews in Lucan and word spread that he had indeed left the house.

Some speculated as to whether he might be on his way to the Supreme Court to lodge an appeal, though it was pointed out that his legal representatives, Mr John Rogers and Mr Patrick McEntee, were both in court arguing other cases.

Then one photographer ran towards the side road into St Patrick's Institution with the news: 'He's in. He's gone in up here.'

A prison guard explained there was a gate between St Patrick's and the main men's prison, though it was, he added, 'very unusual' for prisoners

to arrive through this entrance. Earlier, Mr Lawlor's car was driven towards the entrance, though only his driver was in it. Mr Lawlor is due for release at 1 p.m. on Wednesday. He will be released through the main gate, according to a prison spokesman.

20 JANUARY 2001

Boom Time

Kathy Sheridan

Like an alien dropping in on contemporary Ireland, Ann Marie Hourihane records stories from our brave new world in She Moves Through The Boom

Mullingar features large in Ann Marie Hourihane's book — a place coming down with cosmopolitan accountants and young ones up for a good night out, rampant with wine traders nursing hangovers and who aspire to the Italian way of living. This, writes Hourihane, means 'scooters, men who kiss each other when they're sober, and girls with very long hair'.

Well, we Mullingar folk always said that all we lacked was the weather … Hang on, she hasn't finished: Surely it will be a struggle to get all the elements of Italian life into this country; basil is a terrible price … Yes, she could be laughing at us but she denies it outright. In fact, she set out not to be smart-arsed, she says, only to observe. This is a mistress of the genre, after all, who has seen the inside of a few first-class finishing schools.

After a start with the *Irish Press*, there was the stint as Gay Byrne's researcher on RTÉ ('an education'); Nighthawks ('egos fizzing away in the same saucepan, very productive, satisfying and also very difficult'); Today FM with Eamon Dunphy ('that's a long time ago'), and the *Sunday Tribune*.

But the book is virtually judgment-free, an 'I am a camera' view of the boom, a series of snapshots of 'everyday Ireland at a point of huge change', as she puts it.

So we visit the shopping monoliths of Liffey Valley and Blanchardstown; touch down briefly in Bandon, Finglas, Dundalk and Sligo, with time out for boom-time phenomena such as Red Bull ('the cherry cola that Lola once drank; now her grandchildren call it an energy drink'); Mercedes-Benz sales (did you know that only a quarter of Mercedes buyers now are over 45?); a Montessori school where you can watch your sprog having a tantrum via live video link-up (one parent watches regularly from Scotland and Turkey).

We get a glimpse into holy wells and call centres, house-moving and discos fuelled by one drug or another; meet people agitating over fluoridation and St John's Wort and what it takes these days to be a proper mother. There's a young stock-option millionaire, who finds it vulgar to talk about money, of all things. And a chat with a 'likeable' priest, fresh from a long jail sentence for the sexual abuse of teenage boys, which may well be the first interview of its kind in Ireland.

Now lest that seem like one long romp, there are some profoundly depressing cameos in which Hourihane describes a visit to a nursing home and the horrific injuries incurred by a woman during childbirth which were left untreated for three years.

And still, at the end of it, one gets little sense of how she herself feels about the boom.

'We have to be careful about criticising social change,' she says, 'particularly as you get older and your attitudes age with you, because you could say,

"I am criticising this because my sensibilities are so fine" when, in fact, it could be just that you're a cranky bugger who hates change.'

Has she herself felt the effects of the boom?

'To a great extent, my personal life has been untouched by it — which has left just the traffic jams and lots of messages on answering machines. There's a sense that it has just stressed people out and left them in a sort of free-floating envy. But there have been great things too — like the fact that people don't have to emigrate anymore. In fact, we're now importing them.'

But the way she sees it, we haven't even begun to understand what we've been through because we are still in the centre of it, in a kind of fog.

'The explanations we get from the experts haven't really satisfied us. That's because we think they're partial and delivered in economy-speak. Any-thing written has been either economic analysis or cheer-leading. The word "boom" is shorthand — too short a word to describe what has happened in the past eight or nine years. The change has been so enormous. One of the reasons I wanted to write the book is that we haven't started looking at how we feel about it and I wanted this book to be the first to do that.'

And now?

'My first love has always been writing. I'll certainly do more books.'

And, who knows, the episodic nature of her first book may just translate into television.

29 JANUARY 2001

Getting All Wrapped Up In Chinese Red Tape

Asia Letter by Miriam Donohoe

The other day I had a test for AIDS and syphilis. Not out of concern for my health, I stress, but as a compulsory part of the painstaking process of applying for Chinese residency.

Model Katie O'Brien takes the plunge during a photocall in Jury's Hotel, Ballsbridge, Dublin to publicise the Jury's Wedding Fair at the hotel. Photograph: Frank Miller.

Like many things in this country, this is caught up in layers and layers of maddening red tape. There is no place like China for filling out forms and handing over passport-sized photographs. So far, I have parted with 12 photos between applying for residency, work permit and driving licence.

A comprehensive health check is part of the residency application process, and armed with pictures we arrived at the health clinic in Beijing last Tuesday.

China is only now beginning to mount AIDS awareness programmes, and the first thing we noticed were posters everywhere advocating safe sex. We were shunted from room to room to have a blood sample taken, and an ECG, a lung and heart X-ray and blood pressure tested.

When I indignantly inquired why they wanted some of my blood, the doctor pointed to yet another form where, in English and Chinese, the words 'AIDS and Syphilis' were printed. I held out my arm, too shocked to say anything.

The next day, issued with our clean health certificates (I now officially don't have AIDS or syphilis), we went to the Beijing Public Security Bureau, where you apply for residency permits.

Here, more passport photographs were required for all the family, and after a quick visit to an official photographer in an adjoining office to boost dwindling stocks, we managed to get the paperwork sorted.

Bureau officials kept our passports and told us our residency permits would come through in 10 days' time. As I write, I'm still not resident, which means the contents of the crate we had shipped from Dublin to Beijing last month cannot be delivered to us yet.

Before I get a reputation as a crank, the scourge

Secondary school teachers gather in Molesworth Street at the ASTI rally outside Leinster House.
Photograph: Eric Like.

of red tape is widely acknowledged here, even by the Chinese. Two years ago Beijing was poised to sack up to half its higher-ranking public servants, possibly as many as four million bureaucrats, in a sweeping civil service shake-up.

A report to a session of China's parliament, the National People's Congress (NPC), proposed that 15 ministries be replaced with four new combined departments.

The plan was intended to cut government spending and the stifling red tape that commentators say is retarding economic growth.

So much for good intentions. Signs of reform are few and far between. Writing in the January issue of *Business Beijing*, the chief executive officer of the German Chamber of Commerce here, Dr Jorg-M. Rudolph, pulled no punches when it came to the hurdles facing businesses.

'There are many difficulties in setting up a business in Beijing. For example, if you register a representative office in Beijing, which is the basest form, you have to prepare and produce more than a dozen photographs,' he said.

'People are often turned down because some departments concerned want colour photos, while others want black and white. Then you have to report every year your dealings with government offices of the administration of industry and commerce.'

He went on: 'Every three years you have to repeat the registration process, in our case bringing documents from Germany which require many official stamps.

'If a Chinese enterprise goes to Germany to set up a business, it is much easier. If it comes to a really major investment in China, I know from experience and through German companies that it takes an average five times longer to do it in China than it takes in Europe or the US.'

The heavy hand of bureaucracy also extends to major department stores in Beijing. When you make a purchase, you queue to get a receipt, go to a cashier where you queue to pay, and return to the shop assistant where you queue again to collect the item. Many store employees wear identity tags with a number and, you've guessed it, a passport-sized photograph.

Despite all this red tape, the Beijingers could teach Irish shop and restaurant employees a few lessons about good service.

No fewer than seven eager department store staff converged on me as I checked out a new microwave on Saturday. They even tested the appliance before wrapping it, throwing in a few free containers, and ferrying it down five floors to the car.

And when it came to giving directions to a lost Irish journalist in search of a computer store, the eight staff at the Ritan Hotel deserve a special word of thanks as well.

It may smack of overstaffing, but as long as it's put at my disposal, I won't be complaining too loudly to the Chinese authorities.

Letters to the Editor January 2001

Millennium Spire

Sir, — May heaven preserve us from another deluge of letters to you and complaints in the media about the awfulness of the Millennium Spire.

Sure wasn't the Eiffel Tower derided when it was erected in 1889? A 19th-century, unique design of Meccano-type iron girders is now the epitome of all that is wonderful about Paris. In time the 21st-century spike will surely become the same kind of attraction in Dublin.

If I could be cloned I'd love to be around to witness the reaction to the spike 112 years on, in 2113.

Chic and begorrah! — Yours, etc., Joan Sheil, Embassy Lawn, Clonskeagh, Dublin 14.
5 January 2001.

Sir, — I am a Roman Catholic, and I was saddened to read the statement by a lay Catholic group calling on the Government to abandon plans to erect the 'Spike' in O'Connell Street and asking that a statue of Christ the King or St Patrick be erected instead (The Irish Times, 4 January).

The elegant, beautiful spire will be, for me, a symbol of hope and joy for the third millennium: a beacon of light shining forth over our city. Liturgy speaks frequently of light. 'The light of Christ.' 'Lighten our darkness.' 'Lead, kindly light.' Can this Catholic group not see the significance and potential of this symbol? Were not the great cathedral spires of medieval times a symbolic reaching upwards to the transcendental?

To those who see not beauty but a spike, I would say: 'Lift up your hearts.' A statue, however fine, compared with this beacon of light, is as prose is to poetry.

I do, however, agree with one view expressed in the statement by this group. There has been an odd omission from the various celebrations of the 'millennium'. I would like to see at the base of the spire a quiet reference to what we are celebrating and an invitation to people of all denominations and none to raise their hearts and minds and see this beacon of light as a call to peace and harmony. — Yours, etc., Noel Masterson, Riverside Drive, Churchtown, Dublin 14. 10 January 2001.

British Honours List

Sir, — Is it really necessary to devote practically one whole page (30 December) to covering the British Honours List? — Yours, etc., Michael J. Connelly, Log Na gCapall, South Circular Road, Limerick. 6 January 2001.

Too Many Messiahs?

Sir, — Oh God, Not another Messiah knocker (Arts, 5 December and Letters, 2 January). To be in the National Concert Hall and hear a 100 member choir displaying their range, skill, co-operation, sensitivity and exuberance in 'And The Glory of the Lord', the first chorus of Messiah, was overwhelming. The ripples and waves of sound back and forth across the choir were what Handel had in his head 260 years ago. How it must have thrilled him to hear it performed!

Messiah got its first performance in Dublin, though spurned elsewhere. 'All We Like Sheep' will continue to flock to it and weep. — Yours, etc., Bernadette Heneghan, Breffni Terrace, Sandycove, Co. Dublin. 6 January 2001.

Teachers' Pay Claim

Sir, — As a secondary teacher for more than 20 years I have slowly absorbed all that the job entails; poor pay and conditions of work, little or no prospects of promotion, increasing levels of stress that only those who work with adolescents can understand, 'holidays' spent working to clear the backlog of accumulated debts, and the frustration of working with weak, remedial and difficult children in overcrowded classrooms with no back-up. Add to this the frequent outpourings of contempt from a cynical media and you may agree, it is indeed a thankless job. I can absorb no more, having finally reached saturation point when I opened my most recent pay cheque to find that the Minister had deducted pay for three days on which I worked. The Minister and the ASTI can sort out the rights and wrongs of this event in the courts over the coming months, and it will be entertainment for us all. For myself, I have learned a very valuable lesson and a very simple one: doing work for nothing is a mug's game. On the noticeboard in the staffroom in my school there are two lists. One is a voluntary rota for yard duty, the other a voluntary rota for providing cover for absent colleagues. I will be removing my name from both lists, and I will have to think long and hard before I participate in any non-teaching, unpaid work in the future. Maybe it's the times we live in? — Yours, etc., Bernard Lynch, Glendale Meadows, Leixlip, Co. Kildare. 9 January 2001.

Sir, — I am a 53-year-old teacher. My first permanent teaching post was acquired when I was 44. My P60 for the tax year 1999/2000 shows an income of £23,334.

This is why the strike is happening. This is why the strike is continuing. Fact, not rhetoric, Taoiseach! — Yours, etc., Michael J. Leyden, B.A. (Mod.), M.A. (Liverpool), H.Dip. Ed., Dip. in Caths. (NUI), Ard na Veigh, Sligo. 19 January 2001.

Fine Gael leader, Mr John Bruton, with (from left) deputy leader Ms Nora Owen, Senator Fergus O'Dowd, Drogheda, and John V. Farrelly TD, Meath, after he lost the no confidence motion at last night's meeting. Photograph: Frank Miller.

Sir, — As a former secondary school teacher I am sick and tired of the acres of print that have been accorded to the ASTI dispute in your paper. My sympathies lie with the students and the parents, and with them only.

I chose to leave a lucrative teaching career in the early 1980s during a recession because I had four children under the age of six years. I am now self-employed in the tourist industry. Unlike public service employees, I have no guarantees as regards my livelihood. I have no public service pension rights. I work seven days a week. For me, unlike teachers, bank holidays are normal working days and summer holidays do not exist. December 25 and 26 are the only days I can say with certainty are family days.

I made a choice at a difficult time. Such a choice is more readily available in the Ireland of today. Might I suggest that those disaffected teachers embrace a career change? To hell with the long holidays, to hell with the 22-hour working week, to hell with the weekends and free bank holidays. Join the self employed — it's a much more attractive option! — Yours, etc., Sally O'Brien, Clynagh, Carraroe, Co. Galway. 24 January 2001.

Diary Items

Sir, — I received two interesting items in today's post. My son has been given an appointment in Temple Street Children's Hospital for 3 January 2002. My car has an appointment with the local NCT centre on 5 February 2001. It's a funny old world. — Yours, etc., David Millar, Browneshill Road, Carlow. 13 January 2001.

1 FEBRUARY 2001

Old Guard Is Buried With Full Political Honours

Frank McNally

It was a very civilised coup. After seven hours and 48 speeches, the Fine Gael parliamentary party emerged from its meeting rooms last night having consigned John Bruton's 10 years of leadership to history.

There was no hint of acrimony. The old guard was buried with full political honours, having pledged its loyalty in advance to the new one.

And to the applause of supporters gathered in the courtyard of Leinster House the party proceeded calmly, if with teary eyes, towards a pre-election meeting today.

Mr Bruton had fought the battle of his political life and lost narrowly. But he accepted the decision without rancour, confirmed he would run again in the next general election, and spoke of his certainty that Fine Gael would return to power.

The mood was sombre, but Mr Bruton's infamous laugh — perhaps freed at last from the shackles of the party's image makers — did manage an appearance.

This was when his deputy leader, a tearful Nora Owen, paid tribute to him as a 'convicted politician', before correcting the record: 'A politician of conviction, I mean'.

Liam Lawlor had been among those milling around the courtyard earlier. He looked relaxed and for once was ignored by the media. But he wasn't there to hear Ms Owen's gaffe, as politicians of other parties and none steered clear of intrusion on Fine Gael's private grief.

The grief was real. Richard Bruton, Phil Hogan, Ivan Yates and John Bruton himself seemed close to tears at the press conference.

The sadness affected the winners too. Olivia Mitchell paraphrased the Duke of Wellington: 'The only thing sadder than a battle lost is a battle won.'

The successful challengers were as dignified as Mr Bruton had been, although there was irony in Michael Noonan's comment that Fine Gael was 'a big national family'.

Jim Mitchell didn't blink alongside him, but one of the features of the last four days has been the starkly different stands taken by the Mitchell brothers, Jim and Gay.

A more optimistic note had been struck earlier yesterday by Austin Deasy, when he arrived for his party's leadership showdown asking reporters: 'Do you know what day it is? It's the last day of winter.'

It must have been a hard winter for Mr Deasy. Two months ago, in expectation of mild weather, he planted the seeds for what he hoped would be a new Fine Gael leadership. But a sharp frost hit the parliamentary party, and his fragile plan was nipped in the bud.

Even before yesterday's meeting, he was claiming vindication for his gambit. It was worth losing 'one small battle' to win the big one, he said.

8 FEBRUARY 2001

Calm at First, then Tears Began to Flow

Nuala Haughey

Beverley Cooper-Flynn lowered her head and started crying, her sniffles amplified by the microphone in the witness box.

The Mayo TD's tears began to flow as she recalled receiving a letter from RTÉ's Charlie Bird seeking her response to allegations due to be broadcast about investment schemes she had sold.

Recordings of these news items — played to the court on television monitors — contained allegations that Ms Cooper-Flynn once sold investment products aimed at helping people to evade tax.

The mood of the packed courtroom had been subdued until this point in Ms Cooper-Flynn's evidence, in the mid-afternoon. Earlier, she had related in painstaking detail features of an offshore investment product she sold when she was a financial consultant with National Irish Bank (NIB).

She seemed to lapse effortlessly into sales pitch mode as she described how this personal portfolio product from Clerical and Medical International (CMI) had unique features, was individually tailored and allowed investors' funds to grow tax-free.

'It was a legitimate and very tax-efficient way of investing money,' she said.

Allegations made on RTÉ that Ms Cooper-Flynn sold this product to help customers hide money from the tax man are central to the libel case, which is expected to run for up to three weeks.

Ms Cooper-Flynn, soberly dressed in a black trouser suit and pale gold top, delivered her evidence precisely and calmly, regularly looking directly at the jurors.

Mr Bird, wearing a dark navy suit and blue shirt, sat or stood at the rear of the courtroom throughout, sometimes taking notes. Several members of the jury glanced at him as Ms Cooper-Flynn described how he had become 'hot and bothered' during one of their telephone conversations. RTÉ's special correspondent showed no reaction.

Ms Cooper-Flynn described how Mr Bird pursued her to the Slieve Russell Hotel in Co. Cavan where she was attending a Fianna Fáil conference. She awoke the following morning in room 519 to find a letter from him pushed under the door.

'I was quite shocked to put it mildly, very shocked,' she told her counsel before she broke down in tears and was comforted by her sister, Ms Sharon Dunleavy.

8 FEBRUARY 2001

Worst Accident Kills 3 in Louth

Elaine Keogh

The young woman killed in a car crash which claimed three lives in Co. Louth early yesterday had celebrated her 18th birthday the previous day.

She was named as Marguerita McShane, Monymore, Carlingford, Co. Louth. Her parents

The Taoiseach, Mr Ahern, talking with Mrs Elizabeth Balfe. At 87 and living in Fatima Mansions for 53 years, she is the longest resident living there. Mr Ahern was in the area where he announced the £100 million regeneration plan for the area. Photograph: David Sleator.

and three brothers were distraught after one of the worst accidents in the area in living memory.

Two men originally from Northern Ireland also died when the car they were in went out of control and smashed into a lorry five miles north of Dundalk on the main road to Belfast. One was identified last night as Seamus Donegan (47), Fathom Park, Newry, Co. Down.

The third victim is not expected to be formally identified until this morning.

How the teenager came to be a passenger in the car is under investigation. A Garda spokesman said the car was so badly mangled that 'it looked like the aftermath of a car bomb. It was absolutely horrific'.

Ms McShane had been living between her family home and a flat in Dundalk, and recently started working in the Carlingford Arms pub in the village. Her family is well known in the community, where they run a haulage business. 'This accident was the worst many of the garda had ever seen,' said a garda who was called to the accident scene at 2.15 a.m. Members of Dundalk Fire Service were also horrified by the scene that greeted them. A local photographer who has witnessed many car wrecks said the Toyota Carina in which the three died looked as if firemen had cut it into pieces but, in fact, they had not.

Initial Garda enquiries suggest the vehicle, which was registered in 1988, went out of control, hit a wall and then slammed underneath an oncoming lorry near Feede.

The car slid on its roof across the road into the path of the lorry, which was heading from Dublin to Belfast. The lorry driver was badly shocked but otherwise unharmed. It's believed the car was heading for Dundalk, possibly for the home of one of the deceased, who had moved there a short time ago.

Post-mortems were being carried out in the Louth County Hospital, Dundalk, last night.

Mr Marcel Marceau photographed during rehearsals at the Olympia Theatre where his show runs. Photograph: Brenda Fitzsimoms.

Ms Mary Mulholland, road safety officer of Louth County Council, said there had been a 'substantial' number of accidents along the N1 throughout the county, with 'quite a few' happening on the stretch between Dundalk and the Border.

9 FEBRUARY 2001

An Irishman's Diary

Kevin Myers

It is nearly a year since the car crash which brought unbelievable tragedy to two connected families. At the time, I thought that the State's complicity in the deaths of two married sisters-in-law and one of their daughters would cause such a wave of revulsion that decisive action to prevent young, unqualified drivers from driving unaccompanied would follow.

I was wrong. Our politicians seem to have weighed the electoral consequences of enforcing the law, and decided they would lose too many votes by doing so. So nothing was done, and so more people have died on our roads. At least in death, they will not vote against anyone, unlike the group from which their killers come, and this seems to be the major political influence over the creation of road policies.

Who remembers Josephine Kelly? Who remembers her daughter Lisa? Who remembers Josephine's sister-in-law, Sandra Kelly? Apart from their immediate families, almost nobody. In a couple of weeks' time, Josephine's widower Sammy and his four surviving children, the youngest now aged three, and his brother Pat, and his four children, the youngest now aged eight, will pass the first anniversary of the utterly needless deaths which brought ruin on them all. How have they passed that year? Who has minded their children while they worked? Who has collected them from school? How did they pass Christmas? What will they do on 21 February, to mark the day catastrophe came to call?

The needlessness of the horror which has engulfed them is truly shaming. Josephine, Lisa and Sandra were out walking down a country lane near Castlecomer. A car rounded a bend out of control and killed all three. The driver of the car was 17. He had received his provisional licence only the previous week. He was driving unaccompanied.

And why was he driving unaccompanied? Because, in part, the Government allowed him to. It is just over 20 years since Sylvester Barrett, in perhaps the most cretinous political initiative in the history of the State, decided that people who had failed their test twice would be allowed to have a full driving licence. From that foot so witlessly allowed in the door, the population of people who have not passed the test but are allowed to drive unaccompanied has grown to 250,000. It is now one of the largest special interest groups in the land; and though it slays all around it, no politician dare seem brave enough to take it on. It could even form its own political party: it wouldn't be the first one in the Dáil to defend its right to kill.

Not merely does the State not wish to take this group on, but it seems studiedly determined not to discover statistics about it. Though deaths on Irish roads continue to increase, in violation of undertakings to the EU, according to the National Roads Authority, the status of the licences of only about half of the drivers involved in crashes is actually known, making official figures almost meaningless. Of that known half, 55 per cent are unqualified.

Extrapolating from that criminally small sample, we can make minimal assessments. Since 30 per cent of all road deaths involve drivers under 24, and we know that at least 55 per cent of such drivers have provisional licences only, we can say for sure that no fewer than 70 of the people killed on roads died in crashes caused by unqualified young drivers. The figures might be far, far worse. We simply don't know, because there is simply not the political will to discover the truth. We don't even know how many young drivers have full licences.

This is the sort of fecklessness which tolerates the presence of so many unqualified drivers on the road in the first place. Though the law requiring provisional licence-holders to drive in the company of a qualified driver still stands, it simply isn't enforced. So the actual practice of the law means that a 17-year-old, with no driving experience, can get into a £50,000 sports car or a £20 banger and simply drive away.

There might be some sort of terrible justice involved in young people killing themselves, though I myself don't see it. But what about the deaths of others, such as the blameless Kellys?

How many deaths are directly attributable to the State's refusal to impose the rule of a law which, if enforced, would exclude a quarter-of-a-million unqualified drivers from the road? How many Dáil seats are vulnerable to the electoral rage of excluded provisional licence holders? And how many people this year will be killed on our roads because of the policy of propitiating this group?

And if we are so keen to appease people by a selective application of the rule of law, why isn't such latitude shown towards the abuse of drugs, which kill and maim far fewer people every year? Why does the State say to a teenager, yes you can drive that big lethal car, without any experience or expertise, and endanger the lives of ordinary people around you, but no, you may not inhale that joint, that cocaine, that heroin, which at the very worst, endangers only you, the taker?

9 FEBRUARY 2001

Here's Hoping Chopsticks Are Given the Chop

Asia Letter by Miriam Donohoe

I have a confession to make. What I find most difficult about this job is not the harsh weather, the strange culture, or grasping the geography, politics and economics of one-third of the world's land mass. My problem is chopsticks.

Don't get me wrong, I am trying. As a guest I am determined that, while in this country, I do as the Chinese do. (Within reason, of course.)

But despite hours and hours of painstaking effort, I still can't get the hang of those harmless wooden eating utensils.

To millions of Chinese, they are just two thin splints, snapped apart for use before a meal, and discarded afterwards. My children were experts within a week. To me, they are simply a nightmare.

I am OK with family or friends when I actually manage to get some of the food into my mouth. But in Chinese company, my fingers turn to jelly and I just fall apart.

Take last week, for example. I was in the coastal Province of Fujian in south-east China (two hours' flying time south of Beijing) and guest at a dinner hosted by a high-ranking member of the Communist Party, the deputy mayor of the city of Changle.

With course after course of food being served and the deputy mayor and seven of his male officials looking on, the chopsticks let me down once again. Red-faced with embarrassment, and with my new-found communist friends sniggering at my feeble efforts, the deputy mayor (God bless him) whispered to a waitress who produced a familiar stainless steel knife and fork in seconds.

Chopsticks are in the news in Asia, not because of your correspondent's failure to master their use, but because they are the latest threat to the environment.

China now produces 60 billion pairs of disposable chopsticks a year, cutting down 25 million trees in the process: 45 billion pairs are for domestic use, while 15 billion are exported to Japan and other Asian countries.

According to environmentalists, if this rate of chopstick production continues, China will consume its remaining forests within 10 years.

Chopsticks have been China's primary eating tool since the Shang Dynasty, which began around 15,000 BC. Traditionally they were carved from

Mr Gabriel de Regnauld de Bellescize, the Ambassador of France, inspecting the guard of honour drawn from 12th Battalion, Limerick, assisted by Lt Declan Noone after he presented his letter of credentials to the President, Mrs McAleese at Áras an Uachtaráin. Photograph: Cyril Byrne.

bamboo, cedar or pine. Emperors preferred silver ones, believing they would turn black in the presence of poison.

It was not until the mid-1980s that disposable chopsticks, mass-produced from birch or poplar, appeared in China. This was long after Japan, South Korea and Hong Kong had begun using them. China promoted their use to fight the spread of contagious diseases.

The chopstick gained in popularity as market reforms fuelled China's economic boom. Millions of peasants flooded the cities to find work and higher incomes, and busier lifestyles resulted in more people eating out.

Most restaurants you go into in Beijing and other Chinese cities offer only disposable chopsticks to diners.

But the high volume of use results from the numbers of people who eat takeaway meals.

Every day in China, between 11.30 a.m. and 12.30 p.m. an important ritual takes place. It is called lunch. On construction sites, in offices, in shops and on factory floors, work stops as takeout Chinese meals in plastic boxes are delivered to millions of people, each with a pair of disposable chopsticks.

Last year there was one small step towards change when the Beijing Forestry University canteen switched from wooden disposable chopsticks to ones made from bamboo, which grows fast and can be planted in many parts of China.

A group called Friends of Nature has been established to lobby for a ban on disposable chopsticks.

In Shanghai there is already a partial ban, and the finance ministry in the city is considering a disposable chopstick tax.

South Korea is an example quoted by environmentalists to China. It banned the use of disposable chopsticks after the 1988 Seoul Olympic Games, switching to stainless steel ones. Many are made with designs and carved handles and have become part of that country's culture.

Japan has been criticised by Chinese environmentalists. While it invented disposable chopsticks, it does not use its own trees to produce them in order to protect its forestry. Most of the 25 billion pairs it uses annually are imported.

The Minister for Education and Science, Dr Woods, in China on an official visit, did Ireland proud at a lunch hosted by the Beijing Education Commission last Friday. Officials were taken aback at how proficient he and his officials were in the use of chopsticks. The Minister admitted afterwards the key to his success was years of practice with Saturday-night Chinese takeaways in Dublin.

As for me, I secretly hope that chopsticks are given the chop, for environmental reasons, of course. And then I can eat in peace with the good old knife and fork.

10 FEBRUARY 2001

Iron Mike Promises a Clean Fight 'on Basis of Policies'

Frank McNally

Michael Noonan and Enda Kenny stood on either side of party chairman Phil Hogan, who looked uncomfortably like a boxing referee as he prepared to announce the leadership vote.

Not so many bicycle tracks leading to the city at Fairview, Dublin. Photograph: Dara Mac Dónaill.

Everyone knew what the result would be. Indeed there was relief among his supporters that Enda Kenny's features were still more or less pretty in defeat. Not exactly a featherweight, he had nevertheless stepped up several divisions for his bout with Iron Mike, and there had been no guarantee he would emerge with his smile still evenly distributed.

But this was Fine Gael, so there was never likely to be blood on the floor, or any horrified colleagues shouting: 'Oh no, they've killed Kenny!' Announcing the 44–28 split decision in Iron Mike's favour, the chairman didn't even raise the victor's arm. It was left to Mr Noonan to raise his own, after some prompting, and in a joyous but not triumphalist way.

Even so, when he made his formal speech at the Mansion House, it was fighting talk. His front bench teams — 'commando units' he had called them at the party meeting — would 'take the fight into the Dáil'. Of his even more dramatic idea to refuse corporate donations with immediate effect, he promised 'the father and mother of all battles' if Fianna Fáil tried to 'buy the next election'.

He also took aim at a Coalition soft spot: the Boston v Berlin debate. The US was the country he most liked to visit, he said, jabbing with his right. He spoke fondly of 'Manhattan' and 'the Rockies' and then, before you could say Rocky Noonan, he jabbed his left hook. 'But, if I were old or poor or ill, I'd rather be in France or Germany.'

The new Fine Gael party leader Mr Michael Noonan, right, and the new deputy leader Mr Jim Mitchell outside Leinster House following the parliamentary party leadership election. Photograph: Matt Kavanagh.

John Bruton was on his way to Italy by then. He had voted early before leaving for Rome. Behind him the party was guiltily enjoying the publicity attendant on his demise. Bruton loyalist Brian Hayes wondered if it was the 'bloodbath' element that attracted the media. God love him, Brian has never witnessed a Fianna Fáil heave.

Enda Kenny's promise to 'electrify' the party appeared to be working, as members picked their way around TV cables, trying not to get electrified too literally.

Asked if he had a message for the Taoiseach, the new Fine Gael leader showed clever footwork. Everyone would be expecting them to produce a 'Punch and Judy show', he said. 'So let's surprise them. Let's fight it on the basis of policies.'

10 FEBRUARY 2001

Set Retirement Age Makes No Sense

Garret FitzGerald

Ever since the Arabs invented zero some 12 centuries ago, we have been mesmerised by numbers ending in that digit. But, for some curious reason, we attach importance to dividing figures such as 100 or 1,000 by the figure four — so that, for example, we attach particular significance to figures such as 25, 50 and 75.

Yesterday, I was a beneficiary of this apparent anomaly, because people have made a particular fuss about my 75th birthday. I'm not complaining but I am mildly puzzled by it. But then I'm equally puzzled by the concept of compulsory retirement at 65.

Of course I understand, and am personally very grateful for, the idea of retirement pensions, a concept that we owe to Chancellor Bismarck, who in 1889 persuaded Emperor Wilhelm II of Germany to propose to the Reichstag the introduction of old-age pensions at age 70.

In Germany, this pension age was reduced to 65 in 1916, in the middle of the Great War. And, shortly before that, the old-age pension system that we in Ireland now enjoy had been introduced by a British chancellor, David Lloyd George.

If I may temporarily divert from my retirement theme for a few paragraphs, I would like to point out that by taking this step the man who was later to negotiate that Anglo-Irish Agreement of 1921 — popularly known as 'the Treaty' — had, possibly without realising it, reversed the earlier net flow of resources out of Ireland to Britain.

That outflow had been estimated by a British Royal Commission in the 1890s to have involved some £300 million — perhaps £30 billion in today's money — from the poorer to the richer island during the 19th century. That was because in those days taxation tended to be spent centrally on administration and defence rather than spread around for welfare purposes.

I have often wondered what would have happened to this part of Ireland if the issue of Irish independence had been postponed until a time when, with the further expansion of social welfare, the loss of net transfers from Britain would have cost us between £5 to £10 billion annually in today's money terms. If we had remained in the UK much longer, would we ever have felt able to take the huge short-term financial loss that would have come with independence?

What hope would we have had of creating a viable and prosperous economy if we had remained in the UK — given that our much weaker economy would have become ever more dependent on British transfers?

But back to pensions: the provision of pensions for those who retire does not necessarily entail enforcing a compulsory retirement age. When I recently looked up 'retirement age' in an encyclopaedia I found no reference to the origins of the idea of a compulsory retirement age.

Whence came the idea that people should, regardless of their capacity, be required to retire from many employments at 65 — or at an earlier age in the case of women? Was this a British civil service rule we inherited, then extended to other occupations?

A fixed, compulsory retirement age is essentially arbitrary, for people's capacity to remain

Garret FitzGerald's granddaughters Ciara and Reachbha FitzGerald, giving a 75th birthday kiss to their grandfather at his birthday celebration dinner in Dublin. Photograph: Alan Betson.

productive does not suddenly end magically at 65. For some people that point comes earlier, and for others much later.

We know that in 1991 close to half of men either retired before 60 or else stayed on working after 65. And, as many of the remainder must have stopped work between the ages of 60 and 64, it is clear that only a minority of men retired at 65. As people's lifespans increase, does it make any sense to continue to impose a retirement age which seems to have been arbitrarily fixed in the last century?

Given the changing health conditions of the past century, the effect of having such a fixed retirement age has been to increase hugely the proportion of the average person's lifespan that is spent in a condition of dependency — either in education or in retirement — and thus to impose an increasingly heavy burden on the declining proportion of the population which is working.

For my part, I find the concept of retirement elusive. I suppose I could be said to have retired a number of times — from Aer Lingus when I was 32; from running an economic consultancy when I was 46; from academic life at 47; from being a cabinet minister at 51; from being Taoiseach and party leader at 61; and from the Dáil at 66.

But these were not really retirements — they were simply career changes. No, I'm afraid if I actually retired from work, I might turn out to be one of those who are unable to survive retirement — and I don't intend to take that risk.

22 FEBRUARY 2001

Cardinal Connell Receives Biretta Before 35,000

Patsy McGarry

Ireland's new cardinal received his red biretta from Pope John Paul II almost on the dot of noon at a colourful consistory ceremony in St Peter's Square yesterday.

Cardinal Connell was the 20th of 44 new cardinals to be created by the Pope in brilliant sunshine on the steps of St Peter's Basilica.

An estimated 35,000 people watched from the square, with the church's existing cardinals seated to the right of Pope John Paul, and approximately 400 bishops and archbishops in front of him.

Among the dignitaries present was the Taoiseach, Mr Ahern. He was accompanied by the Minister of State at the Department of the Environment, Mr Robert Molloy, and the secretary to the Government, Mr Dermot McCarthy.

At 9.25 a.m. the new cardinals were led in to the strains of Beethoven's 'Ode to Joy' and took their seats in two lines of 22 opposite the Pope's dais.

Pope John Paul had to be helped by two assistants up the four steps to his chair. He read the names of all 44 new cardinals, in Italian, with each name being greeted by cheers and applause from the crowd.

The American and African cardinals secured the loudest response. Cardinal Battista Re, prefect of the Vatican's Congregation of Bishops, read a warm response to Pope John Paul on behalf of his 43 colleagues.

In his homily, Pope John Paul spoke of the day as 'a great festival for the Universal Church, that is enriched by 44 new cardinals'. He said: 'You will be promoters of communion that will be of benefit to the whole church ... Today you are proclaimed and made cardinals because you undertake, according to your competence, to ensure that the spirituality of communion grows in the church.

'Together we wish to set the sails to the wind of the Holy Spirit, scrutinising the signs of the times and interpreting them in the light of the Gospel.'

Afterwards each new cardinal approached Pope John Paul to have a red skullcap (zucchetto) and biretta placed on his head.

On receiving his biretta Cardinal Connell thanked Pope John Paul on behalf of the people of Ireland for the great honour, which he said was very special for Ireland. The Pope responded: 'Ahh Ireland', of which the Cardinal later said: 'I could detect in what he said his love for the country.'

At this point each cardinal was assigned a titular church in Rome as a sign of his participation with the Pope in the pastoral care of the city.

Cardinal Connell was assigned the Church of San Silvestro in Capite, which is run by Irish priests from the Pallotine order.

After receiving a kiss of peace from the Pope, each new cardinal went to his new colleagues in the College of Cardinals and exchanged embraces. This was followed by a Prayer of the Faithful and the Our Father. The consistory ended when Pope John Paul blessed everyone.

Almost immediately Cardinal Connell set off for the Irish College, where a lunch in his honour was hosted by the college president, Mgr John Fleming.

Among the attendance were Cardinal Cahal Daly, Cardinal Thomas Winning of Scotland, and Cardinal Edward Cassidy of the Vatican's Council for Promoting Christian Unity. He is of Irish extraction and from Australia.

Also there was Archbishop Diarmuid Martin from Dublin who was recently appointed the Holy See's permanent observer at the UN in Geneva.

There, too, were the former papal nuncio to Ireland, Dr Gerada, and Mgr Pecorari, first secretary at the nunciature in Ireland.

The Catholic primate, Dr Seán Brady, led the contingent of Irish bishops, which included Archbishops Clifford of Cashel and Emly and Neary of Tuam. Also there were the Dublin auxiliary Bishops Moriarty, Walsh, Field, Drennan and Ceallaigh, as well as Dr Forrestal of Ossory and Dr Ryan of Kildare and Leighlin.

Other bishops included Dr Murray of Limerick, Dr Boyce of Raphoe, Dr McKiernan, recently retired from Kilmore, and Dr Ben Devlin, a former Bishop of Gibraltar.

The president of St Patrick's College Maynooth, Mgr Dermot Farrell, was also there.

The politicians present were led by the Taoiseach, Mr Ahern, and Minister of State, Mr Robert Molloy. The party included TDs Mr Sean Haughey and Mr Pat Carey, Senator Joe Doyle, and the Lord Mayor of Dublin, Alderman Maurice Ahern.

Members of the judiciary there included Mr Justice Peter Kelly and Mr Justice Dermot Kinlen, both of the High Court. Also there was the former president of UCD, Dr Paddy Masterson.

There was strong representation from senior Dublin archdiocesan clergy as well as the heads of Irish religious congregations in Rome. Cardinal

Cardinal Desmond Connell exchanges the kiss of peace with Cardinal Cathal Daly following his election to Cardinal at the Public Consistory for the Creation of Cardinals in St Peter's Square. Photograph: Bryan O'Brien.

Connell's brother, Jim, his closest living relative, was also a guest.

23 FEBRUARY 2001

Burke Back to Round on Sworn Foe

Paul Cullen

Failed. Rejected. Irrelevant. Vicious. Evil. These were just some of the epithets former minister Ray Burke hurled at his accuser on the first day of his return to the witness box.

The target was former Fianna Fáil colleague, Mr Jim Geraghty, whom Mr Burke repeatedly lashed during his evidence. Mr Geraghty had spent the morning telling the tribunal how he chanced upon Mr Burke and a bagful of cash in the latter's office in Dublin County Council in 1986.

On a second occasion, he was again witness to a bag being deposited in Mr Burke's office. Mr Geraghty claimed Mr Burke threatened to end his political career if he (Geraghty) mentioned the incident to anyone.

'It simply never happened,' was Mr Burke's oft-stated response to the allegation. Mr Geraghty was a 'rejected, failed, one-term politician who blames everybody for his failure except himself'.

He was 'the assassin in the middle of the night' who never expected to have to make his allegations in public. 'Contempt' is the word Mr Burke chose in relation to his neighbour, former party colleague and sworn foe.

Newly emerged from the life of a recluse in north Co. Dublin, Mr Burke was on a short fuse. When Pat Hanratty SC, for the tribunal, asked him something he didn't like, the witness turned to Mr

Justice Flood: 'I've been insulted by experts, and this guy doesn't rate'.

The chairman told him to skip the insults and get on with it.

Mr Burke spent 10 minutes listing the various expenses incurred by the active politician outside election time. Mostly, it seemed to come down to drink. There was looking after canvassers (i.e. buying them drink), visiting sports clubs (and buying drink), entertaining the media (more drink, this time in the Dáil bar) and cumann meetings (you guessed it).

If Mr Burke spent more money than others, and therefore needed more, it was because he was more successful than other politicians. Mr Burke's success in 10 elections was based on organising elaborate and expensive campaigns, he argued.

He ventured an overall figure of £275,000 in contributions over 20 years, but the tribunal is likely to come up with a higher figure. In 1989 alone, for example, we know he got £120,000.

But how much information does the tribunal have? Mr Hanratty admitted that it was unable to identify the source of many of the transactions in his accounts.

Mr Burke did provide a list of donors, but it seems these were all for small amounts of £250 to £400, and related to one specific function only.

Then there's the problem of Mr Burke shifting identity. The man known as Raphael or Ray Burke to the public took on a different guise when it came to forming companies or opening bank accounts offshore.

In these cases, Mr Burke opted for a variety of initials chosen from his full name: Raphael Patrick Damien Burke. The witness called it confidentiality, the tribunal concealment.

Mr Hanratty identified three levels of concealment: the formation of a company in Jersey; the use of unusual forms of his name; and the use of a mailing address in England (his sister-in-law's). Counsel said it was clear Mr Burke had gone to an enormous amount of trouble to ensure that no one would know that he had anything to do with the offshore company.

Monabrogue Tom (left) beats Castlehyde Cash to turn the hare during the Boyle Bookmakers Derby on the opening day of the 76th national Coursing Meeting at Clonmel. Photograph: Alan Betson.

Letters to the Editor February 2001

Penalty Points for Drivers

Sir, — Is it this newspaper or this Government that keeps repeating itself? 'Stringent new measures … to be introduced shortly … which include a penalty-points system' (The Irish Times, 28 July 1998). 'The Government is set to publish … a penalty points system for motorists' (IT, 31 July 1999). 'A penalty points system for driving violations is to be introduced' (IT, 14 July 2000). 'The Government is to introduce a penalty points system for road traffic offences' (IT, 30 January 2001). — Yours, etc., Eric Beasley, Upper Mount Pleasant Avenue, Ranelagh, Dublin 6. 2 February 2001.

Snooker

Sir, — Why all this fuss about the Department of Health sponsoring a snooker event? They have tolerated long queues for years. — Yours, etc., Dr Maurice Gueret, Fortfield Road, Terenure, Dublin 6w. 2 February 2001.

Children's Instincts

Sir, — John Waters (5 February) argues that children have an innate capacity to tell right from wrong, all based on his daughter's fondness for Bob the Builder because Bob apparently represents such masculine virtues as reliability, duty, and hard work.

Although the theory tends to break down when he points out that 'you don't find many cartoons about psychiatrists, social workers or professors of sociology at UCD' (nice one, John!), he may actually be on to something. One of my eight-month-old daughter's favourite pastimes is tearing up The Irish Times *and she does this with particular relish when she gets her hands on Monday's Opinion page. — Yours, etc.,* Harry Ferguson, Professor of Social Policy and Social Work, University College Dublin, Belfield, Dublin 4. 15 February 2001.

The Four Seasons

Sir, — I agree with every word Robert O'Byrne says about that monstrosity called the 'Four Seasons Hotel' (The Irish Times, 19 February). How it ever got planning permission is beyond my comprehension.

It is absolutely ghastly and a total eyesore. Hideous! — Yours, etc., Susan Dempsey, Courtlands, Cabinteely, Co. Dublin. 23 February 2001.

Dr Connell

Sir, — Poor Dr Connell! Ye're at him again. It would never be enough just to put his actual words down in black and white so that your readers could judge for themselves whether to agree to disagree, to applaud or ignore him. No! The media have to jump up and down in an unholy fuss until every mongrel, pup and bitch is yapping, yelping and yowling. Then, affecting more sorrow than anger, you reproach him with, 'Look what you've done to the dogs!' We are used to that. It is what is known as the special position of the Catholic Church. What is hard to understand is how the urbane bishops of another persuasion are so willing to be the hounds that the journalists set on a singularly stalwart exponent of free speech. Can they not find their own offence without the goading of hysterical hacks? I have taken the trouble to read the entire published interview to find the little nugget of acrimony that was pounced upon. What did he say? That if a pastor tries to instil in his flock a reverence for the Eucharist as he conscientiously believes the Lord intended it to be, then it is bad form for a rival pastor to say to the same flock: 'Don't mind him! Come and share the taste of our special eucharist, full of flavour, GM-free and traceability guaranteed from farm to altar.' While some, I suppose, might disagree that it is bad form, no one, rival pastor or otherwise, is forced to agree. But acrimonious? Offensive? Insensitive? Surely that is over the top for anyone protected by the normal complement of cutaneous layers? — Yours, etc. Frank Farrell, Lakelands Close, Stillorgan. Co. Dublin. 23 February 2001.

Noises Off

Sir, — I have recently moved back to Ireland having spent seven years in London. As a regular theatre-goer I have been to most of the theatres there and I plan to do the same in Dublin. I have one complaint, however: can anyone explain to me why theatre-goers in Ireland have to put up with people noisily crunching and rustling sweet packets throughout performances? It does not happen in London theatres and it is irritating to the audience, not to mention being rude and insensitive to the actors who can hear it from the stage.

Two recent performances that I've attended have been marred by people in nearby seats chomping and sucking on sweets loudly and continuously, apparently oblivious to the disturbance they were causing. It doesn't help that some theatres actually have a sweet stall in the foyer, giving the impression that this distracting behaviour is acceptable. We expect high standards from the actors in our theatres. Why does this not extend to the audience? — *Yours, etc.,* Abigail Inmann, Northumberland Road, Dublin 2. 28 February 2001.

3 MARCH 2001

Saying No to Nice Could be a Vote for Democracy

Breda O'Brien

Voting No to Nice could be a contribution to democracy. Having signed the Treaty of Nice, Brian Cowen delivered a broadside on RTÉ News against anyone foolish enough to advocate a No vote in any forthcoming referendum. He declared that marginal groups with a limited vision of where this country's interests lie would suggest we vote No, but that the majority would not be in agreement with them.

Blustering words, considering that 38 per cent of those who voted decided to vote No to Amsterdam, and criticism of the EU is far greater now than in 1998. Some of that may be for the wrong reasons, such as a growing realisation that our new-found wealth means we will be net contributors. Others with a right-wing economic perspective are deeply suspicious of the social democratic model advocated by the EU. Whatever the reasons, Ireland is not the embarrassing, fawning, Europhile country it once was.

There is one difficulty for those looking at Brussels with slightly less rose-tinted glasses. Traditionally, opposition has been spearheaded by Eurosceptics who would frankly prefer to see us out of the EU entirely. They have done us a service by keeping debate alive when all the larger political parties sang from the same hymnsheet, as did the unions, employer organisations, women's groups and so on.

However, total Euroscepticism remains difficult for the average citizen to identify with. We are inextricably bound up with the EU enterprise. In treaty after treaty we have reaffirmed our commitment. We owe much to Europe, though not as much as our European partners would like to think. We have also reached a stage where we can give something back. What is badly needed is a platform for those who hold the middle ground, who recognise that we are part of the EU, but that it does not mean we have to be swept along simply because we are small.

Should we automatically vote Yes to Nice? Certainly not. The Danish ministry of justice has declared there is no need for a referendum in Denmark, much to the fury of Danish Euro-critics. It looks as if we alone will hold a referendum, even if the Government decides to fudge by holding three referenda on that day. That means the eyes of other members will really be on us, instead of our just fondly imagining they are.

This is an important moment. Brian Cowen may have scoffed at what he termed 'marginal groups' but the word marginal might better be applied to Ireland's status after the Treaty of Nice. We did not do too badly, given our population, in the redistribution of votes in the Council of Ministers. Still, Nice represents a move away from

Model Nikki Bonas wearing a stole and skirt from the Liesa O'Keeffe Alchemy Collection, at the launch of The Dublin Woollen Mills Spring/Summer collection, on the new Liffey Boardwalk. Photograph: Eric Luke.

the classic vision of Jean Monnet and the other founding fathers which saw the nation states as equal, to one where the weight of population holds most sway.

This clearly benefits Germany, which managed to insert a veto into the treaty. If a member country can show that a decision made by a qualified voting majority had been opposed by representatives of countries with at least 39 per cent of the EU's population, that decision can be set aside. Thus Germany acting with another large member state and any third member state excluding Luxembourg could block decisions unfavourable to them.

More and more, Germany has become the engine driving the direction of the EU. Insofar as there is one coherent German view, it is towards federalism. Germany itself is federalist, so, for

example, there is no national policy on education. Instead it is decided at the level of each state. Superficially, this appears like an attractive model. However, it requires a degree of integration and interdependence for which there appears to be no popular mandate.

The most cynical of the Eurosceptics would declare that it represents a bloodless 'Germanification' of Europe. Germany would retain the powers it deems essential for its own good, while at the same time dominating the use of the powers which it and the other states would have to cede to the centre. That is somewhat simplistic, but like all simplifications it may well contain an element of truth.

Boston versus Berlin remains the wrong argument. While Mary Harney and others would like to see us embrace the can-do, entrepreneurial culture of the US, there is no appetite here to embrace the lack of social protection which accompanies this model. The true argument is Dublin versus Brussels. What is the nature of national sovereignty? How can we retain distinctively Irish ways of conducting our affairs while contributing to a healthy and democratic EU?

In the midst of a horrific foot and-mouth crisis, it is fascinating to see the appeal being made to concepts such as patriotism to encourage people to make sacrifices to keep the disease out. In spite of Celtic Tiger individualism, the notion of acting collectively for the good of the country still holds sway.

The EU has no such well to draw upon, no such feeling that it is important to sacrifice for the greater good of the Community and that we are all in this together. Witness the French unilateral action in deciding to compensate French farmers for BSE losses. The EU is in many ways a bureaucratic monster, lacking accountability to the peoples of the nations which comprise the Community.

Nice therefore represents a unique opportunity for the people of Ireland to make a symbolic gesture. In Eurocrats' minds, Nice is a foregone conclusion. The focus is already on the next intergovernmental conference in 2004, where 'definition of competences' are the buzzwords. This basically means defining where the powers of the EU versus the nation states begin and end. But should we not be doing this before Nice?

By voting No, Ireland has an opportunity to give voice to the unease of many Europeans. Such a vote should not result from a fit of pique over a Budget reprimand. Centralisation of power, the democratic deficit and the increasing militarisation of the EU deserve centre stage. And maybe we could have a civilised debate this time, where Euro-critics will not be treated as fascist isolationists, but as people wishing to contribute to a more democratic Europe.

5 MARCH 2001

Patrick Sweeney

Appreciation

The tributes at his funeral Mass, both formal and informal, inside and outside the Chapel of St Brendan's Hospital, Grangegorman, by priest and people alike, were heart-warming as they recalled a life of great suffering, faithful friendship, immense goodwill, daily hard work and infectious, and sometimes outrageous, humour. There was little to record of rancour, bad temper or other human blemishes. Who was this person?

Paddy Sweeney's early life is shrouded in mystery. His obituary notice recorded that he never knew his family. He was born in 1943. His mother was Nora Sweeney with an address in the wealthy part of Monkstown, Co. Dublin. The year 1947 found him placed in the care of a convent of sisters in Rathdrum, Co. Wicklow. From there he was transferred to Artane in 1953. He spent six years in the institution and in 1959 was placed by the Christian Brothers as a labourer on a farm near Ballinasloe. His residence in that place was a shed.

After several unsuccessful efforts to abscond, he succeeded and came to Dublin to work on a succession of Crampton building sites, but damage to his back in an on-site accident ended his capacity for heavy work.

Rehabilitation support from St Michael's House eventually brought him to Gurteen Agricultural College in Tipperary for a home and whatever work he might prove capable of. He materialised as a God-sent gift for the cleaning care of hall and changing-rooms during the week and the public areas of the college at weekends. For relaxation he watched television with the rest of the staff and visited the Glue Pot in Ballingarry. The geographical isolation of the college and a change of management style convinced him that the time had come for him to move on.

After an enforced spell in the County Home in Clonmel, he ended up in Dublin in a series of unsatisfactory flats in neighbourhoods where the emerging vultures of a growing drug culture preyed on the innocents. Eventually he found benevolent privacy in a place in the Arran Quay area of Dublin 7, but not before making two efforts at suicide in the Liffey. Those made it easy to conclude that he suffered from some kind of mental illness and he was referred to St Brendan's. That place, so historically despised, became his life anchorage and its staff his respectful friends; for they discovered, as had a few from his earlier existences, just how delightful and rich a personage was concealed within the retiring and self-deprecating exterior.

From first light, Paddy would be at work sweeping the grounds. Later in the day staff cars would be washed and polished to a state of gleaming grandeur. The GAA changing rooms would be kept in order. Nothing of this was required of him. It was of the essence of his nature to work hard, to give pleasure to others, to create order, to celebrate friendship. His contributions to the welfare of the hospital caused him to be treated as an honorary member of staff.

It is time for an interpretation. In recent years, as the horrors of institutional life for children in Ireland began to be disclosed, Paddy took a few of his friends into his confidence. He had been physically abused in both Rathdrum and Artane, and

Eleanor Murray who suffers from Downes Syndrome condition with the family pet Bobby at home in Trim, Co. Meath. Photograph: Matt Kavanagh.

sexually so in the latter. His experience on the farm at Ballinasloe was, to say the least, demeaning in the extreme. In spite of all the educators' efforts by way of physical punishment, he never learned to read or write other than his signature, yet he was a highly intelligent and wise man. These polarised contrasts were bottled up in one person for well-nigh 50 years. Little wonder the cold waters of the Liffey seemed on occasion to offer a decent oblivion.

Paddy Sweeney never hurt anyone. Contrary to the media-communicated model from the reports of court cases, the abused did not become the abuser in Paddy Sweeney. Except on a very rare occasion of outrageous injustice when his temper could momentarily flare, he was both a gentle and a noble man, sharing table fellowship with some of the best-born and best-bred in Ireland without embarrassment to them or him. Noble was a word used to describe him during the last weeks of his life when, in the compassionate care of St Francis Hospice, Raheny, he knew a continuous luxury of existence which in his previous experience had been seldom more than momentary. His senses of appreciation were excited. He commented on the elegance of the furniture design in the hospice. He approved of the quality of the soft furnishings — their matching and complementary colours. He enjoyed the sense of silence and serenity which the place evokes.

He relished planning pilgrimage excursions in the days before his death. He revisited Rathdrum and Artane, St Brendan's, Gurteen and the sandy beaches on the way to Portmarnock and Malahide which recalled from his childhood memories brief moments of golden glory amid the overwhelming institutional drabness. And at the end, in true and faithful reconciliation, he came to be able to accept care and support from the hands of religion, his previous experience of whom in the days of his childhood and youth had been so distinctly otherwise, causing him on more than one occasion to dismiss the practice of religion as being 'for the Indians'. His was a spirit that sought out and even-

tually made some sense of human life and human suffering and we salute him. It was a very great privilege to share his friendship.

Appreciations, published from time to time on the editorial page, are personal tributes to late friends, associates and family members. The author is denoted by initials only. This was written by WSS. Formal obituaries appear each Saturday on the obituaries page.

10 MARCH 2001

New-look FAI may Rise from the Ashes

Emmet Malone

So it ended almost as it had begun. Two years after Eircom Park was unveiled in a blaze of publicity at one Dublin hotel, it died — with the media again looking on — in another.

Over the course of its short life, even those who were critical of the plan for a dedicated soccer stadium admitted from time to time that it was a worthy aspiration. And for much of the time since it was first unveiled it proved a source of pride to those — not least in the many areas outside Dublin where soccer administrators have grown used to envying the strength of the GAA — who gave their time to an organisation that has earned a reputation over the years for thinking small. Finally, though, the projected costs simply spiralled to the point where the majority of people involved in the game here felt that to proceed was to gamble with the future of their sport. Once an alternative materialised, their faith in the project diminished to the point where they were only too willing to abandon it.

On both a personal and political level, the agreement reached with the Government that spelt Eircom Park's end, and the agreement's endorsement yesterday by the FAI's leadership, is a substantial victory for the three men Brendan Menton, John Byrne and John Delaney.

They were the most prominent critics of the assumptions made about the scheme, but even allowing for the size of the stakes, it was surprising at times to hear just how deeply felt the animosity of some prominent figures in the sport was towards them. Having now been vindicated by events, the three will doubtless be increasingly influential voices in the post-Eircom Park era.

As for the chief proponent of the scheme, FAI chief executive Bernard O'Byrne, opinion is divided on whether he can carry on. What is abundantly clear is that he can expect little sympathy from those he has been locking horns with for the best part of two years.

One observed this week that, 'once we get the Eircom Park issue out of the way, we can deal with the Bernard issue'. Things certainly moved quickly yesterday when it was announced that the sub-committee established to look into his usage of an association credit card had had its brief widened to include his role in the stadium debate.

Still, there is a belief in other quarters, which is difficult to argue against, that if Eircom Park had not been pushed so far down the road, nothing close to the deal obtained from the Government for rowing in behind Stadium Ireland could have been achieved. O'Byrne, it is said, must thus receive some of the credit.

Indeed, a senior IRFU source is reported to have commented after seeing the details of the Stadium Ireland deal that 'we should have pretended to have been building a new stadium for the last two years'. The governing bodies of both rugby and Gaelic games will now use the funding promised to the FAI as leverage to obtain more public money for their own sports.

The £30 million matching funds for the development work aspect of the agreement will no doubt also be on offer to these sports. But it is hard to see why Bertie Ahern and his senior ministers would make similar levels of capital funding available, other than a desire to be beloved by all. But then, what better motivation could there be from the point of view of those hoping to benefit from the Government's largesse? Certainly the amount committed to the FAI makes no sense in relation to what will be achieved for Stadium Ireland, a scheme that is itself still wildly out of proportion to the requirements of the city and the country.

Crucially, though, the Government has deep pockets and the FAI does not. Writing the required cheques clearly does not cost the current political leadership a second thought. O'Byrne, on the other hand, as determined as he was that his was the correct road to travel, simply could not continue to convince a sufficient number of those whose support he required that he was right.

'I think to get something like this built you need two things,' said one of his, and Eircom Park's, supporters this week. 'One is a bull-headed leader who can drive the thing forward come what may. The other is a schmoozer, someone who can take people aside, sit them down and really get across to them what's in it for them. In Bernard we had the former, but the latter was lacking right from the start.'

In the absence of such talents the stadium's fate was sealed when, after almost two years of offering almost unquestioning praise, even the representatives of the FAI's junior leagues, so long the backbone of O'Byrne's support, came to bury Eircom Park yesterday.

As soon as their intentions became clear on Thursday night, so too did the fact that the game was up for the long-troubled project.

They finally joined forces with the representatives of the senior clubs, with some of whom they had clashed bitterly at last year's annual general meeting, and this at least holds out the hope that the two sections can now build bridges and forge policies based on mutual interest during what promises to be one of the most important phases in the history of the association.

It is certainly vital that the various levels of the organisation work together now to maximise the potential of the funds that have been offered to

The new Provost of Trinity College, Professor John Hegarty, after his election to office in the Examination Hall at TCD on Saturday. Photograph: Matt Kavanagh.

them. Invested wisely so as to achieve the full potential of the Government's matching funds, the total inflow of capital to the game should greatly exceed the £45 million that is to be paid up-front or the profits that can potentially be generated from advance sales of seats and boxes at Stadium Ireland.

Just knowing that the possibility of substantial backing from the national association exists will provide an incentive to clubs and leagues from around the country to initiate projects and start the process of raising their share of the funding for them. It should be remembered that football is played by more than 150,000 people at its various levels in this country, and some 4,500 clubs will have been looking on with rapidly-growing expectations as the broad outline of this deal became public.

Football, root and branch, is not going to be transformed by this injection of cash — its ills are far too great for that, its under-funding too long a feature of day-to-day life.

After countless years of being poorly treated by governments, however, and after more than a decade of lacking the resources required to cope with the implications of its own success, it finally has a chance to make up some lost ground.

Having embraced that opportunity yesterday, the game's leadership must well know they can ill-afford to squander it.

12 MARCH 2001

Court Rebuke Boosts ASTI Stance

Seán Flynn

T he Labour Court recommendation in the teachers' dispute represents a devastating critique of the ASTI. The court employs honeyed words and nuanced phrases, but the message is clear. It is telling the ASTI to take a running jump.

Stripped to its essentials, the eight-page recommendation asks the ASTI one pertinent question: why is the benchmarking pay review body process good enough for over 30,000 teachers in the INTO and the TUI and not good enough for the ASTI?

The court rebukes the ASTI for failing to present a coherent case against benchmarking. It says that the ASTI's objections are no longer credible. And it refuses to accept the ASTI argument that its case is somehow 'unique'.

A bruising recommendation, from a hugely respected body such as the Labour Court, should be very bad news for the ASTI. It is only the latest in a series of setbacks for a union whose case has already been rejected by the Public Service Arbitration Board.

The ASTI has other problems. It has failed to win the support of the other teacher unions. It has been riven by bitter internal disputes. And its campaign has failed to muster public support.

But something extraordinary has happened since the Labour Court issued its findings. Far from bringing the ASTI to its senses, the court's recommendation has given a new lease of life to the union's pay battle.

Why has this happened? Essentially, because most teachers believed the court was ready to deliver a sizeable bag of money. When it failed to provide what the ASTI president, Don McCluskey, calls 'even one chink of light' to the union, all hell broke loose.

Within minutes of the recommendation being issued on Friday night, ASTI hardliners dismissed its carefully crafted arguments about benchmarking. The court was offering nothing up-front, and that was all that mattered.

When the standing committee met on Friday night and the executive met on Saturday, the moderates within the union — who oppose any plan to disrupt the exams — were on the run. In the words of one hardliner: 'These people had asked us to put our trust in the Labour Court and what did we get? Another kick in the teeth.'

The truth is that unreal expectations built up in the ASTI about what the Labour Court could deliver. The mandate given to the court said that it should consider the ASTI's 30 per cent claim in the context of overall pay policy.

Since the PPF is at the core of public pay policy, was it ever likely that the court would

Secondary school students marching from Leinster House to the headquarters of the ASTI, in Winetavern Street, Dublin. Photograph: Eric Luke.

Dr Michael Casey, assistant director general of the Central Bank of Ireland, announcing details of the Spring bulletin. Photograph: Cyril Byrne.

reward the ASTI for deserting it? Was it ever likely that the court would sound the death knell for the PPF by giving the ASTI a hefty increase outside the terms of the agreement?

On Saturday ASTI executive members were not interested in the finer points of public pay policy. They rejected the court's proposals by 151 votes to 10. The Governnment had hoped a tight vote on the package would open the way for a ballot of the ASTI's 17,000 members. But the scale of Saturday's opposition to the package means this is no longer necessary.

The spotlight has now moved on to the Government. For the first time in the teachers' dispute, there is the sense that it is the Government and not the ASTI which is under pressure.

With the clock ticking towards the June exams, anxious students and parents are wondering: will the Department of Education be able to run the exams? Who will supervise them? Most critically, who will correct them if thousands of ASTI members are unavailable?

The Government moved yesterday to reassure parents and students: the Leaving and Junior Cert exams would proceed 'with or without the ASTI'.

To its credit, the Department appears to have a detailed contingency plan in place. Arrangements have been made for exams without the ASTI. Supervisors for the summer exams will be recruited and given intensive training. Those employed to correct the exams will receive detailed training. And the students can always check their own papers once the results are issued.

Despite this, there is the sense that everyone is crossing their fingers and hoping for the best. The disclosure yesterday that oral and practical exams due to begin in a fortnight have been rescheduled does not inspire total confidence. The results of the Junior Cert exam may also have to be delayed by several weeks.

Despite these practical problems, the Government is digging in. It has been buoyed by the public support for its stance. The most recent *Irish Times* poll showed a clear majority opposed to the ASTI pay claim.

In the coming weeks the Government will again be highlighting the bitter divisions within the union, its failure to win support from the other teaching unions and the implications for the economy of a breakdown in the PPF.

But it will not be all plain sailing. The Buckley report, which gave such generous increases to TDs and civil servants, has undermined its case. And the public mood can change. It may become impatient with the Government's tough line if the exams are seriously disrupted.

The ASTI has problems of its own. Its members stand to lose another six days' pay between now and Easter. And possibly more after that. They will lose the opportunity to receive about £2,000 extra for supervising and correcting the exams.

With the other teaching unions happy to pursue even larger pay claims in a less confrontational manner, they may also come under pressure from public opinion. The public may also be slow to forgive the ASTI for launching strike action at a time when there is a great sense of national solidarity over the foot-and-mouth crisis.

But the bottom line this morning is that the teachers' dispute is now moving into its most critical phase. Over 120,000 students and their parents had better brace themselves. It is going to be a bumpy ride.

The Gilligan Verdict

Editorial

In acquitting John Gilligan of the murder of *Sunday Independent* journalist, Veronica Guerin, the judges of the Special Criminal Court will have disappointed many people. For the murdered woman's family and friends, the closure which might have flowed from Gilligan's conviction, is not to be. For the Garda, whose officers pursued the case with such diligence, it is a reverse, notwithstanding the 28-year sentence imposed on Gilligan for drugs importation.

The verdict must put a question-mark over the viability of the witness protection programme which the Garda has utilised to persuade criminals to testify against their accomplices. It appears that

In rehearsals for the Abbey production of Iphigenia at Aulis, *by Euripides, translated by Don Taylor, Kate Duchene (Clytemnestra) and Justin Salinger (Achilles). Photograph: Pat Langan.*

prosecutions based on the uncorroborated evidence of an accomplice will fall. Many jurists will be pleased that a new and dangerous element, alien to the traditional values of Irish criminal jurisprudence, has been disallowed. But those who believe that the legal system is inadequate to deal with organised, ruthless crime, will be dismayed.

In 1996, the murder of Ms Guerin, along with the murderous attack on gardaí in Co. Limerick which took the life of Detective Jerry McCabe, galvanised the political establishment to action against organised crime. Criminals had become so emboldened that inconvenient lives could be snuffed out at will. The Minister for Justice put legislation through the Oireachtas which enabled the Garda to move with new-found effectiveness, principally through the Criminal Assets Bureau and the witness protection programme.

Yesterday's verdict means that the State has to think again. Convictions are not going to be secured on the basis of accomplice evidence alone. Some gardaí may suggest that this can be seen as reflecting on the force's credibility. But evidence procured by the police through a quid-pro-quo understanding with an accomplice has to be subject to the most rigorous scrutiny and, if it does not pass this test, it must not be admitted. It is, however, incumbent on the State — and society at large — to ensure that all modern aids to criminal inquiry are made available to the Garda and that the law is modified, in whatever degree is necessary, to have evidence secured by these methods admissible in court.

The multi-million pound empire of John Gilligan and his gang may have been broken up, but organised crime is here to stay. It sponsors a deadly web of drugs dealing through every city and large town throughout the State. It has links with paramilitary organisations and, notwithstanding the successes of the CAB, its practitioners increasingly seek to channel its proceeds towards supposedly legitimate businesses. Since the murder of Veronica Guerin, more than 20 men have been murdered,

execution-style, by criminal elements. Once crime gets a grip in a society it becomes virtually ineradicable. When crime bosses are taken out, they are swiftly replaced by others.

The tragedy is that successive governments lacked the moral courage to square up to crime — and, in particular, drugs-related crime — until the murder of Veronica Guerin. It is earnestly to be hoped that the resolution shown in 1996, and the massive efforts of the Garda since, will not now be allowed to dissipate. Criminal methods will continue to change. So must the State's responses. Fewer criminals in the 21st century will wear masks and carry guns. More likely they will wear expensive suits, surround themselves with accountants and lawyers and mix in desirable and influential circles. When the dust settles after the Gilligan verdict, these are the considerations which should inform the State's policy on serious crime.

23 MARCH 2001

Peninsula Braces Itself for an Empty Landscape

Clare Murphy

A crack in the corrugated iron wall showed the bare bulb lighting the shed for Department of Agriculture vets as they carried out their task.

John Wehrly, a native of Ravensdale, Co. Louth, stands a short distance from the shed where his son's sheep are being shot. The lambs, some just hours old, are killed with lethal injection.

'I've said to him to keep your chin up — there's worse off than you. You farm part-time and have another job; it's not your life. My brother has been a sheep farmer for 50 years. He tends them twice a day. Tomorrow when he gets up he'll have nothing to do, he'll have nowhere to go.'

His brother Owen arrived in a four-wheel-drive vehicle but would not comment.

The men were just two of the 24 farmers within a 1 km radius of the Rice family holding in Proleek, Ravensdale, whose animals were killed yesterday after the first case of foot-and-mouth disease in the Republic was confirmed there.

Late yesterday, the Department of Agriculture decided no more animals would be killed on farms but would instead be taken to abattoirs for slaughtering and rendering. However, the animals belonging to Michael Rice (81) continued to be killed on site.

In a brief telephone call, Mrs Teresa Rice said the family were 'coping as best we can'. The lane leading to the family home in Jenkinstown was sealed off by a Garda car with two officers in white overalls at the farm gate.

The local curate, Father Seán Moore, said he had been inundated with phone calls from people asking him to pass on their best wishes to the family who were 'highly respected'.

He felt the experience was worse than a bereavement as that would affect only one family while the outbreak had affected everybody.

'The entire community is in total shock and at this stage it is almost too early for them to see the light at the end of the tunnel. It will be a matter of getting through the next few days and weeks first,' said Father Moore.

The Treanor family, who live close to the Rice family, also kept 180 sheep in Ravensdale which were slaughtered yesterday. Mrs Treanor said she feared the cull would extend to their 115-strong cattle farm in Cooley.

'It would be bad enough to look at our own fields without animals but if every field on the peninsula was without a sheep or a cow it would

A pile of sheep carcasses with foot-and-mouth that had to be slaughtered near Ravensdale, Co. Louth. This is the first case of foot-and-mouth in the Republic. Photograph: Brenda Fitzsimons.

A Department of Agriculture official saturating a mat with disinfectant at a joint Garda/Defence Forces checkpoint at Macshane's Cross on the Louth/Armagh border. Photograph: Frank Miller.

be terrifying,' she said, commenting on reports that up to 40,000 animals would be killed.

'We had a calf born there last night and we're looking at it today and thinking it might not be with us tomorrow.'

However, compensation was at the back of everybody's minds, she said. 'The cows are so sensitive, I was out with them earlier and you'd swear they knew something was wrong.'

The farms of two nephews of Michael Rice are located in Belurgan, on the edge of the exclusion zone. A wife of one of the men said the extended family were devastated but preparing themselves for even further 'heartbreak'.

'Cooley will never be the same again. The shock of the people goes to the core and the whole economy will be plunged back too, just when things were starting to go well,' she said.

24 MARCH 2001

Final Answer to the £2m Question is Yet to Come

Frank McNally

Ms Beverley Cooper-Flynn sat shoulder to shoulder with Mr James Howard's five daughters as the verdict was announced. When the jury's answer to question one on the issue paper was announced, the Howards' expressions turned blank.

When questions number two and three were announced, Ms Cooper-Flynn's turned even blanker.

You could have been forgiven for wondering if there were any winners in the case at all, were it not for the fact that Charlie Bird and George Lee were clasping each other in an emotional (but manly) bear-hug nearby. It was the only display of feeling in the courtroom. Apart, perhaps, from the relief among the jurors as the judge announced that, after adjudicating on the longest libel case in the history of the State, they were excused further jury service for life.

As Ms Cooper-Flynn walked coolly away to the consulting rooms, the Howards stayed behind. Shoulders slumped now, they entered into a huddle with lawyers to have the result interpreted. Then the party moved towards the exit, putting on brave faces.

'Everyone smile,' said one of the sisters as they approached the phalanx of cameras outside. And before you could say 'Howard's Way', they were gone.

Mr Bird had had a quiet word with the family before they left, and the RTÉ celebrations were notably restrained. Standing alongside Mr Lee on the Four Courts' steps, Ireland's best-known journalist looked forward to going back to work, and said he would be 'at his desk' on Monday morning. After two decades of watching him report live from outside Leinster House, and outside anywhere else there was a crisis, it may come as a shock to many to learn he has a desk.

Ms Cooper-Flynn was last to leave, smiling now even as she admitted that it was 'hard to see the good side of this'. She ignored a question about whether the result had implications for her political career. However, there had been an uncomfortable omen earlier when, during the rush into the courtroom for the jury's return, she temporarily lost her usual seat.

Beverley Cooper-Flynn, TD, leaving the High Court after the verdict. Photograph: Dara Mac Dónaill.

Four of the neighbouring Howard sisters were wearing Daffodil Day emblems, but if the Mayo TD felt lonely as a cloud she didn't betray it. She shed tears on several occasions during the case, most recently during the judge's summary on Thursday night. There were none yesterday, however.

During a lighter moment in the day's proceedings, the judge evoked a certain quiz show when he invited comments from the lawyers and, none forthcoming, asked: 'Is that your final answer?'

This case too came down to a set of multiple-choice questions and a large sum of money, although in this case the sum could be nearer to £2 million than £1 million.

The twist here was that the lawyers had already won it and the issue was who would pay. The court did not reach this $64,000 question yesterday, deferring it to the week after next. Viewers will have to tune in then to see what happens.

31 MARCH 2001

Bush U-turn Shows He Is An Honest Man

World View by Frank McDonald

Nobody should be too surprised that President George W. Bush has reneged on the Kyoto Protocol on Climate Change. After all, his campaign for the White House was substantially financed by fossil fuel interests which have most to lose from its ratification and he is their loyal mouthpiece.

Boss Croker, of Tammany Hall fame, once defined an honest man as one who 'when bought, stays bought'. That is certainly true of this puppet President who sold himself very early on to the oil lobby, the coal lobby, the car lobby, the gun lobby, the missile lobby, the logging lobby, the pro-life lobby and the pro-death lobby.

Just five weeks before last November's presidential election, Bush had promised he would require US power plants to cut their emissions, including carbon dioxide — the main greenhouse gas — to tackle what his opponent, Al Gore, had described in 1992 as 'the greatest environmental threat facing humanity'.

Instead, Bush executed a shameless U-turn. Earlier this month, in a letter to four climate-change sceptics in the US Senate, he made it clear he did not now believe mandatory reductions in CO_2 emissions should be imposed on power plants, especially with California teetering on the edge of electricity blackouts.

The President went further, declaring that he was reluctant to curb such emissions 'given the incomplete state of scientific knowledge of the causes of, and solutions to, global climate change'. In this, he was faithfully repeating a tired old line trotted out by the Global Climate Coalition, which opposes the Kyoto process.

The GCC, a consortium of largely US-based multinationals, will no doubt be delighted to welcome such a powerful recruit to its cause. Because the truth is it had been running out of steam as more and more corporations, led by the insurance industry, came to accept that climate change was a very real threat.

Like their counterparts in Europe, US corporations began to see that the Kyoto process represented a business opportunity to get involved in promoting cleaner technologies, such as hydrogen-fuelled cars, solar power and wind energy.

In that context, Bush's knee-jerk reactionary decision to ditch Kyoto is a victory for the old guard. It has also come at a curious time, just weeks after the UN Inter-governmental Panel on Climate Change (IPCC), made up of 2,000-plus scientists from around the world, had issued its latest assessment of the scientific evidence and warned that global temperatures were rising even faster than predicted in earlier reports.

The IPCC said there was no longer any doubt that this was due to human-induced changes in the climate system; in particular, the build-up of green-

A taste of Peter O'Brien. Models Natasha Byram and Gail Kaneswaren photographed in Dublin's City Hall where Eircell announced details of its sponsorship of the Peter O'Brien Couture Collection fashion show in City Hall, in aid of the Dublin Rape Crisis Centre. Photograph: Brenda Fitzsimons.

house gases in the atmosphere. And it forecast much more frequent 'extreme weather events', with predictably dire consequences.

The Bush letter also followed a meeting of G8 environment ministers in Trieste, attended by a representative of his administration, which expressed concern about 'the seriousness of the situation'.

Bush has now decided that even the minimal steps required by the Kyoto Protocol are too much for his country to stomach. And so it will not do anything to curb its greenhouse-gas emissions, which amount to a quarter of the global total, until developing countries such as China also agree to take action.

This cuts Kyoto to the quick. For it was a fundamental principle of the protocol agreed in December 1997 that the rich industrialised countries, which caused the problem in the first place, must take the lead in addressing it. And even George W. Bush must know that there is no way China, or India for that matter, will let them off the hook.

The EU is dismayed by Bush's decision to renege on Kyoto, but it is unlikely to be deflected from its commitment to ratify the protocol so that it can take effect next year.

Even the Japanese and the Canadians have expressed regret about Washington's U-turn.

The Rev. Ian Paisley addresses a crowd of eight thousand people during a service in the Odyssey Arena, Belfast, to celebrate the 50th anniversary of the Free Presbyterian Church in Ireland. Photograph: Ann McManus.

However lukewarm, Japan's support for the protocol negotiated in its old imperial capital is critical if it is to secure the 55 per cent of industrialised countries necessary for ratification.

If the resumed summit in July does manage to cut a deal that preserves the integrity of the protocol, as the EU has demanded, the US will find itself isolated and under tremendous moral and political pressure to fall into line.

Otherwise, George W. Bush will increasingly be seen as a modern Nero who plays the fiddle while the planet burns.

Taken together with other anti-environmental moves, such as the proposal to open up Alaska's wilderness to oil exploration, it may even provoke such a backlash at home that Bush may find — as the Minister for the Environment, Noel Dempsey, suggested this week — there are 'more environmentalists than oilmen', even in Texas.

Letters to the Editor March 2001

Church Matters

Sir, — How dare the Rev. Stephen Neill call on Catholic priests to speak out against our Cardinal (The Irish Times, 26 February)? Is it not enough to seduce lay Catholics — who are motivated largely by politeness, not theology — away from their faith, without inciting the clergy to heresy as well? So much for not telling ministers of other denominations what to say. No priest I know disagrees with Cardinal Connell's recent restatement of core Catholic doctrine. We are all appalled, however, by the sheer bitterness and impudence shown by Church of Ireland personnel at all levels. Let us recognise so-called intercommunion for what it is: false-tongued, back-door proselytism. Do Anglicans also offer ham sandwiches to their Jewish guests — in the spirit of 'inclusion', of course? As I observed three years ago, it used to be soup — now it's sherry. — Yours, etc., Rev. Fr David O'Hanlon, CC, Parochial House, Kentstown, Navan, Co. Meath. 2 March 2001.

Sir, — Father David O'Hanlon's letter (3 March) is profoundly offensive. I am a convert to Anglicanism from Roman Catholicism. I was not seduced, proselytised, duped or bribed, but met in Eucharist hospitality the God to whom I have prayed all my adult life. That Love bids us welcome is the foundation of Anglican faith and worship, even if that leads to vilification by those who seek to make exclusion a sacrament. — Yours, etc., Maria Jansson, Beechdale, Co. Meath. 6 March 2001.

Teachers' Pay Dispute

Sir, — As a secondary teacher I am deeply depressed by the latest turn in the ASTI dispute.

The Labour Court, a neutral and honest broker, has conceded that we have a legitimate pay claim and argued that it can be achieved through the benchmarking process. Is there any reason to believe that much of what we claim will not be won by the INTO and TUI through benchmarking? Furthermore, because all teacher salaries are common we will eventually get what they achieve. If this is so, why are we threatening this year's certificate examinations?

The current campaign has been a public relations disaster. We have alienated students, parents, fellow teachers and popular support. We have seen our profession and every facet of our working lives subject to scrutiny, much of it hostile. Our cause has not been served by some of our representatives, who have come across as insensitive and inflexible.

Some facets of this action were ill-advised from the beginning. We abandoned the support of our colleagues in the INTO and TUI. By withdrawing from Congress we forfeited the support of fellow trade unionists. At a time when the Government was desperately trying to shore up the PPF, we chose to threaten it. Our failure to make concessions to Leaving Cert students has been, at the least, a tactical error.

Should the present course of action continue, any resulting victory will be pyrrhic. Nothing will compensate for the alienation of our students, the undermining of our professional status, the loss of public esteem and the resulting collapse in morale.

Our dispute is not with our students or their parents. It is with Mr Woods and the Government. Let us redirect our energies at the source of our problems — not at our allies. Our cause is just, our tactics must be likewise. Let's begin by lifting the threat to this year's State exams. — Yours, etc., Joe Coy, Kilbannon, Tuam, Co. Galway. 16 March 2001.

Sir, — In regard to the silly little charade that is the students' strike, has so much changed in the year since I took my Leaving Certificate? Has secondary schooling suddenly become the place to be at? Has secondary school become fun or enjoyable? Does the normal school day now consist of love lessons, football and disco bars, as opposed to long lessons, eight minutes of sport and a dodgy canteen? Hardly. As ever, the school bell remains a starting gun for a sprint to the classroom door, and most teenagers think the teachers' strike is fantastic. The only students who are genuinely worried are those appalling, do-goody, must-succeed-at-everything types, who have in turn arranged a mini-strike of their own. The rest of the students are merely in for the laugh of getting one up on their teachers, with the bonus of a half-day and potential telly appearance thrown in. The real cause of Leaving Certificate stress syndrome is over-expectant parents. Some of them have been coyly whispering the phrase 'Trinity College' into the ears of their beloved children since age nought, and now have Marian Finucane on speed dial. This teachers' strike is not about this year's Leaving Cert, but all future Leaving Cert examinations, and the future of the teaching profession. So if any of you goody-goody two-shoes students can stop thinking about yourselves for a second, then maybe you'll cop on and realise that the teachers' strike is in the students' interest (for both dossers and kissups alike). — Is mise, Seán Kerr, Bothar Mín, An Uaimh, Co na Mí. 26 March 2001.

Repressed?

Sir, — Vincent Browne says he's a repressed Catholic (Interview, 17 March). Vincent repressed? Who's he kidding? — Yours, etc., Seamus McConville, Tralee, Co. Kerry. 22 March 2001.

5 APRIL 2001

Cabinet Shivers as Mandelson Spins Back

London Letter by Frank Millar

He hasn't gone away, you know. So watch out, Clare. Mind your back, Jack. The Home Secretary, Jack Straw, had fair warning. When Peter Mandelson bowed to the verdict of that 'kangaroo court' back in January, Mr Straw calmly explained his colleague's second enforced resignation from Tony Blair's cabinet.

The then Northern Ireland secretary had had to go, said Mr Straw, because he had told 'an untruth'. Once Mr Mandelson had recovered from his moment of madness he confidently predicted that the Hammond inquiry would clear him of lying or wrongdoing in the Hinduja 'cash for passports' affair.

And 'friends' let it be known that in that event Mr Mandelson would expect an apology from the Home Secretary.

Hammond duly cleared Mr Mandelson, and Mr Straw may now be wishing he had similarly obliged. Likewise the Overseas Development Minister might be ruefully reflecting on her very public glee at Mr Mandelson's fall. As Labour MPs reportedly drank Commons bars dry of champagne, Ms Short exulted: 'Peter Mandelson is over.'

Well, by all accounts he's back. Incredibly, sensationally, the twice resigned minister is back by Mr Blair's side — or, at any rate, by the Prime Minister's ear. 'Delay to election shows Mandelson still has Blair's ear' ran the headline over an article by Peter Kellner, whose known inside track to the Blair camp suggests this is indeed the state of the world as viewed from inside Number 10.

Elsewhere, too, an abundance of clearly-informed articles tell us that it was Mr Mandelson — alongside focus group guru Philip Gould, Lord Falconer and the Blair gate-keeper, Anji Hunter — who prevailed against the majority view within the cabinet, and the overwhelming instinct of Labour MPs, that the general election should have gone ahead as planned on 3 May.

Meanwhile Andrew Rawnsley, whose brilliant book *Servants of the People* laid bare the personality fault lines at the heart of the New Labour project, explains why there is suddenly 'a cold shudder around the cabinet table'.

According to his account, Mr Mandelson's judgment about himself may be terribly unreliable, 'but Tony Blair continues to invest great weight in his estimation of what is best for Tony Blair'. The Prime Minister apparently once said that if a third World War broke out he would first ring Peter because he would offer advice 'with a coolness, clarity and acuteness' unmatched by anyone else he knew.

Closeted in the pre-election bunker, drawing ever closer to that 'loneliest' decision, it seems Mr Blair was true to his assessment of the former sultan of spin, consulting Mr Mandelson two or three times a day on the hotline.

'It really is incredible,' confirms another close observer of the New Labour scene. 'Peter does rise from the dead more often than Dracula.'

Indeed, as Easter approaches, this political resurrection has stunned many at Westminster who cheered Mr Mandelson's descent into outer darkness, to the background noise of Mr Blair's spokesman questioning his sanity and cheerful predictions that he might even stand down as an MP before the good people of Hartlepool had the chance to dump him.

But there should perhaps be no surprise. Whether or not spun by Mr Mandelson, there was good reason to note one early report casting Mr Blair as increasingly isolated in a cabinet in which the Chancellor, Gordon Brown, was said to be 'rampant'.

Crucially, the report identified Mr Blair's fear that the loss of Mr Mandelson could endanger New Labour's modernising project. Mr Mandelson subsequently raised hibal-based politics.

And it was probably fidelity to the project which ensured Mr Mandelson's victory over those urging the Prime Minister to proceed on 3 May.

As that keen observer explains: 'Blair would have been receptive to the One Nation argument. He knows it makes no difference to the outcome, he's still going to win on 7 June. But he would be more worried about how he would govern after that if he'd alienated large parts of the country in the way Thatcher did. That's not the Third Way.'

But the result, he ventures, is potentially very damaging for the Labour Party, 'not least because it seems clear that Blair values Mandelson's advice over that of Alistair Campbell'. Pre-resignation mention of Mr Mandelson immediately opened up questions of Blair/Brown, Blair/Mandelson and Mandelson/Brown.

To which now may be added Mandelson/Campbell. It is not clear to what extent Mr Mandelson holds the Prime Minister's official spokesman responsible for his summary dismissal from the cabinet.

But Mr Campbell will hardly be thrilled by suggestions that Mr Mandelson now thinks himself secure as 'the most important unofficial influence behind Mr Blair in a second term in office'. Mr Blair likes to dismiss all such talk about New Labour's personality battles as so much froth. He may expect plenty more of it.

7 APRIL 2001

All Saint

Patsy McGarry

It was in the mid-1980s during yet another winter of disbelief. A popular colleague was losing her mother to cancer. Slowly, and with that merciless inevitability which is its style, it sipped at her mother's existence as though it were a cocktail. Her only comfort through this casual savagery was St Thérèse of Lisieux. She prayed to the saint constantly.

So did Cathy, our colleague and her mother's only child. Cathy told us there was a belief that when a devotee died, St Thérèse would shower the

RTÉ reporte, Charlie Bird gives a victory salute; pictured with Ed Mulhall, Head of News at RTÉ, left, and Kevin Healy, Head of Public Affairs, after RTÉ won costs against Beverly Cooper-Flynn in the libel case she took against RTÉ and Charlie Bird. Photograph: Collin Keegan, Collins, Dublin.

room with the smell of roses. This, she said, was a way of letting the bereaved know the death had been a happy one. Cathy's mother wanted this, for Cathy. We, her sceptical colleagues, heard the story as an illustration of Cathy's desperation and that of a still-young woman, grieving for the grief of her child.

Cathy's mother died. We gathered after the burial at their home. We were standing around talking when I got the distinct smell of roses. I dismissed it as imagination, but it persisted. I went searching, but could find no roses anywhere in the room or outside. I was astounded and somewhat embarrassed. Any previous experience I had which might even be remotely described as 'paranormal' would have been associated with drink or a mix of that heady trinity of 'sex and drugs and rock 'n roll'. But there I was, sober as most judges, and suddenly everything was coming up roses.

My impulse was to stay silent. The last thing I wanted was to be lumped in with the growing moving statues brigade, then burgeoning all over the country. But I couldn't keep it to myself.

I gestured to another colleague, a doughty Londonderry (as she insisted on calling it) Presbyterian, who was particularly close to Cathy. She was also a no-nonsense, down-to-earth, commonsense woman. 'Sheila …,' I beckoned. I knew immediately by the recognition in her eyes that she smelled the roses too. 'Do you smell them …?' I asked. She just nodded and began to cry. 'I must get Cathy,' she said and left the room.

What was most surprising was that Cathy did not seem surprised at all. She just wept calmly, assured her mother was at peace.

I have wondered many times since about that experience. Whether it was inspired by some deep, sub-conscious suggestion/need to console a distraught colleague. I don't know. I have never been able to explain it, and I learned long ago to live comfortably with the inexplicable. But neither do I doubt what my senses told me that day. I smelled roses there in Dublin 4, where there were no roses, and so did others as sceptical as myself. It did happen, even if it did not dispel that winter of disbelief.

Tomorrow week, on Easter Sunday, the remains of St Thérèse of Lisieux will begin a 75-day tour of the island of Ireland, following similar visits all over the globe. Between 15 April and 28 June the remains will be brought to all 26 Catholic cathedrals and every Carmelite institution on the island, to Mountjoy Prison, the Army camp at the Curragh, Knock shrine, and Lough Derg. The ghoulish parade of saints' bodies and body parts by the Catholic church is something many, both within and without the Church, find disturbing, whether it be events such as the procession of St Oliver Plunkett's head through the streets of Drogheda every year or, now, the grand tour of what's left of St Thérèse throughout the length and breadth of Ireland. To many, the practice seems medieval, primitive, belonging more to a *Silence of the Lambs*-type script, the graveyard scene in *Hamlet* or Michael Jackson's *Thriller* video than, for instance, in the Cathedral of the Annunciation, Ballaghaderreen (on 6 June).

But, as Father Joe Ryan said, 'it comes down to faith. We [believers] see beyond [the bones].' People of faith don't see the bones, so much as the things they are emblems of. Some expect the Thérèse visit to be the biggest Catholic event in Ireland since Pope John Paul visited in 1979. That is what prompted the slogans of a recent teaser outdoor poster campaign. 'She will attract more people than U2 at Slane' or 'Soon you'll get to meet one of the real All Saints.'

The Relics of St Thérèse arrive here at the invitation of the Irish Catholic Bishops' Conference; in February, 1999, they issued the invitation to the authorities in Lisieux through the Catholic Primate Archbishop, Seán Brady.

A committee to organise the visit was set up with Bishop Brendan Comiskey as chairman. He and Cardinal Cahal Daly, separately and together, have led the annual Irish pilgrimages to Lisieux in recent years.

The Carmelite priest Father Joe Ryan was appointed national co-ordinator and most work has been voluntary, with subscriptions paying remaining costs.

The reliquary containing the remains will be taken on the tour of Ireland in a privately-sponsored 'Thérèse-mobile'. They will be met at Rosslare at 10.30 a.m. on Easter Sunday by an Army ceremonial unit, which will transfer the 400-lb reliquary ashore from the Irish Ferries vessel the *MV Normandy* (indicating a degree of State or Army involvement). The relics return to Lisieux 'courtesy of Irish Ferries' before departing for Lebanon by air.

Not much — just bones — is left of Thérèse since she died (of TB) in 1897. She has been exhumed three times, once as part of the canonisation process — to verify the remains' existence — and later to allow for greater public access. However, her habit had not completely disintegrated at the first exhumation, while a palm buried with her was intact. At the second exhumation a habit, placed over her after the first exhumation, was found to have decayed also, but a white silk ribbon on it was intact, bearing Thérèse's words: 'I intend to spend my Heaven doing good on Earth. After my death, I shall make a shower of roses rain down.'

Recent visits by Thérèse's remains to the US, South America, and Russia took many by surprise. 'The saint who stopped the traffic on 5th Avenue' was a headline in the *London Independent* over an article on last year's visit to the US. After the Brazil visit, the bishops there issued a statement expressing their astonishment at the crowds that had turned out. When the remains were brought to Russia in 1999, they were carried through Moscow by the Kremlin Guard, past the old KGB building to the Church of the Immaculate Conception.

Thérèse's military connections were strong. Both her grandfathers were in the French army. Her cult received a terrific boost during the first World War when, it is said, hundreds of thousands of young soldiers on all sides went to their graves carrying her badge. She became known as 'The Angel of the Trenches'. It continued in the second World War. As poet John F. Deane has written:

They drew strength from her in Auschwitz
they made her protectress-saint in Russia.

The same poet also wrote:

I had thought of her as an insipid saint standing
demurely within her coign of dimness;
they had fenced her round with a dissonance of candles …
But I have come to see
how she was an island of pain, how God enjoyed
whittling and refashioning her so he could tell
how we are breakable and mortal, how suffering is a
grace and pain a lived pearl.

So who was this saint who became known as 'The Little Flower' and is venerated by armies? Thérèse was a young Carmelite nun who died of TB in 1897 at the age of 24 in the provincial French town of Lisieux where she had lived in a convent since she was 15.

Members of A Company of the 10th Battalion FCA, Wexford, carry the gold casket bearing the remains of St Thérèse of Liseaux from the MV Normandy after it docked in Rosslare Harbour, to begin a nationwide tour of 74 places of worship. Photograph: Bryan O'Brien.

Carmelite sisters from New Ross welcome the remains of St Thérèse of Liseaux after their arrival on the MV *Normandy at Rosslare Harbour. Photograph: Bryan O'Brien.*

Her extraordinary passage from obscure death to such esteem is attributed primarily to her one book, *Histoire d'une Âme* (*The Story of a Soul*). In it, she democratised holiness, teaching that it is for all, not just the exceptional, and is lived through the ordinariness of life. She affirmed the body and feeling, as opposed to over-intellectualised spirituality /theology. As Father Ryan has said, 'she felt more than she reasoned'.

This, after all, was a saint who said her school-days were 'the saddest of my life'. She also slept through sermons and prayer services, explaining that just as parents continued to love their children while they slept, so God loved her even while she dozed off during prayers.

Her fellow nuns saw her as in no way exceptional, but she pioneered a return to a simple living out of the gospel commands of love.

'What matters in life is not great deeds, but great love,' she said.

Within 10 years of her death, she was described by Pope Pius X as 'the greatest saint of our time'. She was beatified by Pope Pius XI in 1923 and canonised by him in 1925; she would then have been 52 had she lived. In 1997, Pope John Paul made her a Doctor of the Church, the youngest of just three women in that small group of 33 which includes saints such as Thomas Aquinas. The other two women are Catherine of Sienna and Teresa of Avila. Equally extraordinary is that she is the only Doctor of the Church to be so declared by Pope John Paul, a minimalism not generally associated with this Pope who has canonised more and beatified more than all his predecessors put together.

But Thérèse's great appeal for many in Church circles today is that she suffered in a thoroughly modern way. Away from the realms of cultish, popular piety, as well as the physical pain that went with her illness in latter days, she was plagued by disbelief. 'Temptations against faith', as she described it, particularly in her final 18 months of life. As the Jesuit author Father Michael Paul Gallagher said in a 1997 address in Dublin on the centenary of her death, 'her insight into the lived actuality of atheism leads her immediately to see unbelievers as her brothers', to an identification with them in a void of feeling which she embraces in a missionary spirit on their behalf. She lost the 'joy of faith', but continued to make acts of faith. 'My madness is to hope,' she said, Fr Gallagher recalled. Some suggest that as such she could be described as 'the patron saint of unbelievers'.

Father Gallagher continued that 'the tone of unbelief … has shifted over these last centuries from seeing God as an unnecessary hypothesis (the scientific denial of faith) to seeing God as an insult not just to human intelligence but to human freedom (the humanist-nihilist dismissiveness). In our own day, the tone is a less angry mixture of apathy and lostness, where God is made culturally unreal by lifestyle and the assumptions by which we live,' he said.

'There is an argument to be made that she, Thérèse, is strangely "postmodern" in her response to her encounter with unbelief: she cultivated a mature, feminine trust in her deepest experiences of tenderness as capable of overcoming the emptiness on the level of mind or meaning. She would live — and love — what she could no longer think,' he said.

He quoted from an essay by novelist Georges Bernanos who imagined an agnostic preaching in a cathedral. Addressing the congregation the agnostic said: 'I cannot help feeling that this is your last chance. Your last chance and ours. Are you capable of rejuvenating our world or not? The New Testament is eternally young, it is you who are

old … The remarkable fate of an obscure little Carmelite girl seems to me a serious sign for us all. Christians, hurry up and become children again, that we unbelievers may become children too. It can't be so very difficult. If you do not live your faith, your faith stops being a living thing. It becomes abstract — bodyless.'

Thérèse, Fr Gallagher concluded, was the opposite of abstract, where that imagined agnostic was concerned. She was an incarnation of childlike freshness, a gospel glimpse of salvation for our tired world and culture.

'No doubt her authenticity can provoke hope and healing in others who think they cannot believe in God,' he said.

The Relics of St Thérèse arrived in Ireland on Easter Sunday and visited 74 places (from Tuam to Falcarragh, from Mountjoy Prison to Knock and Lough Derg) between 15 April and 28 June.

11 APRIL 2001

Hit Single

Hugh Linehan

It ain't exactly Cannes, but this is as near as Dublin gets. On a wet, windy Friday evening, the crush barriers are in place outside the Savoy Cinema for the Irish première of *Bridget Jones's Diary*. Stretch limos are backed up to the Gresham Hotel, flurries of PR people regiment the press photographers in their corral, and a gaggle of unfortunate young women loiter about the foyer, dressed as cans of Diet Coke (the film's official sponsors — welcome to the tacky world of media synergy). All here for the eponymous Ms Jones herself, the film's star Renée Zellweger.

Whisked in and out of the cinema in a matter of seconds, she's back on the other side of the river, in a suite in the Clarence Hotel, within 10 minutes, job done and ordering a glass of champagne.

Classic French designs from Pia Bang Spring/Summer 2001 collection shown by Una Gibney, left, and Andrea Roche at a fundraising Central Remedial Clinic ladies' luncheon held in the Four Seasons Hotel, Dublin. Photograph: Matt Kavanagh.

Looking a lot more waifish than the slightly chubby character she plays in the movie (Guinness and chocolate helped in putting on the pounds), her Texan twang is more pronounced than in any of her US films, as she recalls the last time she stayed in the Clarence. 'My girlfriend and I were running around here a couple of years ago, and had the best time. We started at six o'clock in the evening and didn't stop till dawn.'

For the past few weeks, Zellweger has been riding the promotional rollercoaster, as the movie opens in the US and Europe simultaneously — this is her third première in the space of a week. So is she sick of talking about the Bridget Jones experience yet? 'No! I loved this experience,' she protests. 'I loved this character, and I'm having so much fun with it, even still.' What she's tired of, she says, is 'talking about myself. I'm bored to death with me.' Well, alright then, let's talk about Bridget — diarist extraordinaire, enthusiastic consumer of booze, ciggies and fattening food, daydream believer and romantic disaster.

Had she heard of Helen Fielding's creation before the film script arrived on her doorstep? 'Oh yeah, I'd read about the book, and I'd stayed away from it, because I'm very suspicious of pop culture. Then the reviews kept coming in and my girlfriends kept telling me how excellent the book was. So I went for it, and laughed my ass off. Then, I suppose about a year later, I heard they were going to make a film version in England, with an English film company, and here was the list of English film actresses who would potentially be playing the part. It was just information to me. So when quite a while later I got the phone call from my manager asking if I knew what *Bridget Jones's Diary* was, I thought he was looking for a recommendation as to whether or not he should pick the book up. He asked whether I'd be interested in getting involved, and I was wondering in what capacity.'

The Hook Lighthouse, which dates from the early 13th century, and is one of the oldest working lighthouses in the world. Photograph: Pat Langan.

The casting of a Texan in this most English of roles has elicited predictable howls of outrage from some sections of the British media, but was an astute move on the part of the film's producers. Not only does Zellweger bring a little more Hollywood glamour to the mix, she also makes a charming Bridget, although quite different from the character in Fielding's book — rather more upper-crust, slightly less air-headed and (crucially) considerably more attractive to eligible members of the opposite sex, as represented by caddish publisher Hugh Grant and dour-but-decent lawyer Colin Firth.

'It was very exciting for me — the Britishness of it, and how I'd have to change a lot and learn a lot of things,' she says. 'It's the appeal of this job, to be able to be creative in such an extraordinary way, but also to grow as a person. To completely change your lifestyle and learn about a culture from the inside is a dream come true. Although this character isn't culture or gender or age-specific. It applies all over the world. That's a testament to Helen Fielding's ability to capture the truth about humanity in what she writes. The cultural and social references are obviously British, and they're obviously from a female perspective. But the more substantial underlying theme of her journey is one of self-acceptance and self-discovery. Learning to differentiate between what's going to make you happy in life and other people's expectations.'

Oh dear. This all sounds a bit earnest and dewy-eyed for what is essentially a laff-a-minute slice of harmless romantic comedy. Surely one of the better things about the Bridget Jones phenomenon, especially for an American, is its anti-puritanism and sense of fun about booze, fags and other unhealthy pursuits? 'Absolutely. I love the honesty and humour with which this character faces those challenges everyday, and those failures and mishaps. Everyone can relate to that feeling of: "Oh, I know I shouldn't. Maybe I'll give up tomorrow." That's just an expression of our humanity.'

But you don't see it very much in modern movies, I suggest. 'No, you don't, and as someone who loves movies, it's very exciting. Maybe even more for the men than for the girls. We'll have a good laugh about things like the wax strip in the bathroom, because we all know about that. But guys don't, and it's a wonderful peek for men, to learn about those very intimate moments a woman has before she arrives all fabulous for your date.'

'It's a complete accident,' she says when asked about the trajectory of her career. 'There are so many elements which feed into what you end up doing. What's available is a big element; whether they want to work with you is another. You do get a feel for what's right to do next, rather than checking off a list, saying "well I've done that; now I'm going to do this". I'll see if they ask, and then I'll see if it's right for my life.'

It's been an interestingly odd sort of career to date for the 31-year-old Zellweger, daughter of a Swiss father and Norwegian mother, who grew up in the Houston suburb of Katy — several years of TV movie roles, followed by supporting parts in a couple of less-than-memorable mid-1990s Generation X comedies (*Reality Bites*, *Empire Records*). Then, bang into the limelight with her performance as single mom Dorothy Boyd opposite Tom Cruise in *Jerry Maguire*, where her gamine good lucks and crinkle-eyed smile suggested a young Shirley MacLaine. But a couple of commercial duds, such as the underrated Meryl Streep tearjerker *One True Thing*, and one absolute stinker (the unwatchable romantic comedy, *The Bachelor*, with Chris O'Donnell) meant that her profile dropped considerably over the following years. The past 12 months have been much kinder: she didn't have to do very much except look sweet and bewildered in last year's Farrelly Brothers comedy, *Me, Myself and IRenée*, where she co-starred with her then fiancé Jim Carrey (the two have since split up); but she won critical plaudits for her performance in the title role of Neil LaBute's *Nurse Betty*, as a woman who can't distinguish the difference between her favourite soap show and reality.

While it might seem that her greatest strengths

are as a comic actress, she's reluctant to agree. 'I wouldn't classify *Nurse Betty* as a comedy, although some people did. It was much more complex than that. *Bridget Jones* is funny, but I wouldn't call it a comedy either. It has more dimensions than that. I didn't really do comedy until relatively recently, until the last couple of years, really, and I'm now in my 13th year in this business. The questions I ask myself about a film if I'm offered a role are: "Do I care? Do I want to see this? Is there something to say?" I've been very lucky, in that I've had a very, very full professional experience, very interesting. There have been extraordinary journeys and transitions in my characters' lives, during which they undergo serious challenges. Which for me as an actor makes it appealing.'

You get a lot of this slightly gushy but clearly heartfelt stuff from Zellweger, which becomes a trifle wearing after a while. I can't resist the temptation to refer to her 'Raging Bull-style' weight gain and method preparation for the role. That fattening diet, and several weeks spent working incognito in a London publishing company to get the accent right, suggest a Robert De Niro-esque commitment to the role.

'Well, that comparison is very flattering and a bit exaggerated,' she responds drily. 'I think Robert De Niro had a few more meals than I did. Actually, I got ripped off. I thought it would be much harder to maintain that, how should I put it, "particular quality of physicality". I appreciated it while I had it, though.' She brought home all the clothes she wore during the shoot, she says, but they just don't fit any more. 'They're very pretty, but they're rotting at the bottom of the drawer.' As to whether she might have to put on the pounds again, she says she hasn't read Fielding's sequel. 'I haven't read it on purpose, because I didn't want it to find its way into this performance.'

You sense that the relationship with Carrey in particular, and the ensuing media glare, has made her wary of giving too much away. 'But that's what people want, because that's what's fun. The rest is boringly professional. It's a job, it's about figuring how you fit into this technically complex co-operative effort. How to be a professional. It's such a drag when it becomes about one particular person on the set and nurturing their ego to get them to do their part.'

Does she think women are shortchanged by the stick-insect or pneumatic doll stereotypes which dominate most Hollywood movies? 'Well, maybe there's something going on that I don't know about, but people go to see those films,' she says. 'I suppose it's a myth that's perpetuated by its own success. But the guys that I know seem to like a girl who's a girl. They don't want a washboard stomach on a girl.'

It is still disappointingly rare, she agrees, for big-budget movies to feature strong female characters in the central roles. 'I honestly wonder why that is, especially with Julia Roberts proving that there is a market for stories about women that are not made for an exclusively female audience. This film is not a girlie movie. Women will absolutely relate to it, but so will men. When I did *One True Thing* a few years ago, every man was bawling their eyes out by the end of it. It's such crap that there's not more of that, it's such a shame, because the guys need to be able to close the door and have a good cry as well.'

21 APRIL 2001

Vulture's Plight Is Ignored By An Post

Mary Hannigan

Truly, life is one long learning experience, with every day throwing up spanking new, revelatory, 'well, I never knew that' moments. For example, did you know that it is illegal to post beef hearts and chicken necks from Dublin to Rio de Janeiro, even if you wrap them in tin-foil and put them in a well-sealed jiffy bag?

A member of the Army Ranger Wing Rapid Insertion Team absails on board the naval vessel **LE Róisín** *during a demonstration at the launch of the Defence Forces Recruitment Campaign 2001. Photograph: David Sleator.*

It's these kind of pernickety rules, regulations and red tape that leave An Post's customers not a little exasperated (and result in ugly scenes in local post offices, with some customers departing the scene in the back of a squad car) and now leave me with a fine for a public disorder offence and an unposted jiffy bag full of animal bits for which I have no great use.

Meanwhile, in a Rio de Janeiro zoo there's a peckish vulture who would kill for a beef heart or a chicken neck. It's senseless. The goods of this world are unevenly distributed, as they say, like the way some clubs have three half-decent left-backs and Manchester United have divil a one.

Anyway. You will be unaware of this vulture's plight if you have a life and are not a regular visitor to South American football websites. Brazilian club Flamengo are nicknamed 'The Vultures' and, so, two years ago the club's wizard PR department decided that it'd be a cute move to sponsor the vulture in Rio de Janeiro's zoo and pay for all his grub.

That, 1999, was also the year Flamengo was listed as the 11th richest club in the world, in a survey by accountants Deloitte and Touche. It is estimated that the club has 25 million supporters (mercifully, not all turn up for home games), so if you take it that even half of them buy one replica shirt every season you have yourself a healthy bank balance.

But? But now they're up to their eyes in debts (with corruption allegations filling the air) and are more pre-occupied with paying players' wages than paying for the vulture's five-course meal of beef hearts, chicken necks, rats, live guinea pigs and a cappuccino. In fact the club has failed to pay up the 500 Reais ($260) a month it had pledged since the start of the year. The rumbles from the vulture's tummy can be heard in Mullingar.

Why so much concern about happenings at a South American football club (and neighbouring zoo)? Lots of reasons. The main one being there's never a dull moment with Flamengo, on or off the pitch, and so many reasons to love them.

The average headline from a match involving Flamengo? 'Mayhem — Six sent off, two shot in Brazilian game'. On that occasion, four of them were Flamengo players, including Beto who wasn't best pleased when Vasco da Gama's Pedrinho began playing keepie-uppie when his team led 5–1. Beto was red-carded, Pedrinho is still being stitched together.

Tánaiste, Ms Mary Harney, launching the Stena **Forwarder** *at Dublin Port. Photograph: Brenda Fitzsimons.*

And? Their supporters are a smidgen passionate, bless 'em. When Vasco da Gama, whom they, um, dislike, lost to Real Madrid in the World Club Cup final a couple of years ago, thousands of Flamengo's die-hards poured on to the streets of Rio in celebration. The party lasted all night. All week, in fact. And the club bought large advertising spaces in leading newspapers to taunt Vasco over their defeat.

Best of all — in 1902, Fluminense, Rio's rich man's club, was established by the son of a well-to-do British immigrant. Early club members were said to travel to games in dinner jackets. In 1911, a bunch of Fluminense lads had enough of this lark and walked out on the club and formed their own — Flamengo. The Fluminense aristocrats gave them the nickname 'urubu', which means vulture. Why vulture? Because the vultures that hover over the shanty-towns of Rio are black and so, the Fluminense toffs observed, were most of Flamengo's supporters.

Meanwhile, Fluminense's traditional emblem is po-de-arroz — rice powder. Eh? Well, their supporters used to throw rice powder or talc at visiting black players to 'lighten' their skin. (Read more in Chris Taylor's sublime 1998 book, *The Beautiful Game — A Journey Through Latin American Football.*)

See? Any wonder we have a soft spot for Flamengo? And any wonder we worry about that hungry urubu in Rio de Janeiro's zoo? And any wonder we were a mite aggravated by the An Post official's wanton disregard for the urubu's empty tummy?

'I appreciate that you didn't pack rats and live guinea pigs in to the package but, for the 14th time, you are not allowed post beef hearts and chicken necks to Rio de Janeiro,' he blustered. A Bohs supporter if ever I saw one.

The vulture's plight, of course, is being ignored by the European media, too pre-occupied are they by events in Munich on Wednesday night. As I write, they're still trying to discover the identity of the man pretending to be a footballer in that Manchester United pre-Bayern Munich photo. Lads? Hello? His name? Mikael Silvestre.

24 APRIL 2001

We're Doing Nicely Down Here, Thank You

Alva MacSharry

I loved my work in Dublin. I miss the job a lot. I miss my colleagues and I miss the way I could walk into work and instantly become a brighter, more focused, more purposeful person. And I miss the structure of starting and finishing tasks to immovable deadlines in *The Irish Times* — I was never one of life's self-starters, and I still see housework as urgent only when I should be writing.

But I'm starting to believe we may be more than a couple of eejits who thought they could beat the system. For one, the telecommunications industry has lived up to its promise. With minimum effort and at a reasonable cost, I can produce entire newspaper pages from my desk and send them down a high-speed phone line to Ireland. For another, it is proving possible to balance home life and work in a sensible, sane manner.

It is three months since we arrived at our whitestone haven in Tarn, near Gaillac, in the south of France, leaving great jobs, supportive families and, much less reluctantly, the Celtic Tiger behind. Even as we made them, our plans to come here sounded, well, idealistic. Sell up the overpriced Dublin home and head south, where the heating bills would be lower; get control of our life as a family, swapping the stress of the daily grind of créche-work-sleep-créche for the challenge of a new life and a new language.

Nobody is more surprised than me to find it's working. I haven't regretted our move for one minute.

Starting again like this, we are designing our life as we choose — this amount of family life, that amount of work time, this amount of money. I work evenings and early afternoons, while my two-year-old sleeps, or while she is at play-group three mornings a week. It takes a bit of planning and discussion, but it is proving a lot easier to combine work and a family than a job and a family.

With bills fewer and lower, I simply don't have to work so hard. Houses here are — to us, anyway — cheap. A four-bedroom house on nine acres

Alva MacSharry and family — husband Julian Kindness and daughter Sarah Kindness — enjoy life in the south of France.

costs £150,000. Childcare costs £1.50 an hour. The house, the car and the new cooker are all paid for: no credit, very novel! And with the south of France outside the door, the rewards for not working are high.

What work is done has to be done well and on time, however — I can't stick my head round the door to apologise for late stories or a misplaced picture — so we need the best communications we can get.

Our equipment is sophisticated, and France Telecom is impressive. It takes a day to get a telephone line, a week to get a high-speed computer line. As well as the household phone lines, we have two mobile phones, a high-speed computer line, two Internet service providers and two satellite television services. I can read Irish newspapers every day; I listen to Marian Finucane and Pat Kenny on RTÉ Radio 1 in the morning and catch the main news bulletins.

And all of this living in the countryside, which wasn't part of the plan. A true Dubliner, I never envisaged living without street lighting, 24-hour petrol stations and public sewerage. But this is very tame countryside — rolling hills in a patchwork of vineyards and fields, full of bird life — and it seduced us. It is well populated, too: there are houses within holler in every direction of most homes I know. Also, only as I have lived here for a while have I come to realise how the weather plays a more important role than distance in isolating people. In sunshine, everyone within sight is a neighbour, and we get a lot more sunshine here.

Life has been seductively easy, and I have to admit to a certain amount of survivor guilt after the winter you've had in Ireland. It's not just the better weather, the better infrastructure, the better views; it is also the fact that people are friendly and helpful and that we appear to be interesting to them. I don't know if that's because they are country people, because they are French people or because they are French country people.

If I were asked to pinpoint the biggest difference between Irish society and French society, I would point to the way France is aware of its own nature. We've had fêtes, flower marches, classic-car rallies, community omelettes, pan-village tripe breakfasts, and officially organised car boot sales in the surrounding villages in the past week.

Everything attracts funding from the mairie, the local administration. And everyone joins in, because everyone believes these things are important.

I have long believed the French instinctively put people first and let business or foreign interests follow. I see evidence at all levels of life. France is leading the way in reducing working hours in the EU. Before and after school care is free in our nearest city. Our hamlet is too small to support a shop, but it has a committee to organise fêtes.

As for us, we begin to see the same faces every day. We have a favourite baker, we ask for Paul in the France Telecom office, we have made friends, we know both doctors at the local surgery, we know the names of the staff at the playgroup. This makes me feel a lot more settled.

And my French is, well, perhaps not improving, more stretching. There have been ample opportunities to feel stupid and make daft mistakes, but none so far has proved permanent, and every small success lends me even more confidence.

Sentencing May Bring Peace to Inishbofin

Lorna Siggins

Alan Murphy (27) stood tall and still as he received a 14-year jail sentence from Judge Carroll Moran in Galway Circuit Criminal Court yesterday. There was hardly a murmur in the heated, packed courtroom as the waiter from Newcastle, Co. Down, was led away after being sentenced for the manslaughter of three elderly sisters who died in a house fire he started on Inishbofin in July 1999.

Sitting in court were his parents, Frank and Bridie Murphy, who had been present throughout last month's trial.

At the rear, a daughter of one of the women who died in the fire dabbed her eyes as she heard the judge consider the evidence.

On the island, the two-storey house at Middle Quarter is still a burnt-out shell, and the events of 6 July 1999 have had a 'devastating effect' on the population, as Superintendent Tony Dowd told yesterday's hearing.

Up in 'the gods' of St Colman's Church near the harbour, cans of paint are stacked neatly against the wall. The interior has been redecorated recently in all of 10 colours — shades of red, pink, cream, blue and yellow catch the Atlantic light streaming through the stained-glass windows. The floor has been sanded and varnished, the sanctuary has a new carpet, and the church also has an improved sound system.

The cheque to cover the work, costing about US$10,000, is pinned to the notice board. Dated 5 December 1999, it was raised by friends of St Colman's Church in Brooklyn, New York, in memory of the three Concannon sisters — Eileen Coyne (81), Bridget McFadden (80) and Margaret (72), who never married.

Alan Murphy being escorted from Galway courthouse. Photograph: Joe O'Shaughnessy.

Eileen had lived on the island all her life; her two sisters were visiting her from England at the time of the fire.

Eileen was a daily Massgoer, as were her sisters. Bridget, who was married and had three children in Slough, loved coming back for summer visits, as did her sister Margaret, a qualified air traffic controller. They would spend time with three brothers, Matty, Christy, and Martin who died last year, and they would tend their parents' graves.

Flanked by Inishark and High Island and lying 8 km off the north-west Connemara coast, 'Bofin' has attracted many callers — welcome and otherwise — from 7th century monks to Cromwellian soldiers to the Spanish pirate, Don Bosco, who was an ally of the O'Malley clan.

Alan Murphy was a visitor in July 1999. He had worked in the Derryclare restaurant in Clifden for over a year, and was, as his former employer, Mr Peter Heffernan, told yesterday's hearing a 'very loyal, honest, good-hearted, good-humoured' member of the staff.

On the evening of 5 July the sisters had a meeting with a family member, David Concannon, who had come in search of roots. When they returned home to bed, they saw no need to lock the door.

That same night, Alan Murphy was well into one of 10 pints. He had travelled out to Inishbofin on the ferry from Cleggan — just 15 minutes from Clifden — earlier in the day and had booked into a hostel on the island.

As the evening wore on, his behaviour was described as bizarre, and he was ejected from Day's pub on the island at 1.45 a.m. 'I was mad at the way I was treated since coming on to the island,' he told gardaí later.

Returning to the hostel, he saw a porch light in Eileen Coyne's two-storey house. He walked up the narrow path and found the front door unlocked. He started lighting papers.

Afterwards he said it did not bother him that there might be people in the house because he was in a bad mood. 'I felt everyone was against me. This was a way of expressing my revenge.'

The alert was raised in the early hours, and valiant efforts to save the women were made with scant resources — garden hoses and fire extinguishers from the hotel. Afraid of people's reaction, Murphy jumped off the pier, ended up waist-deep in water, and refused assistance from those who tried to pull him out. He was later assisted from the water and taken into Clifden.

It was the first time there had been three coffins in the church, and it was the worst tragedy to hit the island since 1927 when 25 fishermen perished off Cleggan. The Western Health Board offered counselling.

Everybody knew the trial would be difficult, but its collapse on the second day of hearing in late February — after it emerged that a garda had taken tea with the jury — exacerbated the trauma. The hearing resumed with a new jury on 27 February and ran for nine days. The jury of six women and six men returned a unanimous guilty verdict on seven charges, after three days' deliberation.

Mr Noel Schofield, development officer with Inishbofin Community Development Company, says most people now just want to try to get on with their lives.

But the lack of proper fire services almost two years afterwards — and a staggering 23 years after the initial request to the local authority — is a particular concern on the island. On 12 March last, Galway County Council told the development company that the Department of the Environment was deciding on 'standards of fire equipment' for the islands.

Mr Schofield disputes the claim by Galway County Council, made immediately after the fire, that there would be a difficulty in recruiting volunteers. 'There are plenty of people who are willing to get involved,' he says, and water supply is good in most areas.

Ms Margaret Day, of Day's Hotel, wonders if the island will ever get over it.

Although there is uncertainty over the family's plans for the house, she and others would like to plant a memorial garden to mark Mrs Coyne's love of flowers.

Father Declan Carroll, the island priest, hopes the sentencing will mark the end of a sad chapter. But, as he said at the funeral Mass, 'the morning of the 6th of July is one I will probably never forget for the rest of my life.'

28 APRIL 2001

Hanging on the Telephone

Regarding Ireland by Nuala O'Faolain

Hello? May I speak to Alfie Kane, please? A man to whom I had never, up to this, given one minute's thought, apart from thinking to myself that he's the second-least-rewarding interviewee I've ever heard on RTÉ. (All right. The cyclist, Seán Kelly.)

I came home to the west of Ireland, pushed open the door after two months and thousands of miles, switched on the light. All well, thank God. No dead bodies in room, but phone not working. Found the flashlight and went down the lane to ask my neighbour for the use of her telephone to report a fault. Oddly enough, at 10 p.m. on Good Friday, I got a human, and one who managed to imply by

her tone of voice that the phone had been disconnected. This was impossible, since I pay the bill by
direct debit. However, I had to go to bed phone-
less, email-less, and with no way of sending copy.

There was indeed a letter, early Easter Saturday
when I collected my mail, from the Eircom Direct
Debit Section, which said AIB had told them my
account was closed. Why AIB did this I do not
know and shudder at the thought of trying to find
out. Eircom's letter didn't mention disconnection.
They disconnect without writing, much less phon-
ing, to warn you. A quite gratuitous provocation,
but I let that pass.

I paid the phone bill within one minute of the
post office opening. I then intended to report to
Eircom that I had paid the bill. I mean — the lady
in the post office scans it into some central data-

base: there's no reason why that shouldn't activate
restoring your service.

'Don't hold your breath,' the post-office lady
said. 'Eircom is gone to hell.' And she told me harrowing tales of elderly people trying to cope with the
new, cost-conscious Eircom — tales full of passages
like this '… so they told her to bring the appliance
to her nearest Eircom sales centre. But she's 80 and
she lives six miles from here, never mind a sales
centre. So she ordered a taxi into town …'

I trudged up the town to find a phone to
report that I'd paid my phone bill. None of the
public phones was working. 'No, they never
work now,' a man in a shop said cheerily. 'Sure,
everyone has a mobile.' I drove a few miles to yet
another neighbour. 'Could I use your phone to
phone the phone company?' I said.

*A young member of the colour party looks out from behind his flag as he stands in front of the GPO in O'Connell
Street, Dublin, during the 32-County Sovereignty Committee Easter Sunday Commemorations. Photograph: David
Sleator.*

'Good luck to you is all I can say,' she said. 'I had to get the phone moved across the room the other day and when I rang Eircom they told me they didn't do that any more — I could buy that yoke that the phone comes out of myself. And then what? I asked them and they said any handyman would put that in for you.'

Anyway, Mr Kane, when you dial the number for Faults, a menu, after the sales pitch, directs you to press 2. But if you press 2 you're cut off. By Eircom! This happened five times, so I went through to sales.

'Are you on "T" or "P"?' the woman there said. 'You might have to turn the little switch from "T" to "P" or from "P" to "T".' 'What?' 'Is the phone you're using a tone or a pulse phone?' 'How would I know?' I said. 'Well, is your phone a Slaney or an Avoca?' 'What?' 'Look underneath it,' she said. 'It's an Aisling,' I said. 'It's up to the customer themselves to know whether they're on a tone or a pulse phone,' she said smugly. 'The Faults number cuts off if you're on the wrong kind of phone. It's to avoid the customer having to wait.'

Eventually I got on to someone else in sales who kindly got me someone in accounts. It was 12 o'clock on a working Saturday.

'You'll have to ring Limerick on Tuesday,' they said. 'Tuesday!' I said. 'I need the phone,' I said. 'I'm nervous at night without it. And my job depends on the phone. Is there anyone at all at Eircom I could talk to about this?' 'On Tuesday. The credit controller in Limerick won't be in till Tuesday. It was him that cut you off.'

Well, I couldn't stay on my neighbour's phone forever. There wasn't anyone to say things to, such as: 'I haven't been a day late paying a phone bill in 30 years — could Eircom not take a look at your record in the software before it cuts a person off?' I couldn't say 'I see in the paper you're cutting another 3,500 jobs to shore up your share price — what are the chances that the "service" will be better after those job losses than it is now?' All I could do was wait for Tuesday.

Mr Kane, have you ever stood in a phonebox in a north wind trying to get your people to say when a disconnected phone will be reconnected?

'A few hours, maybe,' is as precise as I could get. I waited beside my phone for four hours. Nothing. Then I got into the car again to drive to a friend's to inquire. That was three days and four hours since I paid the bill AIB should have paid. Eircom's 1901 customer service person made me rehearse the whole thing: said I owed some further sum I hadn't ever had a bill for, put me through to credit control, and while I was waiting I was cut off. The next 1901 person made me rehearse the whole thing again: came up with some new sums; said he wasn't sure if they were bills; and said he'd recommend I get my phone reconnected. 'Tomorrow sometime.'

'Tomorrow?' I asked to speak to the supervisor. 'She's on her lunch.' Cutting-edge technology my arse, Mr Kane.

Letters to the Editor April 2001
Beckett on Film

Sir, — I did not have time to read Sinéad Egan's letter of 29 March. I am too busy taping and cataloguing, for future viewing, Beckett's 19 plays on RTÉ 1. I have, however, carefully cut the letter from the paper and pasted it into a scrapbook for future reading. I hope to study the letter when I get around to viewing the tapes sometime before I die (sine die). Perhaps I will do so during Breath, *time and longevity permitting. — Yours, etc.,* Brian D'Arcy, Broadford Walk, Ballinteer, Dublin 16. 3 April 2001.

Sir, — Sinéad Egan (29 March) wonders if we are watching or taping Beckett on Film. *Of course, we are all watching … and waiting … — Yours, etc.,* Cormac F. Gaynor, Dunboyne, Co. Meath. 3 April 2001.

The Taoiseach Mr Ahern delivering the oration at the annual Fianna Fáil commemoration to honour the leaders of the 1916 Rising in Arbour Hill, Dublin. Photograph: Matt Kavanagh.

Sir, — I can confirm Sinéad Egan's suspicion that people are taping the Beckett films: I overheard my son complaining that the last tape was Krapp. — Yours, etc., Iggy McGovern, Gledswood Avenue, Dublin 14. 3 April 2001.

Policy on Sports Stadiums

Sir, — I see bribery is alive and well in Leinster House. I can't think of another term to use to explain the 60 million of taxpayers' money being given to the GAA on my behalf to make them use the stadium.

I wonder how many people could be taken off housing lists with all the money being spent, either directly or indirectly, on Bertie's Bowlerama? For all it costs, it can't be that good if we have to bribe people to

use it! — Yours, etc., Garry Clarke, Spricklestown, The Ward, Co. Dublin. 11 April 2001.

Sir, — The money being proposed for financing a national stadium in Abbotstown would be equally well spent on a submerged clock counting down the 998-plus years, second by second, to the next millennium. — Yours, etc., Jerry Twomey, Woodlawn Court, Santry, Dublin 9. 24 April 2001.

Sir, — I would like our Taoiseach to complete the following sentence. I believe that £1 billion should be spent on a national stadium and not on our ailing health service because … — Is mise, Ciaran MacAonghusa, Baile an tSratha, Tír Chonaill. 24 April 2001.

Except for Son, Everyone Sings from Kim Sheet

Miriam Donohoe

It couldn't have been more ironic. As the heir apparent of reclusive North Korea was under arrest yesterday for trying to sneak his son into Disneyland, the rest of its children were having their daily dose of anti-Western brainwashing.

The indoctrination of this state's children into what can only be described as the 'Kim cult' starts as soon as they can talk and, God forbid, think for themselves.

Little were the children of North Korea aware that the son of their leader, Mr Kim Jung-il, had been detained at Tokyo airport for reportedly attempting to bring his four-year-old to see Mickey Mouse. But how could the next generation of one of the most closed societies in the world have been aware of the stir caused by the arrest in the West? Little touches North Korea from outside. Radio, newspapers and books are controlled by 'The Party'.

Even those privileged to own a television set can view only light entertainment and patriotic drama on either of the state's two channels.

Thirteen-year-old Kim Chol Min is a soccer fanatic. He plays for the Pyongyang No 1 Senior Middle School team. But he has never heard of Manchester United. Asked who his favourite player was, he replied 'Pele'. His favourite European team was 'Brazil'.

Asked how he felt about the World Cup soccer finals being hosted partly in the bordering 'enemy' territory of South Korea next summer, he looked at me blankly. He had not known.

It is impossible for the youngsters of Pyongyang to escape the Kim cult. Millions of dollars have been spent in this show-piece city on building

A near-empty street in the centre of Pyongyang yesterday. Photograph: Miriam Donohoe.

A young North Korean boy pictured in the doorway of a near-empty shop in Pyongyang. Photograph: Miriam Donohoe.

massive monuments to the state's founder, Kim il-Sung, and his son, Kim Jung-il, while thousands starve in the countryside.

At the 30-metre bronze statue of the deceased 'great leader' yesterday, a group of primary school children marched forward, bowed reverently and quickly marched away again.

A visit to the No 1 Senior Middle School was stark evidence that North Korea's schools are one of the main channels of instilling loyalty. One pupil said Kim il-Sung was as important to the state as was the sun.

A 14 ft by 12 ft colour portrait of Kim snr and jnr was hanging in the hallway. Every one of the classrooms in the school, with 1,500 pupils, had pictures of father and son.

There is even a special party meeting room for the students who have joined up.

Miriam Donohoe was the first Irish journalist allowed into North Korea.

Fiesta Time as Revellers Sway to Dizzy Cuban Beat

Kevin Courtney

Arriba! It's Saturday night in Smithfield and there's a fiesta in full swing. The former marketplace has become Dublin's Latin Quarter, and nearly 10,000 revellers are dancing to the Cuban beat.

OK, they're kind of swaying from side to side a bit, and some are even swinging their elbows, but for an Irish crowd that's tantamount to complete abandon. If only the babysitter could see us now.

The Buena Vista Social Club travelled from Havana to play for us as part of the Heineken Green Energy Festival and, thoughtfully, they brought the sun with them. As dusk faded on a warm May day, a troupe of veteran musicians arrived on the Smithfield stage, and it would probably take a quantum mathematician to calculate their combined ages.

As soon as they began playing the bright, Latin rhythms of salsa, samba and merengue, however, the years fell off, and we were transported back to the halcyon days when Cuba was young and Havana was the hot spot of the world.

The Buena Vista Social Club is a loose collective of Cuban musicians, famously gathered together by Ry Cooder and captured on celluloid by Wim Wenders. The world caught on and musicians who had plied their trade in relative anonymity for most of their lives suddenly found themselves performing to sellout crowds around the world. Talk about an Indian summer.

This team of 15 or so veterans performed on stage for two-and-a-half hours, leaving most of us young 'uns exhausted. The main man is 70-year-old Ibrahim Ferrer; in true showbiz style, he waited till nearly halfway through the show before making his entrance. The whole evening was superbly paced, building nicely to a festive finale.

It only remained for Dave Fanning to present the Buena Vista Social Club with two platinum discs for Irish sales in excess of 34,000.

The Buena Vista Social Club was undisputedly the highlight of the Heineken Green Energy Festival, but there were other events worthy of celebration. On Friday night, Welsh band The Manic Street Preachers entertained the faithful with incendiary tunes such as 'Everything Must Go', 'Motown Junk', 'You Love Us', 'So Why So Sad', and 'A Design For Life'. French dance act, St Germain, brought the trendy punters to the Olympia on Saturday night, and few of them needed a babysitter.

The Divine Comedy acquitted themselves well at Dublin Castle on Saturday night, performing tracks from their excellent new album, 'Regeneration', while Elbow confirmed their next-big-British-thing status with a Saturday gig at the Temple Bar Music Centre. The dull-but-worthy Travis packed in the punters at Dublin Castle last night, and they will be doing a second show tonight.

While the sun shone outside, a panel of music industry types selflessly shut themselves indoors to chair seminars on such subjects as touring, public relations, copyright and independent labels. In various pubs around town, young hopefuls battled it out in the Heineken Hot Press Band Challenge. The final takes place at the Music Centre tonight for a £20,000 prize.

Buena Vista Social Club musical director Demitrio Muniz performing in Smithfield, Dublin. Photograph: Joe St Leger.

7 MAY 2001

Marine Leisure Growth Puts Pressure On Safety Body

Out of the West: Lorna Siggins

Not many of his Galway West constituents may know this, but the Minister of State for Housing and Urban Renewal, Mr Bobby Molloy, almost lost his life in the water as a child.

Mr Molloy, who holds the highest satisfaction rating among five TDs in the constituency, doesn't like to make too much of it. 'I was drowned and was revived when I was seven years old,' he told *The Irish Times*. 'I took a special interest in competence in swimming and lifesaving from there on.'

He qualified as an instructor with the Irish Red Cross's water safety section — the first body to be responsible for that area from 1945 — and when he became a minister in 1971 he was only waiting for an opportunity to establish it on a firmer footing. The Irish Water Safety Association was set up — a separate entity responsible to his own department.

Mr Molloy says he never agreed with a decision taken by government more than 15 years ago to amalgamate water, fire and road safety into one body as the National Safety Council. He was glad to re-establish the identity just over a year ago. When the Irish Water Safety Association's new national headquarters opened on Long Walk, near Spanish Arch and on the banks of the Corrib, it was, in a sense, coming home.

Mr Molloy's involvement is not the only link with Galway. A former chairman was the late Mr Des Kenny, who, with his wife, Maureen, set up the successful bookshop and art gallery in the city. He had become involved after a swimming incident when his son, Tom, narrowly escaped drowning.

A loyal following and the commitment of people such as the current chairman, Waterford garda Mr Frank Nolan, ensured there was no major trauma when the body was re-established. But there are challenges ahead, which the new office, run by chief executive Lieutenant Commander John Leech, recognises.

The rapid growth of marine leisure has put extra pressure on, and stretched the goodwill of, people who have a strong volunteer ethic. Lifeguards recognised by the Irish Water Safety Association don't accept payment for what they do.

Moves have been made by the Government in the past three years to regulate safety in adventure and outdoor pursuits centres, but there is no such regulation in leisure centres. Many of these were built as extensions to hotels in the past decade. There is nothing to force a hotel or leisure centre to provide a qualified lifeguard — or any lifeguard — if it so chooses.

The water safety association estimates that there are 1,000 active volunteers, and some of these people received recognition at an awards ceremony in Galway recently attended by Mr Molloy and by the president of the International Life Saving Federation, Dr Klaus Wilkens, who said Ireland has a 'triple A' record when it comes to water safety effort.

Sometimes, the worst is prevented, and that is why five people who demonstrated acts of bravery were presented with Seiko 'Just in Time' rescue awards in Galway by Mr Molloy. Certificates for

25 and 10 years' service respectively were also presented to volunteers. Mr Kieran McAllister from Ennis, Co. Clare, received his award for rescuing a man from a river in Ennis in a strong current last December, while Mr Ollie Cahill saved two children in distress in the water at Goresbridge, Kilkenny, last July.

Corporal Tommy O'Neill pulled a man from the Shannon in Athlone, Co. Westmeath, last October — and the previous year he rescued a six-year-old boy in a hotel swimming pool in Portugal. Ms Siobhán O'Connell saved the life of a man at Ballydwane Cove, Co. Waterford, last July; and Mr Seamus Monaghan fought strong currents and freezing temperatures in the Boyne river at Drogheda to rescue a man last January.

Captain Dave Courtney, longest-serving

A cheetah cub in Fota Wildlife Park, Co. Cork, after the park reopened its gates to the public when foot-and-mouth restrictions were eased. Photograph: Michael Mac Sweeney, Provision.

The Northern Ireland Minister for Health, Social Services and Public Safety, Ms Bairbre De Brún, accompanied by the Minister for Health and Children, Mr Martin, in Merrion Square, Dublin, for the launch of the Physical Activity Campaign, 'Get A Life – Get Active'. Photograph: Joe St Leger.

captain with the Irish Coast Guard helicopter at Shannon, received an International Life Saving citation, as did Captain Geoff Livingstone, chief of operations with the Irish Coast Guard, Mr Frank Doyle, secretary-general of the Irish Fishermen's Organisation, and Mr Pat Costello, former chief executive of the Irish Water Safety Association.

At the ceremony, the chairman, Mr Frank Nolan, appealed to teachers to avail of resource packs sent to schools, which are aimed at raising awareness about the dangers of bathing and swimming during summer months. One of a new series of posters and leaflets produced by the Galway-based body deals with hypothermia, and is in both English and Irish. It was written by an Irishman who is the world expert on the subject, Surgeon-Admiral Frank Golden, who now lives in England.

10 MAY 2001

In Pole Position to Capture Earth's Images

Weather Eye: Brendan McWilliams

For the last few days, you may recall, Weather Eye has been reporting live from inside the Arctic Circle, from the Norwegian island Spitzbergen, as near the North Pole as makes no difference.

And what could tempt anyone to brave these frozen, barren wastes, to suffer disorientation from the midnight sun with intermittent blizzards, and risk attack by hungry polar bears? The answer is weather satellites.

Bord Fáilte promoted the reopening of national parks and visitor centres throughout the country. Pictured at the official opening of Glendalough National Park are models Roberta Rawat and Victoria Lefroy. Photograph: Patrick Bolger, Inpho.

'Polar-orbiting' satellites travel around the globe from pole to pole, about 500 miles above the ground, following as it were the lines of longitude. They photograph the whole globe bit by bit from directly overhead, as the Earth revolves on its axis underneath.

Now it is obviously convenient if, when taking images, a polar-orbiting satellite is deployed in such a way that the ground beneath it is always bathed in sunlight. Ideally, then, the north-south track of the satellite should shift westwards with the daily sun. This arrangement, a so-called near-polar sun-synchronous orbit, can be relatively easily achieved, and it is precisely what EUMETSAT, the European Organisation for Meteorological Satellites, proposes a year or two from now with Metop-1.

But this clever, sun-synchronised solution makes it difficult to retrieve the pictures from the satellite. A ground station in Ireland, for example, could receive pictures from the satellite as it passes overhead, but six hours later the spacecraft's southward swoop will take it over Canada. To collect data at all the different longitudes would require a string of ground stations dotted around the world at frequent intervals along, say, the 50th parallel.

The solution lies in the fact that the lines of longitude converge towards both poles. Polar-orbiting satellites, therefore, always pass near the North Pole every 100 minutes as they circle around the Earth. If it is arranged, therefore, for the satellite to store the images it takes throughout an orbit, all the pictures can be downloaded in one go

Enjoying the sunshine in Herbert Park, Ballsbridge, Co. Dublin. Photograph: Eric Luke.

to a single ground station near one or other of the poles.

In the case of EUMETSAT and Metop-1, a ground station will be built on the island of Spitzbergen, whose ultra-northern location makes it uniquely suitable for receiving data from a polar-orbiter. From there, the information will be relayed by other means to forecasting offices all around the world.

And that's why I am here. A EUMETSAT meeting has been arranged in Spitzbergen so participants can view the site on top of a local mountain, where the ground station will be located.

11 MAY 2001

Billy Bandwagon and the Final Frontier

Frank Millar

Enter Planet Hague. The title is a spin-off from Planet Tory, a photographic exploration of the Tory Story currently showing in London.

It depicts today's Conservatives as 'almost in a parallel reality, completely unlike the people you meet in your everyday life'.

The captain's set is obviously intended to look futuristic. A hangar for alien aircraft? The strange Dalek-style podium has survived October's party conference.

Thankfully, Mr Hague's head no longer sits disembodied above it.

On the contrary, the 40-year-old, would-be prime minister is very much all there, fit, confident and happy in his own skin. The man Labour dubbed 'Billy Bandwagon' arrives on stage with a cocky swagger and a knowing nod to pals (well, pals for the moment at least) Widdecombe, Portillo and Maude.

His opening line is hardly crafted to counter charges of negative campaigning.

'My greatest fear for the country that I love is that we will wake up one day and find that something very precious has been lost without our ever quite realising how or why we let it happen.'

And, no, he definitely is not talking about his leadership.

The message is at once apocalyptic and re-assuring. The spirit of enterprise is under fire from

Séamus Mallon, SDLP, MP, Deputy First Minister, canvassing in the Chestnut Grove area of Newry, Co. Down, giving some information to Peter McParland (sitting in his garage) with Peter McEvoy, SDLP, Newry Town candidate for the Newry and Mourne Council election. Photograph: Dara Mac Dónaill.

high taxation, regulation and conformity. The streets are becoming more threatening. The United Kingdom's power to run its own affairs is being surrendered to the European Union.

'And the greatest danger of all is that people begin to think all of this is inevitable.'

But there is a choice, a vision of the country when true to itself, 'proud of what makes us distinctive as a nation'. Conservative principles, and 'the commonsense instincts of the mainstream majority'.

More police on the streets and more criminals in prison. Taxes cut. Doctors, nurses and head teachers set free. One million pensioners lifted out of tax.

The unborn (and those not yet 11) beneficiaries of a new married couples' allowance that rewards the family. Freedom and responsibility. And respect — for all the people, whatever their race, religion, colour or sexual orientation.

Tony Blair said the Dome would be a vivid symbol of Labour's Britain. It was.

'Step inside and you could be anywhere. It was banal, anonymous and rootless. It lacked a sense of Britain's history or its potential.'

The Tories would halt the erosion of Britain's independence, argue for a different kind of Europe and, above all, keep the pound.

Taxes down. Streets and inner cities made safe. Respect for pensioners. In Europe, not run by it. Grip got on the crisis in the countryside. Schools that parents want. Support for marriage and the family. People freed to shape their own lives.

A time to choose 'between a Labour Party that trusts government and a Conservative Party that trusts people'.

Mr Hague was maybe overegging his claim to have produced the most radical Tory manifesto in a generation. But there was no doubt this would play well on Planet Thatcher.

As for the rest of the country?

A departing colleague wondered about that set. Doesn't it remind you of the *Titanic*? No. 'Well, whatever it is, it's still going down,' he said with terrible certainty.

12 MAY 2001

Yes Campaign Bogged Down in Eurobabble

Drapier

I n a surprisingly low-key week, the most low-key event of all was the launch of the Nice referendum campaign. Never mind that the Government's referendum schedule was very nearly a casualty of a Seanad handbagging a week ago, or that the most eloquent and forceful advocate of the Treaty, Brian Cowen, is temporarily hors de combat — there was something a shade ominous about the downbeat tone of the campaign's launch.

Drapier knows that every Euro referendum to date has been won and won decisively and that when the leaders of the three main parties, not to mention the captains of industry, trade union leaders and farming organisations all join forces, most people respond in a positive way. And so it will be this time, though Drapier detects an underlying unease, indeed nervousness, among those charged with delivering a Yes vote.

There is good reason to be nervous. The Yes campaign, in spite of being about some of the most momentous and far-reaching developments in

Rocky Horror helped at the launch of the Sixth Heineken Green Energy Festival at Pearse Street Train Station. He is sitting beside Ms Jane Gaughran and Ms Anne Sherwin, from Drogheda. His costume is part of a set which will be on exhibition commemorating the life of our most celebrated street artist, The Diceman. Photograph: Dara Mac Dónaill.

Actor Donal O'Kelly reading a statement from the James Connolly Monument at the launch of the Afri booklet detailing the military implications of the Treaty of Nice. Photograph: David Sleator.

modern European history, lacks passion and commitment. Is it that the idealistic Europeans of the Garret FitzGerald vintage have all grown old or shuffled off the stage to be replaced by smooth-talking Eurocrat specialists who speak largely to themselves in a language few understand?

Maybe it's a measure of national maturity that we now take these major European developments in our stride, but familiarity can breed complacency, and that is exactly what is happening.

There is very little effort made to spell out the issues, to persuade people that what is good for Europe is good for Ireland and to talk in a straight way about our responsibilities as well as our rights. Instead we get Eurobabble.

The No side does not lack passion. Never mind that many of the arguments are off the wall, that scare stories and conspiracy theories are the order of the day, the language used is making an impact. For some of the No groups, especially the

Greens and Sinn Féin, the campaign offers a useful dry run for the general election.

However, that said, the No campaign on its own will not do much more than raise a gallop. The real danger to the Yes vote is that the voters who are in a sour mood — and there are many such disgruntled groups around — will use the referendum to register their protest, to teach the Government and all political parties a lesson.

Drapier has no doubt the Nice Treaty will be affirmed. But unless the Government gets its act together, gets its message into clear and understandable language and shows a bit of passion, then we will have a low poll and a high No vote.

Meanwhile, the past is ever with us, or at least the Arms Trial part of it. There is no doubt 'Prime Time' stirred up a hornet's nest with its first programme, but as the controversy unfolds Drapier suspects the hornet's biggest sting may be reserved for the programme itself.

Mr Justice Rory O'Hanlon, right, guest speaker and patron to the 'No to the Nice Treaty' campaign that was launched in Buswells Hotel yesterday. From left are Mr Manus Mac Meanmain, National Organiser, Mr Justin Barrett, PRO, and Mr Denis Riordan, Chairperson. Photograph: Brenda Fitzsimons.

From the outset, Drapier had reservations about basing an entire revision of a major historical episode on a single document. It may work that way in spy thrillers, but most sane historians would want to see all available documents before rushing to judgment.

The strange thing is how many people did rush to judgment on the basis of a programme that was as much polemic as documentary. The accepted view of Des O'Malley was turned on its head, amid much gloating and sniggering. For some observers, O'Malley was guilty as charged and Captain James Kelly was the blameless hero, the Dreyfus of Irish politics.

It was as if the normal rules of evidence were suspended and no painstaking examination of the facts should be allowed get in the way of a good story. Old scores were being settled. New conspiracy theories emerged and, for some, Dessie all but ranked alongside Piggott the Forger of Parnellite days.

The second 'Prime Time' programme in particular left a great deal to be desired. Drapier has argued from the outset that we need to have all documentation made available so that people can make up their own minds on the basis of verified information, though no amount of information, new or old, will change some minds, which will forever remain closed.

Drapier found O'Malley's own statement this week persuasive. Already the nit-picking has started, but to Drapier at least he faced up to the main issues in a fairly convincing way, and Drapier looks forward to the 'Prime Time' response.

There now remains the reports from the Attorney General and the Department of Justice. From what Drapier hears, Michael McDowell has adopted a hands-on approach and is determined to ensure the AG's office will produce a report independent of the Government Departments.

The Justice report will be the interesting one. John O'Donoghue can be in no doubt that his Department — maybe for good reasons — is not noted for its openness or self-scrutiny.

The publication of these two reports may satisfy the needs of the immediate controversy. Or may not, and then the question of a wider inquiry will be on the cards once more. Indeed, as things are unravelling, a wider inquiry may be inevitable.

The O'Malley television series suffered from the lack of a hard critical edge. Few of those opposed to O'Malley chose to put their point of view, with the result that it is his version which holds the stage. He has got his retaliation in first, and it is this version that is likely to prevail, at least in the short run.

The whole episode is a diversion from the problems of real politics — the daily unravelling of the PPF in face of strikes, wage demands, job losses, hospital waiting lists and a general sourness of mood.

Mary O'Rourke has been uncharacteristically quiet all week in face of the rail chaos, but then what choice does she have? CIÉ on its own is enough to destroy any minister, and Mary is wise enough to know that when there is nothing she can usefully do, it is best to shut up.

Finally, back to where we started. Brian Cowen was very lucky last Friday. A second or two earlier or later and the accident would have been very much worse. Drapier's advice is to take it easy. Don't rush your recovery, let the world look after itself. It generally does.

Misjudged State Reception Was an Invite for Disaster

Patsy McGarry

One thing at least is certain, the protocol section of the Department of the Taoiseach could not have made such a 'misjudgment' six years ago.

The divorce referendum was in November 1995 and, considering the church's stance on the issue, there was no room then for the luxury of getting it wrong, if such was the case.

Then, in a country almost evenly divided on divorce, a Taoiseach favouring change had to be seen to be as committed to his marriage as was John Bruton.

But it is an indication of how rapidly attitudes changed that in 1997, when he became Taoiseach, Mr Ahern felt he could come clean about his failed marriage and his relationship with Ms Celia Larkin.

It is not coincidental that over that same mid-1990s period the people of Ireland first became aware of Bishop Casey's son, the Father Brendan Smith affair and a deluge of child sex abuse cases. Crucially, it was the church's handling of these matters that seemed to make most impact on public perception. A trend was accelerated, by years.

Combined with growing wealth, the comparative youth of our society, a high level of education and a growing tolerance for diverse arrangements/relationships, the time was ripe for a 'misjudgment' of the magnitude we had on Monday.

The wording of the invitation to the State reception for Cardinal Desmond Connell could also be seen as an indication of the degree to which the State no longer feels it has to indulge church sensitivities. Some will welcome this, but it was just bad manners.

The Taoiseach Mr Bertie Ahern, with his partner Ms Celia Larkin, photographed at Dublin Castle at a reception in honour of His Eminence, Desmond Cardinal Connell. Photograph: Brenda Fitzsimons.

It is not a sign of advance in any society when we feel free to ignore or tread on what is dear to others. Even when, especially when, we disagree with them. It is just crude to place people in positions which can only cause them embarrassment.

This is not by any means a comment on the Taoiseach or Ms Larkin. It has to be difficult enough for them. But those who made the arrangements for last Monday night's reception in Dublin Castle did nobody a service.

It should be recognised that the churches have handled the Taoiseach's extramarital relationship with great sensitivity. Not one senior church figure on the island commented publicly on it until Dean MacCarthy did so in last Monday's *Irish Times*.

And in many ways he and other clergy had no choice. The dean has been refusing such invitations since he took office 18 months ago. He and others would probably have maintained their discreet silence had the invitation to a State reception for the Cardinal not been seen as such an overt challenge to what they believe in.

And it placed the Cardinal himself in an impossible position. As a churchman his views on most subjects, including marriage, are well known. Despite this he has never commented on the Taoiseach's relationship with Ms Larkin. And despite reports that he was 'distressed' by the wording of the invitation, he has never said so.

It is also clear he and the Taoiseach belong to something of a mutual admiration society, which makes it all the more perplexing that either should have been placed in such an uncomfortable position.

Ms Larkin was not in Rome, for whatever reason. There was no embarrassment to anyone then. Which also makes it even less clear why, on

Monday night, she was placed in a position which had (the realised) potential of making her suffer unnecessary humiliation before all and sundry.

If Dr Connell was a victim, most certainly she was the one deserving of most sympathy. Surely a 'misjudgment' too far?

23 MAY 2001

Punishment Shootings, Beatings Rise Sharply

Clare Murphy

The number of 'punishment' shootings in Northern Ireland is up by more than 40 per cent this year compared to the same period last year.

According to RUC statistics a total of 73 'punishment' shootings have been carried out from 1 January to 20 May this year compared to 51 for the same period last year.

Loyalist paramilitaries have been blamed for 48 of the incidents, with republicans responsible for 25.

The total for the whole of last year was 136 gun attacks, which was the highest annual figure since 1975. Figures for punishment beatings also increased, with 41 beatings in loyalist areas and 30 in republican areas from 1 January to 30 May this year. The figures compare with 33 loyalist beatings and 22 republican beatings for the same period last year.

The number of 'punishment' shootings has risen steadily in recent years after falling to just three in 1995 (a total of 217 'punishment' beatings were carried out the same year).

Last week 16-year-old Eamonn O'Boyle was shot in both ankles in an attack in Newry, Co. Down. It later emerged his family had moved to the town from Larne, Co. Antrim, a year ago following sectarian attacks by loyalist paramilitaries.

Eight masked men shot the teenager with a low-calibre weapon in the ankles and hit him on the head with a hatchet.

Over the weekend loyalists were blamed for attacks in the Tiger's Bay area of north Belfast and in Newtownabbey, Co. Antrim. Both victims were shot once in the right leg.

The Ulster Unionist Party leader and First Minister, Mr David Trimble, called on the North's Human Rights Commission to focus on the human rights abuses being perpetrated by the paramilitary groups on their own communities. He said the attacks 'raise very serious doubts about the intentions and objectives of paramilitary organisations'.

The Sinn Féin president, Mr Gerry Adams, described the attacks as 'the community responding in exasperation to the fact that there are elements who disregard any sort of acceptable norm and who simply prey upon other members of the community'.

However, he added: 'Any sort of physical punishment of those involved in criminal or anti-social activity does not work. If it worked the problem would be solved.'

Mr Billy Hutchinson of the Progressive Unionist Party, the political wing of the Ulster Volunteer Force, said his party believed anti-social behaviour should be dealt with by the police, not by 'punishment attacks'.

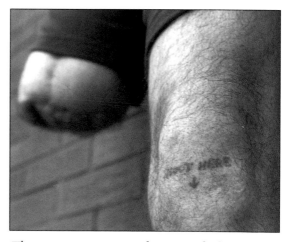

The victim of an IRA punishment squad who shot their victim in the leg with a shotgun in West Belfast. He had a tattoo on both knees which read 'Shoot Here'. Photograph: William Cherry, Pacemaker, Belfast.

Dumas and his Lover Convicted

Lara Marlowe

Light filtered through shutters in the stiflingly hot courtroom, and the prison sentence hit the former foreign minister Roland Dumas like a physical blow. The 78-year-old lawyer sank onto the front row of the tribunal, then his silver-maned head jerked backwards. After regaining his composure, Dumas twirled his cane and stared at the ceiling.

Dumas, a statesman known for friendships with Picasso and Giacometti as well as François Mitterrand, a ladies' man famed for his elegance and powers of seduction, yesterday became a convicted criminal. He was sentenced to six months in prison, a two-year suspended sentence and a 1 million francs (£120,000 sterling) fine for receiving property embezzled from the French national oil company.

Since the trial of Dumas and six co-defendants ended in March, all France waited to see whether a man once considered untouchable would go to prison. Dumas's former mistress, a former lingerie model 25 years his junior named Christine Deviers-Joncour, received an even tougher sentence of 18 months in prison and a 1.5 million francs fine.

Deviers-Joncour has called herself 'the whore of the Republic'. She was convicted of receiving 65 million francs (£7.8 million) including 'salary' for a fictitious job at the then state-owned oil company Elf, commissions for 'lobbying' Dumas to accept an arms sale to Taiwan, a 17 million francs (£2.04 million) apartment near the Eiffel Tower and unlimited use of a company credit card.

Although she never had an office at Elf, Deviers-Joncour said during the trial that she was 'proud to have done this work; it was good for Elf and good for France'.

Three judges concluded that Deviers-Joncour was in fact 'hired' by the former Elf chairman, Loik Le Floch-Prigent, and his deputy, Alfred Sirven, to thank Dumas for asking President Mitterrand to appoint Le Floch as chairman of the oil company. Le Floch says exorbitant commissions and phoney jobs for friends and relatives of politicians were common practice in France.

Le Floch was sentenced to three and a half years in prison and fined 2 million francs. Sirven, whose arrest in the Philippines and dramatic repatriation to France provided some of the most colourful moments of the trial, received a four-year prison sentence and a 2 million francs fine. An estimated 3 billion francs (£360 million) disappeared from Elf coffers while Le Floch and Sirven ran the company, not all of which has been recovered.

Gilbert Miara, another Deviers-Joncour lover who helped her transfer embezzled funds to Switzerland and the Caribbean, received an 18-month sentence and a 1 million francs fine. Two Elf executives who processed payments to Deviers-Joncour through company accounts were cleared.

The five defendants convicted of graft yesterday announced they will appeal, a process which could take up to two years.

Dumas's illustrious career looks set to end in prison and French politicians may now think twice about doing favours and receiving gifts.

Letters to the Editor May 2001

Savings Scheme

Sir, — This morning I heard a cuckoo! It was on Morning Ireland and he was saying that a couple who have £400 a month to spare will be given an extra £100 by the Government. Those who have no cash to spare get nothing.

Is this a record? If so, can it be switched off? — Yours, etc., Garry Clarke, The Ward, Co. Dublin. 3 May 2001.

Mr Cowen's Accident

*Sir, — I am sure every right-thinking citizen will be as delighted as I am that Mr Brian Cowen's injuries were not so serious as to require a stay in hospital (*The Irish Times, 5 May).

Seve Ballesteros playing a tee shot on his knees at Druids Glen to publicise the launch of the Seve Trophy. Photograph: Peter Thursfield.

What I'd really like to know, however, is how long he had to wait in Accident and Emergency before he was attended to. — Yours, etc., Ian Blackmore, Shanid Road, Harold's Cross, Dublin 6W. 10 May 2001.

Blissful Ignorance

Sir, — *Miriam Donohoe, on her recent visit to Pyongyang (The Irish Times, 4 May) described meeting a 13-year-old soccer player who had never heard of Manchester United. It seems that there is something to be said for Stalinist repression after all.* — Yours, etc., Terry Dolan, Station Road, Dunboyne, Co. Meath. 12 May 2001.

A Punt on the Euro

Sir, — *Spotted today at the entrance to Blanchardstown Shopping Centre: a sign inviting customers to 'visit the euro information centre'. The incentive? 'You could win £100.'* — Yours, etc., Peter Fitzpatrick, Dublin 15. 14 May 2001.

State Reception for Cardinal

Sir, — *The refusal by the Dean of St Patrick's Cathedral of the invitation by Bertie Ahern and Celia*

Sunglasses reflecting the crowds out to enjoy the sunshine at Sandycove, Co. Dublin. Photograph: Eric Luke.

Larkin to a State reception honouring Cardinal Connell serves as a timely reminder to those of us who are in a second relationship of just how hypocritical and excluding is the society in which we live. Is the sin of being in a second relationship on a level different from the sins of others whose hospitality is freely enjoyed by the great and the good? Surely it is possible to encourage the 'principle' of marriage, without at the same time insulting in such a public way those whose experience of marriage has prevented them from remaining within it. Most people unlucky enough to have experienced separation, for whatever reason, would not choose the path on which they find themselves. They do not need to be reminded by more fortunate people of how difficult it was to make the decision to separate, and how excluded they now are from the Church to which they formerly belonged as a penance for having again found happiness.

I do not recall hearing the hierarchy of any Christian church announce that members of their clergy who may be in improper relationships, or who have offended morality in other ways, may not distribute Holy Communion to their flock or perform the other sacraments. Perhaps if insults and humiliations were publicly administered in a more even-handed way, this sinner would not have felt compelled to put pen to paper. — Yours, etc., Michael D. Peart, Stillorgan Grove, Blackrock, Co. Dublin. 17 May 2001.

Sir, — *A senior Church of Ireland clergyman refuses to attend a reception for a senior Roman Catholic clergyman hosted by the Taoiseach of the day because of the nature of the politician's relationship with his partner. Are you sure it's not the other way around? I had to check the date to see if it wasn't 1 April. I suppose this is progress, after a fashion.* — Yours, etc., Ronan McDermott, Georgetown, Guyana. 17 May 2001.

A chara, — *I won't be inviting Cardinal Connell to my next soirée as, like all party poopers, he seems to have this great ability to clear the hosts off the premises before things get into full swing!* — Is mise, Dara Lynch, Glendale Meadows, Leixlip, Co. Kildare. 17 May 2001.

Most Rev. Robin Eames (left), Archbishop of Armagh, and Most Rev. Walton Empey, Archbishop of Dublin, during a photocall at the Church of Ireland Synod at UCD Belfield. Photograph: Peter Thursfield.

Sir, — Ruairí Quinn has said that one day Ireland might have a gay or lesbian Taoiseach. What chance a gay or lesbian Cardinal? — Yours, etc., M. Magill, Howth, Co. Dublin. 19 May 2001.

2 JUNE 2001

The Witness Who Never Gets His Signals Crossed

Frank McNally

He may have made his fortune out of mobile telephony, but Mr Denis O'Brien knows that giving evidence before a tribunal is essentially a fixed-line business.

His line yesterday was that the Telenor donation to Fine Gael in 1995 was never anything to do with him or Esat. And although he experienced some difficulty getting through to the tribunal on it, he stuck with it throughout.

Counsel for the tribunal didn't think it was a very good line, and several times invited him to hang up and try again. At one point, Mr John Coughlan SC even appeared to suggest the line was out of order. But Mr O'Brien would not be shifted.

Matters came to a head when the witness spoke disparagingly of the 'ring-a-ring-a-rosey' of invoices by which the Norwegian company had attempted to re-route the $50,000 donation back to Esat, disguised as consultancy fees.

Mr Coughlan didn't like this ringing tone. And when, soon afterwards, the witness suggested Telenor had 'made' Esat take responsibility for the donation during negotiations on a shareholders' agreement, counsel finally cut him off.

He invited the witness to 'reflect' on what he was saying. 'We are in the world of serious business people now, not school children,' he snapped. Mr O'Brien duly reflected and, for the only time yesterday, changed his line a little. Esat hadn't been 'made' to claim the payment, exactly; the two companies had 'agreed' this.

Not for the first time in Irish history, Norsemen were getting the blame for a lot of things — even if, apart from his 'ring-a-rosey' jibe, Mr O'Brien's strongest comment was that the company's invoicing for the Fine Gael donation was 'chaotic'. To which Mr Coughlan replied drily: 'It may be chaotic. It may be something else.'

Mr O'Brien said he suggested Telenor as a possible donor to the Fine Gael fundraiser Mr David Austin, because it wanted to get involved in 'Irish affairs'. Did he mean just business affairs? counsel wondered. 'Yes,' said Mr O'Brien with a pause, 'and to become more involved in Ireland'.

The company has certainly achieved that ambition. Earlier, its chief executive, Mr Arve

Johansen, resumed the witness stand to say that Mr O'Brien asked him to make the payment on Esat's behalf to avoid causing a 'fuss in the media'.

The sequence by which the money was paid into an offshore account and then reimbursed to Telenor seemed strange, the Norwegian admitted. But: 'A lot of firms and a lot of private persons in Ireland had onshore and offshore accounts. So in my mind I said: well, this is another one.'

Mr Johansen was going offshore himself by the time Mr O'Brien took the stand, chasing a flight back to Oslo. However, he has made one significant contribution to this inquiry. His first name has two syllables, with a stress on the final 'e'. So when the ballad of the Moriarty tribunal finally comes to be written, at least we now have a word that rhymes with Charvet.

Mr O'Brien spoke of other political donations he had made 'since my windfall 18 months ago'.

The £230 million profit blown his way by the Esat sale was more like hurricane damage than a mere windfall. Yet, with all the stormy weather around him, Mr O'Brien has remained unflappable. True, at one point yesterday, he spoke of the need, prior to Esat's flotation, for 'dotting all the Ts'. But perhaps this was Norwegian punctuation.

4 JUNE 2001

Marina At Galway Docks Planned

Out of the West by Lorna Siggins

St Malo, Dieppe, Lisbon, Seville, the West Indies and Newfoundland. Hard to imagine now that the port of Galway once had these links, as the hub of international

Denis O'Brien jnr (right) and William Collatos, at the press conference outlining details of the eIsland bid for Eircom. Photograph: Eric Luke.

Jim Costello from Drimnagh, a foreman with Fleeton Watson Façade Refurbishment, says farewell to 'Mucky Duck' whom he and his fellow workers befriended while refurbishing 30/31 Wicklow Street in Dublin. The bird nested with its eggs between chimney pots, a most unusual habitat for a duck. Photograph: Bryan O'Brien.

trade, importing wine, iron, lead, spices and silks and exporting wool, fish, hides and tallow.

The zenith was the first half of the 17th century, when it could be compared with any British port — and when Henry Cromwell, son of Oliver and former Lord Deputy, could describe the city as inferior only to London.

However, so mixed have been the port's fortunes over the past four centuries — as recorded in a recent history by Dr Kieran Woodman — that this may explain why no one remembered to mark out the maritime limits.

Thanks to the current mayor, Mr Martin Quinn, this has now been resolved. Using a spear (reportedly, a broomstick and two makeshift arrowheads), the mayor recently reclaimed the waters of the port.

The platform for the ceremony was the deck of the naval patrol ship, LE *Aisling*. Councillor Quinn had been informed that as admiral of

Galway Bay this was his prerogative, similar to his counterparts in Dublin and Cork. Lieut Cdr Tim O'Keeffe, captain of the ship, was delighted to facilitate the historic event.

If the current Minister for the Marine and Natural Resources and Galway West TD, Mr Fahey, has his way, the dockside area where he is himself a registered property owner, will become a haven for leisure craft.

Plans for a 26-berth marina at Galway docks are expected to proceed very shortly, following application for a foreshore licence.

The first phase of the £450,000 project will involve installation of finger jetties, pontoons, a fuel berth, a floating breakwater, fresh water and closed-circuit television cameras. The second phase will involve construction of shower and yacht club facilities on reclaimed land, according to the harbour master, Capt Brian Sheridan.

The initiative is expected to receive 75 per cent funding under the National Development Plan, which has earmarked £20 million for marine leisure developments.

The beauty of the project is that much of the infrastructure is already in place and very little civil work will be involved, according to the harbour master.

Over to the east, in Oranmore Bay, Galway Bay Sailing Club is expanding rapidly and has its own plans. It has just received £45,000 in State and local authority funding to carry out a feasibility study for a marina there.

It also plans to construct a marine leisure centre. The centre and marina would be held in public control. The estimated cost of the project is £4.5 million, and the club is hopeful of National Development Plan support — given that the £20 million is weighted towards projects in the Border, Midlands and Western region. If approved, the first phase will involve construction of a breakwater, marina and foreshore works in time for the 2003 sailing season, and the marine centre will be built in the second phase.

Unlike the docks project, which is expected to be completed by next sailing season, the marina at Renville will have 24-hour access. It is not bound by tide. The project 'represents an important western element' in the NDP. Out west, the new marina at Roundstone is currently proceeding, as one of four flagship projects announced by the Minister last January at a total cost of £4.5 million. Cahersiveen and Kenmare in Co. Kerry and Rosses Point in Sligo also benefited by the tranche from the last Budget.

The Department of the Marine, therefore, will be kept busy with foreshore licence applications … and the author of a guide to marinas and mooring buoys around the coastline will have to produce a second edition. *Cruising Ireland*, by Brian Keane, is a very useful guide which lists over 70 safe landfalls for yachts, along with details on water, fuel, showers, banks, shops, repairs, restaurants and pubs.

The guide features an introduction from Mr Justice Robert Barr, who quotes Ninian Falkiner — 'of immortal memory, who sailed the seas of Western Europe from the Arctic to southern Portugal for many decades'. He was of the opinion that the ultimate cruise was an odyssey around Ireland. The judge did just that, undertaking two circumnavigations of Ireland in recent years.

9 JUNE 2001

Seven Deadly Sins That Sank Yes Campaign

Deaglán de Bréadún

All is changed, changed utterly. Hopefully, not a 'terrible beauty' but a new and more people-friendly Europe will be born. It would be a pity if the Nice referendum result were to be glided over and ultimately airbrushed from political discourse by our masters, because it contains important lessons in both domestic and European terms.

Among the seven deadly sins of the Yes campaign, sloth is the first that comes to mind. Apart from a noble and selfless few, the supporters of the treaty did not come out and knock on doors. The so-called 'flatearthers' on the other side were working flat out.

Two images: the night before the vote I saw two young men shinning up a lamp-standard to place one last placard urging a No vote, and a colleague taking the train from Balbriggan before 7 a.m. one day encountered Trevor Sargent of the Green Party handing out leaflets against Nice. Anger was another besetting sin on the Yes side. The usual nice, conciliatory Taoiseach we all know was replaced by Bertie the negative campaigner, putting out a shrill message to the effect that the No crowd were an extremist rabble and that Europe expected everyone to do their duty.

Envy: The Yes people made the funding of the other side the main issue in the last days of the campaign, diverting attention from the substance of the treaty. Allegations were made about British Tories giving large amounts to the National Platform and American Bible thumpers backing the No to Nice campaign, but there was a paucity of supporting documentation.

Pride: The feeble Yes campaign generated a feeling on the ground that these people were too haughty to request a vote for the treaty. Maybe they were just shy. The legendary Tip O'Neill explained to a disappointed aspirant for office that he hadn't supported him because he hadn't been approached. 'You've got to ask,' O'Neill said.

Complacency: All the organs of the establishment from the political parties through most of the trade unions and many of the bishops issued a variety of statements explicitly or implicitly supporting the treaty. It was all a little too neat and tidy and lacking in spontaneity. No doubt unfairly, the punters smelt a stitch-up.

Arrogance: This mainly came from a variety of senior EU figures who made unhelpful speeches and comments about their plans for our future without taking the likely effect on the Irish electorate into account.

Impatience: It was a mistake to allow such a short time for the debate. Calls for a Forum on the Future of Europe after the referendum were seized on and exploited by the No side who said this was like closing the door after the horse had bolted. Vote now and you can ask questions later seemed to be the message.

Just as the strength of the anti-Nice campaign was underestimated in advance of the vote, so the

Green Party MEP, Nuala Ahearn, and TD Trevor Sargent celebrate as the Nice Treaty votes were being announced at the RDS in Dublin. Photograph: Frank Miller.

Ruth Whitty, Michele McLoughlin and Bríd Ní Chionaola read from Ulysses *on Sandymount Strand during a picnic of gorgonzola and burgundy for Joyce enthusiasts who travelled on the Ulysses Vintage Bus Tour of Dublin landmarks. Photograph: Matt Kavanagh.*

power and influence of the No lobby is being exaggerated after the result. Most of them are small groups of part-time activists who worked on the campaign in their spare time. It was not so much a case of the No campaign winning the referendum as the Yes side losing it.

The possibility of a second referendum now looms. The Peace and Neutrality Alliance (PANA) has indicated that it would probably stand aside if there was a protocol that clearly excluded Ireland from participation in, or funding of, the Rapid Reaction Force. In theory, therefore, the current majority against Nice could be reduced, but we do not know how many people voted No because of the neutrality issue.

Secondly, a Pandora's box of issues has now been opened and the number of people concerned about, say, Enhanced Co-operation, may have increased significantly. The PANA group is only one faction in the informal anti-Nice coalition and a spokesman for the No to Nice Campaign claimed his organisation had exerted far greater influence on the referendum result. The No to Nice group essentially wants the process of European federalism stopped in its tracks. Its spokesman also called for the resignation of Mr Ahern and Mr Brian Cowen from their current positions. 'We do believe in a European Union of co-operating independent states,' he said.

The Green Party has done well out of the referendum campaign. Mr John Gormley and Ms

Patricia McKenna in particular have raised their political profiles. Mr Gormley, who rides a bicycle, seems to be trusted by more members of the public on European issues than many who travel in State cars.

The Green Party has its own set of priorities which differ from every other faction including Sinn Féin. It was no accident that No votes tended to be higher in constituencies where Sinn Féin was active. The party was clearly using the referendum as a dry run for the general election. Why the established parties could not do the same remains a mystery.

Europe's democratic deficit has come home to roost. Eurocrats careering down the fast track to integration need to pull into the next lay-by and take the time to explain the grand plan in ordinary language to ordinary citizens.

It should be said that there was little or no evidence of xenophobia in the Irish campaign and both sides expressed their support in principle for enlargement. There will be disappointment in the former communist countries where many people will be dismayed at the prospect of further delay in their admission to the EU. Most Irish voters would regard this as an undesirable side-effect of the referendum result: people here did not vote No in order to keep out the Poles and the Czechs but because they were concerned or confused about other issues.

This is possibly the most remarkable and unexpected result since the 1977 general election when virtually no one read the public mood accurately. A little humility from Government leaders and their European counterparts is now in order. Instead of lecturing and berating the voters they should indicate that they have been given food for thought and that the various messages implicit in the result will be carefully studied and sensible conclusions drawn. But a tactical, spin-doctored humility will not suffice: the conversion to a listening approach must be genuine. Repent ye sinners, before it is too late.

SDLP and UUP Face Major Battles To Regain Ground

Suzanne Breen

It's hard to know which party should be happier — Sinn Féin or the DUP. Sinn Féin doubled its Westminster seats and displaced the SDLP as the North's major nationalist party. The DUP went from 14 to 23 per cent support to become the second-largest party in the North, with three new Westminster seats.

So how did Sinn Féin and the DUP do it? First, their candidates are generally more dynamic than their opponents. In North Belfast, the DUP ran Nigel Dodds (42), one of unionism's most articulate and intelligent figures. The sitting UUP MP was Cecil Walker (76), who made weak television performances and repeated vote-losing comments about a united Ireland. The UUP vote fell 40 per cent and the DUP beat Mr Walker by almost 12,000 votes.

Sometimes, one party presents a more youthful image than the other. SDLP leaders are in their 60s while Sinn Féin leaders are in their 50s, yet Sinn Féin presents a more modern, dynamic image. When the SDLP runs young candidates, many are from prominent party families but are relatively unknown in the wider community.

The party predicted its Mid-Ulster candidate, Eilís Haughey — daughter of SDLP junior Stormont minister Dennis — would increase its vote. She was no match for Martin McGuinness and actually polled 3,000 votes fewer than her father's tally in the 1997 election.

Both Sinn Féin and the DUP are dedicated constituency workers on social and economic issues. The UUP and the SDLP suffer from bourgeois images and poor internal organisation. They became complacent during the Troubles; the IRA campaign ensured Sinn Féin would never overtake the SDLP. The UUP took it for granted that a majority of unionists wouldn't prefer its fundamentalist rival.

But apart from the Rev. Ian Paisley's denunciation of line-dancing, the DUP has considerably changed the tone — if not the content — of its policies. During the Westminster campaign, it talked of 'renegotiating' the Belfast Agreement. A few years ago, the slogan would have been of 'smashing' it.

Sinn Féin's changes have gone beyond linguistics. It has shed much of its traditional republican baggage. It has stolen SDLP clothes but wears them in a livelier and sexier fashion. As with Fianna Fáil in the 1930s, its leaders have the whiff of past revolutionary deeds while on the constitutional road.

The ending of the IRA campaign has strengthened the nationalism of Catholic voters. 'You can be as green as you like and nobody thinks you're a Provo,' says an observer.

In the unionist community, there is considerable opposition to the Belfast Agreement. Voters are unhappy about Sinn Féin in government without IRA decommissioning and about the proposed changes to the RUC. The DUP is in tune with this mood. UUP candidates who increased their vote — Jeffrey Donaldson, the Rev. Martin Smyth and David Burnside — were notably anti-agreement.

In terms of internal organisation, Sinn Féin and the DUP are well in front of their rivals. Television pictures from the count centres showed the camaraderie in both parties. In terms of the party leaders, Dr Paisley's vote went up while David Trimble's fell. Gerry Adams and Martin McGuinness both scored higher personal votes than John Hume and Séamus Mallon, whose votes decreased.

While Dr Paisley took a lesser role during the election, allowing Peter Robinson and Nigel Dodds to appear on high-profile television programmes, Mr Hume remained at the forefront of his party's campaign. Anecdotal evidence suggests some nationalist voters were disappointed with his performances.

While policy or leadership changes could improve the UUP's position, the SDLP is in far greater danger. It emerged from the 1998 Assembly elections as the North's largest party. At Westminster 2001, it was relegated to fourth place.

During the election campaign, the SDLP refused to acknowledge that nationalist voters were increasingly identifying with Sinn Féin policies and candidates. Instead, it concentrated on opinion polls showing it comfortably clear of its rival.

The SDLP will have to face up to reality if it wants to halt the growing drift to Sinn Féin.

11 JUNE 2001

McVeigh Sorry For Pain, But No Regrets

Patrick Smyth

'I am sorry these people had to lose their lives,' Timothy McVeigh has written to his hometown newspaper, the *Buffalo News*, and published yesterday on the eve of his execution. 'But that's the nature of the beast. It's understood going in what the human toll will be.'

The April 1995 bombing of the Murrah Building in Oklahoma in which 168 died was 'a legit tactic' in his war against an 'out-of-control' government.

In a series of letters written from his death-row prison cell before and after the postponement of his original execution date, the condemned mass murderer declared that his bombing was in defence of the right of Americans to personal freedom and a reaction to government atrocities at Waco, Texas, and Ruby Ridge, Idaho.

Acknowledging that millions of Americans despise him, the decorated Gulf War veteran said he hopes his countrymen eventually will come to view

Participants in Tesco Ireland Evening Herald *Women's Mini Marathon leave the starting line in Merrion Square in Dublin. Photograph: Bryan O'Brien.*

him as a 'freedom fighter' who died for his cause. He compares his bombing to the actions of John Brown, who fought slavery in the mid-1800s by leading raids that killed men, women and children.

Unrepentant, still in his own eyes a righteous soldier, his victims the hapless casualties of war, McVeigh last night prepared for the certainty of his own death this morning.

At 7 a.m. local time (1 p.m. Irish time) he will be strapped to a table in the federal prison of Terre Haute, Indiana, and receive his first of three injections, sodium pentathol, to make him unconscious. Then follows pancuronium bromide, to paralyse the lungs and muscles. Finally, potassium chloride will be administered to stop his heart — the subject usually dies in 10 minutes. McVeigh will be the first person to be put to death by the federal government since 1963.

Last night, McVeigh was confined to the 9 ft by 14 ft isolation cell in the execution building only a few yards from the room where he will be killed, with a few books, a black-and-white television set, and the prospects of a $20 last meal from the restaurant of his choice. He made final calls to friends and his father who will not be attending the execution.

His death will be witnessed at the prison by 10 victims or survivors of victims, 10 media representatives and four people McVeigh had invited, including two of his lawyers. The fifth of McVeigh's guests, the novelist Gore Vidal, said he could not attend. About 300 victims of the blast or family members of those killed are due to watch by closed circuit television in Oklahoma City.

McVeigh has turned down hundreds of reporters' requests for interviews in recent weeks.

He told the *Buffalo News* he had also turned down a request from the FBI for a 'final debriefing'.

And he told the paper that he might have chosen another tactic for expressing his hatred of the federal government. McVeigh said he sometimes wishes that, instead of a bombing, he had used his gunnery skills for a series of assassinations against police and government officials who crack down on the rights of gun owners.

He has made clear that after his death he is to be cremated and his ashes will be scattered at a secret location. 'I don't want to create a draw for people who hate me, or for people who love me,' McVeigh wrote.

He continues to get letters in prison from people who admire his political stance, though most do not condone the bombing. Some of the letters are bizarre. 'Timmy even got a letter from a woman who said she would have his baby if he could somehow get his sperm smuggled out of prison,' his father, Mr Bill McVeigh, told the *News*. 'She even said her boyfriend told her it was OK.'

Protests for and against the execution started last night and prison officials gave both sides separate but equal sites on the green meadows surrounding the US Penitentiary just south of Terre Haute, fenced-in areas with portable floodlights and temporary toilets where they could begin to gather at midnight, seven hours before the execution. Prior to that, they could assemble at two city parks. Some 1,500 journalists have gathered.

In this Indiana college town, some regular Sunday church services were devoted to the execution. The First Unitarian church brought in a speaker to discuss capital punishment.

At St Margaret Mary Catholic Church, a centre for those opposed to capital punishment, protesters planned a late afternoon march to the prison just outside town.

At nearby St Mary of the Woods College, nuns from the Sisters of Providence order planned a silent prayer vigil for the victims of the bombing and the man who brought it about.

The latter has few plans to prepare to meet his maker. An agnostic, he wrote to the *News* that he will 'improvise, adapt and overcome' if it turns out that there is an afterlife, and he winds up in heaven or hell.

'If I am going to hell,' he said, 'I'm gonna have a lot of company.'

He should know this morning.

16 JUNE 2001

Office Of Taoiseach Is Effectively Vacant

Dick Walsh

Bertie Ahern is a dangerously likeable man. Standing beside him in a pub, you'd swear he was one of the lads. The trouble is he isn't just playing the part: he is one of the lads.

The office of Taoiseach has been vacant for some time and will remain so, at least until the general election; longer if Fianna Fáil is returned to power. A Taoiseach worth his salt wouldn't have had to wait for his minister to tell him what a state the health services are in. And he certainly wouldn't have contradicted official evidence by pretending that all was well.

A Taoiseach who was serious about reforming local government would not have allowed four Independents to block a reform his minister considered essential. He would have accepted Labour's offer of support and got on with the job.

A Taoiseach who'd negotiated the Treaty of Nice would have shown his commitment to the development of the European Union and led the campaign to have the treaty ratified. He would not have confined himself to firing the odd insult at the electorate as the Coalition's efforts went down in disaster and woe.

And he would have accepted Ruairí Quinn's proposal of a forum in March, when it might have prepared the ground for an autumn referendum.

Instead, he ignored the offer and blundered ahead as if he were building a football stadium.

Don't take my word for it — ask Micheál Martin, Noel Dempsey and Brian Cowen about the vacuum in Merrion Street. Get them to tell you about the dangerously likeable man who keeps his head down while they struggle with the affairs of state. Ask about the disaster of a Government that looks as if it's being run by some fellow at the corner of a bar with a pint in his fist and an eye on the box.

Anthony Coughlan of the National Platform wrote an open letter to Ahern this week in which he said that Éamon Ó Cuiv had 'upheld the best values of the Fianna Fáil party' of Éamon de Valera when he voted No to Nice.

The unconscious humour of it may be lost on those who need to be reminded of old Dev's opposition to the oath of allegiance to the King in 1922.

And how he overcame his scruples by calling it an empty formula and marching his party into the Dáil.

And there was Dev's grandson, 80 years on, explaining to Philip Bouchier Hayes on Radio 1 why there was nothing odd about supporting the Yes campaign and voting No. Political consistency and the collective responsibility? Empty formulae.

Not only did Ó Cuiv vote No, he then told the people who'd been persuaded to vote Yes what he'd done. Ahern found nothing wrong with this. It probably reminded him of the bould Ned O'Keeffe, another junior minister who 'upheld the best values of the party' by campaigning against BSE while the family firm manufactured bonemeal, a suspected source of the disease.

Fianna Fáil and the coalition it leads now have three different lines on the European Union. Ó Cuiv's approach is traditional nationalism — straight, as it were, from the horse's mouth.

The Minister for Finance, Mr McCreevy (left), and the Minister for Consumer Affairs, Mr Kitt, at the Euro Press Conference, hosted by the Central Bank. Photograph: Eric Luke.

Junior Minister, Liz O'Donnell, with Reuben on Grafton Street, Dublin, where she joined the PD leader, Mary Harney, to canvass for a Yes vote to the Nice Treaty. Photograph: Bryan O'Brien.

Then there's the Harney-McCreevy line, not just suspicious of Brussels but of the centripetal force it represents. Mary Harney and Charlie McCreevy prefer big business and small government to European social democracy.

As for the third way, FF-style: that's where you'll find Ahern. Waiting, as ever, to see how the cat jumps. Willing, if need be, to ride two horses at once.

This all but leaderless condition is a very dangerous one for the country at a time of confusion of which the post-Nice shout-in has been the most obvious — by no means the only — example. In an early debate on how we'd get used to our European identity, an English writer made light of the problem by pointing out that somebody from, say, Wigan, would be European in a peculiarly English way just as somebody from Grenoble would be European and still unmistakably French.

Listening to callers tell Joe Duffy on RTÉ Radio 1's 'Liveline' programme this week why they'd voted No, it occurred to me that we too are European in a peculiarly Irish way. Never mind the

contradictions, feel the grievance.

For centuries we'd blamed Britain for all our troubles; now it was Europe's turn. The EU was becoming more militarised, callers said. But Sinn Féin, among the leaders of the No campaign, is in partnership with the paramilitaries of the IRA. There were objections to secrecy and faceless bureaucrats. As if the members of the IRA army council, one of the most influential groups in Ireland, appeared daily in the media on their way to meetings about decommissioning.

There were complaints about privatisation, the concentration of ownership and control in a few hands. As if the European Union were responsible for our notorious tax system in Cayman Ireland. As if we hadn't our very own Sir Anthony Berlusconi, to whose power and influence there appears to be no limit.

The EU was even blamed by some for our health services. The cruellest cut — in a week in which we hear yet again that ours is the worst service in the EU and the poor are the people who suffer most from it.

A Taoiseach serious about local government reform would not have allowed Independents to block it. Fianna Fáil and the coalition it leads now have three different lines on the European Union.

21 JUNE 2001

EU Enlargement Is Possible Without Nice, Says Prodi

Denis Staunton

The European Commission President, Mr Romano Prodi, has said EU enlargement can proceed even if the Nice Treaty is not ratified. But he expressed concern at Ireland's rejection of the treaty and promised to listen closely to the Irish people during a three-day visit beginning today in Dublin.

In an interview with *The Irish Times*, Mr Prodi said the issues of enlargement and the ratification of the Nice Treaty should be treated separately. Under the Amsterdam Treaty of 1998, the EU can accept up to five new members, making a total of 20.

However, the Commission President maintained that the EU could accept more than five new member-states without ratifying Nice.

'Legally, ratification of the Nice Treaty is not necessary for enlargement. It's without any problem up to 20 members, and those beyond 20 members have only to put in the accession agreement some notes of change, some clause. But legally, it's not necessary.

'This doesn't mean the Irish referendum is not important. But from this specific point of view, enlargement is possible without Nice,' he said.

Mr Prodi will attend a State dinner in his honour in Dublin Castle this evening and during his visit will meet leaders of the No to Nice campaign as well as Government ministers, opposition leaders and representatives of the social partners. At University College Cork tomorrow he will make a speech clarifying his vision for Europe's future.

Insisting that the primary purpose of his visit was to listen, Mr Prodi said he would not advise the Government on whether to call a second referendum on Nice. And he said there should be no pressure from Brussels in the meantime.

'You must feel yourselves free to choose and there cannot be pressure or arm-twisting or blackmail,' he said.

Mr Prodi rejected suggestions that a speech he made a week before the referendum, in which he called for an EU tax, had influenced the result. He said that a decision by Ireland to block the Nice Treaty would send an important signal about the direction of Europe.

Romano Prodi, President of the European Commission, is greeted by the Taoiseach, Bertie Ahern, at Government Buildings. Photograph: Cyril Byrne.

'Of course this is a serious problem even without impeding enlargement. Also because it was a referendum in which the Nice issues were mainly absent. I tried to observe the campaign and it was a campaign on sentiments, so the problem is, has the Irish attitude towards Europe changed? This is my real point. It is even more serious than a No to Nice,' he said.

The Commission President suggested that Ireland's new-found prosperity could have played a role in the referendum in so far as people who are doing well fear change.

'It's not different from the situation in some other countries in a very good situation economically and in terms of vision for the future, in terms of social equilibrium, in terms of not having any big dangers. In this situation people say, why change?' he said.

Mr Prodi declined to comment on remarks by the Minister for Finance, Mr McCreevy, describing the referendum result as a healthy development for democracy. But he dismissed a suggestion by the Attorney General, Mr Michael McDowell, that the EU was taking on the attributes of a superstate. Mr Prodi insisted that pooling sovereignty in some areas was the only way nation states could retain influence in the modern world.

Admitting that the referendum result surprised him, Mr Prodi said he was worried it may express a deep feeling of resentment towards Europe.

Limerick fans on the terrace at Páirc Uí Chaoimh where their team were victorious over Waterford in the Munster Senior Hurling Semi-final in Cork. Photograph: Eric Luke.

30 JUNE 2001

Nobody Should Be Writing Trimble Off Just Yet

Frank Millar

Observe the Loyal Son of Ulster. Last night he and his wife, Daphne, were due at the opera for a performance of 'Le Nozze di Figaro' — a satire on French politics heralding the end of an era. This morning he sets off for France and a Somme commemoration of those who knew no fear of death.

Mr Trimble is set to fly out still First Minister of Northern Ireland, and return tomorrow plain leader of the Ulster Unionist Party. The Presiding Officer, Lord Alderdice, might observe strict sabbatarian rules and not read Mr Trimble's letter of resignation until the Assembly convenes on Monday morning. But the trappings of ministerial office are due to begin their graceless fall from the Ulster Unionist leader tonight on the stroke of midnight.

He was intent on going, and the British government — denied any option by the IRA — has seemingly bowed to his determination. Hence, apparently, the absence of any pre-emptive move this week to suspend the Stormont Assembly and other institutions of the Belfast Agreement in an effort to keep Mr Trimble in play.

Assuming nothing happens to avert his resignation in the next few hours, London and Dublin, of course, will still hope to see him restored. The British Prime Minister, Mr Blair, and the Taoiseach, Mr Ahern, have not accepted the IRA's latest emphatic No as the republican movement's final word on decommissioning.

Indeed, Mr Trimble has said he would anticipate re-election as First Minister should the IRA comply with the second deadline — a statutory six weeks which Mr Blair and Mr Ahern have decided means an effective cut-off point at the end of July — which flows inescapably from his first.

In truth, however, Mr Trimble does not expect to resume ministerial office in mid-summer. He does apparently believe that the IRA will eventually move to put weapons beyond use, because Sinn Féin's political project ultimately requires it. But his best-guess scenario is believed to be predicated on the expectation of a second suspension of the agreement and its institutions, to be followed by a fresh negotiation in the autumn.

At this point we enter into the world of the unknown and the unknowable. For if there is no basis for assuming how the republican movement will respond in the coming month, nor is there any for the assumption that Mr Trimble will still be around to pick up the pieces come September or October.

Not that anybody should be writing him off just yet. 'For a dead man walking, he's got a remarkable number of people dancing to his tune', observed one of Northern Ireland's shrewdest commentators the other day — this in reference to the DUP's offer to 'resign' its ministers if Mr Trimble's three colleagues also quit the Executive, and to the Taoiseach's decision to place primary responsibility on the republicans to break the political deadlock by moving first on decommissioning.

Having conspicuously refused to dance to Mr Trimble's tune, Mr Blair and Mr Ahern plainly hope that the IRA might now make a move in response to the legislative deadline requiring the election of First and Deputy First Ministers six weeks after a vacancy occurs.

Others in both capitals fear republicans will instead regard the invocation of the statutory deadline as but the consequence of the imposition of Mr Trimble's own ultimatum. Moreover, they point to the worrying evidence of recent days, weeks and months that (as Mr Gerry Adams has, in fairness, always maintained) the public and private positions of the republican leadership have been, and remain, 'one and the same'.

Two facts shine out from the enveloping gloom. First, for good or ill, unionism has made IRA decommissioning the litmus test of Sinn Féin's democratic bona fides. Second, Sinn Féin — buoyed rather than intimidated by electoral success — has effectively told Mr Trimble, Mr Blair and Mr Ahern to get lost and think again.

The Taoiseach is said to have been shaken by the tone and demeanour of Sinn Féin leaders in the afterglow of their June 7th triumph. This, in turn, is cited in explanation of his hardline decision to abandon the careful policy of never placing the onus on any one party. At their meeting in Downing Street on 18 June, Mr Ahern and Mr Blair are understood to have concluded that a successful resolution of the issues threatening the Good Friday accord would not be found in time to prevent Mr Trimble's resignation. The assessment of the two premiers was also that the situation following Sinn Féin's electoral success was actually worse than they had left it back in March.

In other words, all that talk about votes translating into greater republican flexibility on arms had been so much pie in the sky. What one source describes as the 'extraordinary caution' of republican leaders on the weapons issue — which Mr Blair and Mr Ahern well recognise, even if they cannot understand it — was simply unaffected by votes cast for the peace process in West Tyrone or anywhere else.

Yes, Mr Adams continued, and continues, to tantalise. In this newspaper on Thursday he rehearsed Sinn Féin's strategy for putting IRA weapons beyond use and again asserted his confidence that the weapons issue 'will be successfully resolved'.

But that strategy is evidently not for here and now. Not for this moment in history. And certainly not for compliance with any timetable prescribed by a modernising unionist leader now drowning in the bitter denunciations of so many in his own community that he should have taken so much on trust.

So, if they have refused to act to prevent his resignation, will republicans move in the short and potentially explosive weeks remaining to bring Mr Trimble back to political life? Or will they calculate that they need expend no capital on a unionist leader whose days, in any event, might very well be numbered?

Such calculation might well help fulfil the prophecy. If it proves to be so, then we may this weekend be witnessing the end of the current phase of political life and development in Northern Ireland, and the beginning of the end of the Belfast Agreement, at least as we have known it.

Certainly, if the IRA's last word should prove its final riposte (at least for now), it might seem reasonable to assume that the Sinn Féin leadership will have built this possibility into its calculations. Troubled unionists — including some of those most passionately committed to the agreement — are likely to be doing the same.

For some time now — indeed virtually since the 1998 Assembly elections — Mr Trimble has been battling against the reality that a majority of unionists do not in fact consent to the present dispensation in Northern Ireland. He has been fortunate in the quality of his opposition, and in the reluctance even of the Democratic Unionists to lose the devolved dimension of the Good Friday settlement. However, the two governments might be foolish to suppose Mr Jeffrey Donaldson or Mr Peter Robinson — putative leaders in a post-Trimble world of realigned unionism — would or could break faith with their constituency over decommissioning in order to claim the top prize themselves.

No. If Mr Trimble is forced out in the coming months over the failure to secure decommissioning, it is more likely that that lack of unionist consent will be made manifest and explicit — and that a succeeding unionist leader would risk all on a return to the drawing board and a wholesale renegotiation.

Letters to the Editor
June 2001

Nice Treaty Rejection

Sir, — When we agree with the Government we are told that the people have spoken. When we disagree we are accused of being confused. That I find very insulting. — Is Mise, Luke 'Ming' Flanagan, Lower Longford, Castlerea, Co. Roscommon. 11 June 2001.

Sir, — If I don't like the result of the next general election can I have it re-run until the parties I support get elected? — Yours, etc., Frank Barr, Glasnevin Woods, Ballyboggan Road, Dublin 11. 12 June 2001.

Sir, — When all the explanations (and excuses) for Ireland's failure to ratify the Nice Treaty have been exhausted, there remains one inescapable fact. When we were asked to send a clear signal to countries in Eastern Europe that we supported their right to gain access to the same opportunities for social and economic prosperity that have been so beneficial to us over the past 30 years, we refused. It should be remembered that many of these countries have a history as poverty-stricken as our own and our failure to support European enlargement last Thursday says much about our current priorities and our development as a modern European nation. — Yours, etc., Kevin Kenny, Roseburn Maltings, Edinburgh. 12 June 2001.

Sir, — The declaration by EU leaders that the Nice Treaty ratification process will continue, and that the treaty will not be renegotiated, is a direct insult to the

The Labour Party leader, Ruairí Quinn, being heckled by 'No' campaigners as the Nice Treaty votes were being announced at the RDS. Photograph: Frank Miller.

Irish Government and the Irish electorate. We cannot claim to have even one shred of sovereignty remaining if our democratic decisions are not respected. Where is closer EU integration leading us if the decision of the electorate is swept aside as if it were of no consequence whatsoever? — Yours, etc., Patrick Kenny, Kill Avenue, Dún Laoghaire. 14 June 2001.

Sir, — Unfortunately the Irish people answered the Nice Referendum question incorrectly. However, after intensive grinds, we may be allowed to repeat. — Yours, etc., Ray Monahan, Castlegregory, Co. Kerry. 14 June 2001.

Sir, — If the Irish electorate were to approve the Nice Treaty in a second referendum, would it mean that the treaty could be ratified by Ireland? Shouldn't we at least make it a best-of-three? — Yours, etc., Rachel Quinlan, Rialto, Dublin 8. 14 June 2001.

Sir, — Revenge is sweet. The Irish electorate has given a 'Harvey Smith' to Europe. That's what it gets for throwing us out of The Eurovision Song Contest! — Yours, etc., Brendan M. Redmond, Hazelbrook Road, Terenure, Dublin 6W. 14 June 2001.

2 JULY 2001

Roaring Lions Tear Apart The Wallabies

Gerry Thornley

Australia 13, The Lions 29

As has become custom on this tour, after the hosts took exception to earlier post-match pitch invasions, there were repeated warnings at the Gabba that any spectators encroaching onto the playing surface would receive a minimum Aus$500 fine. For the first hour or so, it seemed there was a case for fining the Wallabies.

No one really knew quite what to expect on Saturday, but pretty much no one expected this.

Enjoying the sunshine at Curracloe, Co. Wexford. Photograph: Pat Langan.

Even in their most optimistic moments, the Lions may well have envisaged putting together such an all-embracing performance of their own, but not that the world champions would be so off the pace, especially their famed defence.

It was no surprise that the volume of support for the tourists was even greater than officially forecast, or that the Lions would try to take the game to the Wallabies by attacking them out wide as well as targeting the home pack in the scrums and lineout drives.

But the extent of the double whammy was still quite something and left Australia reeling.

All day long it was as if Brisbane had become a little corner of England, and Wales and Ireland and Scotland too. They had camped outside the bars, drinking and singing good-naturedly from late morning. No one needed directions to the ground: just follow the crowds.

The Gabba was awash in gold and red, but mostly red. Contrary to official forecasts of 12,000, the barmy red army must have numbered at least 20,000 of the 37,460 attendance with the help of the expatriate community. It certainly looked that way, and it sure as hell sounded that way.

Keith Wood had tried to warn the Lions' debutants of the wall of sound they would encounter, that it was greater than anything in the Six Nations. Supporters had saved, sometimes for years, for what might also be the biggest trip/holiday of their lives. Whatever, they would give it the full blast.

One local, who'd seen Aussie Rules, cricket and league at the Gabba, sitting in front of me at pitchside, said he'd never heard noise like it at the old ground.

Quite what the world champions thought of being booed onto their own turf, heaven only knows.

Then, as we suggested they might, the Lions made the bold statement of intent by moving the ball to O'Driscoll with their first play for him to breach the famed golden line. To then move the recycle on to that other game-breaker, Jason Robinson, for him to transfix Chris Latham to the spot and then do his Billy Whizz around him — well, psychologically, Australia were on the back foot for the rest of a remarkable night.

When asked in a contemplative moment in a corridor underneath what he would savour from this game, the normally taciturn Graham Henry couldn't bottle up his immense satisfaction any longer.

'Probably the first try,' he purred. 'We took them on, got over the advantage line right away through O'Driscoll, and then scored wide out. It was a magic start. Unbelievable.'

All the coaching staff could feel reasonably well pleased — not that they'd show it too much, mind.

The set-pieces were, unsurprisingly, a source of Lions strength. The scrum was offensive (it's hard to see how the Wallabies can buy one of them in the next week) and the lineout was even better, as the Lions drove the Wallabies back.

The Lions pack had the measure of their hosts; the only nagging doubt was that this superiority wasn't reflected on the scoreboard as Andrew Walker and Jonny Wilkinson traded penalties. But something else was happening.

The Wallabies weren't penetrating the Lions' swarming defence. The big rumblers were generally rumbled at source by excellent first-up tackling. Even when Nathan Grey or someone else might break one tackle, he was quickly smothered.

The organisation and communication must have been excellent. The numbers were always there, until the Lions lapsed into defensive mode and were reduced to 14 men with the game well won.

They'd also kept a few tricks up their sleeves, and when O'Driscoll and Robinson strutted across field to exchange places with Wilkinson and Matt Perry to the narrower side of that 40th-minute scrum on half-way, you sensed they were up to something. The Wallabies didn't react, and O'Driscoll cut inside Stephen Larkham and Robinson provided the link for Dafydd James' try.

When O'Driscoll turned on the afterburners at the start of the second-half, it was party time. All night 'Bread of Heaven', 'Molly Malone' and 'Flower of Scotland' had intermingled easily ('Swing Low'? Well, there are limits.)

Now it was time to chide the locals. 'You're not singing anymore,' echoed around the Gabba.

Viewed now, the Aussie propaganda war can almost be viewed as fear, and with good reason. They looked dangerous after multi-phases against 14 men, but otherwise they looked very patterned and certainly lacking the individualism of O'Driscoll.

There were blemishes. Scott Quinnell was the leading culprit at the breakdown, and Corry was unlucky to receive the yellow card the Welshman deserved. Iain Balshaw looked ropier than Perry, but the good thing about Wilkinson's unexceptional performance is that he'll probably be exceptional next week.

SCORING SEQUENCE: 4 mins: Robinson try 0–5; 22: Walker pen 3–5; 40: James try, Wilkinson 3–12; (half-time 3–12); 42: O'Driscoll try, Wilkinson con 3–19; 45: Wilkinson pen 3–22; 52: Quinnell try, Wilkinson con 3–29; 76: Walker try 8–29; 79: Grey try 13–29.
AUSTRALIA: C. Latham (Queensland); A. Walker (ACT), D. Herbert (Queensland), N. Grey (NSW), J. Roff (ACT); S. Larkham (ACT), G. Gregan (ACT); N. Stiles (Queensland), J. Paul (ACT), G. Panoho (Queensland), D. Giffin (ACT), J. Eales (Queensland, capt), O. Finegan (ACT), T. Kefu (Queensland), G. Smith (ACT). Replacements: M. Burke (NSW) for Latham (half-time), M. Foley (Queensland) for Paul (56 mins), E. Flatley for Larkham (56 mins), B. Darwin (ACT) for Panoho (68 mins), M. Cockbain (Queensland) for Eales (73 mins), D. Lyons (NSW) for Finegan (83 mins).
LIONS: M. Perry (England); D. James (Wales), B. O'Driscoll (Ireland), R. Henderson (Ireland), J. Robinson (England); J. Wilkinson (England), R. Howley (Wales); T. Smith (Scotland), K. Wood (Ireland), P. Vickery (England), M. Johnson (England, capt), D. Grewcock (England), M. Corry (England), S. Quinnell (Wales), R. Hill (England). Replacements: I. Balshaw (England) for Perry (half-time), C. Charvis (Wales) for Quinnell (69 mins), G. Bulloch (Scotland) for Wood (75–82 mins), J. Leonard (England) for Smith (82 mins). Sin-binned: Corry (68–79 mins), Vickery (85–91 mins).
REFEREE: Andre Watson (South Africa).

7 JULY 2001

Beachcomber Charm

Another Life by Michael Viney

The natural bric-à-brac that crowds our window-sills leaves little room for fussy housekeeping. From time to time, shamed by its patina of museum dust and cobwebs, I take it all down, hoover the sand away, and even wash a few things, gently, as with delicate china, reviving the violet-and-rose of a sea urchin's globe, the gleam of a seabird's bill.

Most of these objects were picked up at the tide-line, that shifting aperture on ocean life and death where skulls, carapaces, shells, worm-tubes, things forged of calcium and carbon, make a defiant landfall, their fragile irreducibility a part of their charm for the beachcomber.

After that, perhaps, the wonder at nature's creating, quite by the way, colours, textures and forms that fill us with delight. There seems no functional reason the global skeleton of a sea urchin, normally quite hidden by its spines, should glow with such radiant hues (or why, for that matter, so many deep-sea creatures are brilliantly scarlet and yellow at depths which filter just those wavelengths from the sunlight). Yet the colours of the bigger urchins, plus their exquisite proportion and five-fold geometry, make them some of the most satisfying structures in nature, at once seamed and seamless.

The worm-tubes I speak of shelter colonies of minute animals at the sea-bed. They extrude their homes in a swirling, brilliant white on flat surfaces of stones that, later, in storms, get lifted ashore in the clasp of kelp. The sun reveals them as calligraphers, cameo-carvers, Old Wedgwood potters, the Italian stuccodores of Georgian ceilings — whatever one's culture calls to mind. In the same associative way, a vertebral disc from a Risso's dolphin, with its intricate radial engraving, can demand to be worn on a fine chain: an ivory medallion for a druid.

The beauty of drift-objects can be inherent or referential ('like' or 'as if'). It takes an artist to make connections that brought you to the tide's edge in the first place, to pace the thin, dark line between sand and wave. Even in the unnatural calm of a city-centre art gallery, the magical bone boats of sculptor Alan Counihan must reach far into the urban imagination, searching out whatever is left of its animistic soul.

I first met this remarkable Dubliner on the wind-swept terraces of Kilcummin Head, on Mayo's north coast, chipping at great stone slabs with a mason's hammer and chisel. This was his original trade, learned in part while labouring on Charles Haughey's home on Inishvickillane. Now, to the same, deep sea-sounds, he was shaping stone to build 'a holy place' on the cliff. This sheltering gable of a sanctuary, pierced by a passage for the wind, was his contribution to Tír Sáile, the sculpture trail spaced out between Killala and the tip of the Mullet peninsula.

Another of his stone sanctuaries, couched in mountain bedrock above a bay at Allihies, Co. Cork, appears in the richly collectible catalogue of his current exhibition, Prayers before Dying (which finishes tomorrow in the Temple Bar Gallery).

The evening sunset provides a backdrop to the masts of boats moored at the new marina in Dún Laoghaire, Co. Dublin. Photograph: Eric Luke.

There are pictures, too, of some of his big organic works, such as the rough-husked 'fruit' of granite, with polished beach stones at its heart, that stands outside the civic offices in Greystones, Co. Wicklow.

After the large, hard-hewn forms of this public sculpture, both here and in the US, the toy-like structures of his new bone boats come as an intimate revelation. Crafted from bones and feathers gathered on long, lonely walks round Achill Island, they are held together by tiny pegs and horsehair and the spring of one bone against another; above all, by an almost shamanistic vision of them whole.

Even a zoologist might be hard pressed to trace all their skeletal sources. Dolphins, sheep and seabirds offer sternums, ribs, wingbones, backbones, feathers, to build vessels poised on tiptoe, ready to fly. Counihan spent many months rowing a currach in the Blaskets, and the dancing buoyancy of his boats is keeled in a fine illusion of seaworthiness; spirits crowd out of a mythic past to set sail behind a gannet's beak or the fanged skull of a stoat.

As he trudged the eroding shores of Achill, he came upon a litter of very old, iron-stained, human bones, including a skull in two halves, scattered among beach stones and sea-wrack. With no one rushing to bless their burial, he carried them high into the hills, fitting them at last into a niche of rock perched above bog and forest. His photograph of the broken skull as 'vessel of the imagination', gilded by a failing sun and cupping empty air, is a richly meditative image.

Meanwhile, lichens crust the slabs of 'Tearmon na Gaoithe' ('the wind house' as locals prefer) on its perch above the waves at Kilcummin. It is certainly one of the most successful and popular of the 14 land-art sculptures of the Tír Sáile trail, completed in a hectic 'symposium' in the summer of 1993. The sculptors had just three weeks, with local helpers and even mechanical diggers, to realise on the ground what had started as sketches on paper. The atmosphere was that of a meitheal, the work-gathering of Mayo tradition, but one spiced with accents from Japan, Denmark, Germany and America.

The works, spaced out along some 80 kilometres of coast and moorland to either side of Céide Fields, have immense variety, each project inspired by the site itself. Thus, limestone sheep graze gently beside the river at Bellanaboy bridge, but the bare sweep of hill above Blacksod was given the dramatic, granite henge it seemed to need.

The continuing community involvement in Tír Sáile (even to the donation of land) made it easier to hope that the trail would achieve the essential durability of its brief, free of neglect or obstruction, and this, with the help of FÁS, has been bringing a welcome trickle of tourists to many out-of-the-way corners.

Tír Sáile, the Mayo Sculpture Trail, is published by Dealbhóireacht 5000 Teo (4). Website: www.mayo-ireland.ie/tirsaile.htm

7 JULY 2001

Bad Politics and Bad Law

Editorial

It must be rare for a Government to put a Bill through the Dáil against the advice of its Attorney General. It must be equally unusual for a Government to ignore and suppress all legal advices — oral and written — presented to it. And it surely must create something of a precedent that a Government proceeds, nonetheless, to force through an amendment to a Bill, without debate, on the second last day of term when it knows that a former Attorney General, Mr Justice John Murray of the Supreme Court, the present Attorney General, Mr Michael McDowell, and an independent legal opinion have advised that there could be constitutional difficulties.

Despite the Taoiseach's attempt to waffle his way around the report in yesterday's editions, this is precisely what has happened. Seizing the opportunity presented by Fine Gael last Thursday week, the Fianna Fáil/Progressive Democrats Coalition has, knowingly, drawn the guillotine down on an amendment in the Dáil which bans the carrying out and publishing of opinion polls in the seven days immediately before polling day. All of its legal advices are that this proposal could interfere with Article 40.6.1 of the Constitution: the right of the citizens to express freely their convictions and opinions, subject only to 'public order and morality'.

The proposing Minister of State, Mr Robert Molloy, maintains that the ban on polls has been considered by the Government on a number of occasions in the last year. How strange that it did

vested interest of the media. The Government should know by now that it is the citizens who hold the constitutional right to express freely their convictions and opinions. What must follow is an implied right for the newspapers to publish them.

Opinion polls today are merely a modern tool of political science. They have been used in general elections over the past 20 years. They have never been shown to have distorted the results. They are, in fact, the most independent material to be put before voters towards the end of a campaign as truth often becomes the casualty of the spins of politicians and parties.

not find its way into the Electoral (Amendment) Bill, 2000, when it was first published. How strange that it did not surface when the Bill went through the Seanad. And how opportunistic that the Government only ran with the ban after Ms Olivia Mitchell of Fine Gael proposed it in a Dáil committee last week. Then the legal advice was withheld, not just from Seanad and the Dáil, but from their prohibition partners, Fine Gael.

This is bad politics and bad law, pushed through in an unseemly scramble to manipulate the nature of information given to voters as they prepare to exercise their franchise. It is not just a

The Taoiseach insists that the Bill will not be revised. Mr John Bruton, a member of the Council of State, has suggested that the President, Mrs McAleese, should convene a meeting to discuss it. The National Newspapers of Ireland has decided to petition the President to exercise her powers to refer the Bill to the Supreme Court for a test of its constitutionality. In all of the prevailing circumstances, this would be a wise move. The Government's speed to suppress opinion polls stands in sharp contrast to its paralysis on reforming the laws of libel and contempt.

10 JULY 2001

Ireland 18th On UN List For Quality Of Life

Paul Cullen

'Could do better' is the clear verdict of this latest report on Ireland's performance in creating an equitable, prosperous place to live in.

The UNDP's Human Development Report is the best measure we have of quality of life, and its publication each year is eagerly awaited throughout the world. This year, after six years at the top, Canada loses its position as the country with the highest quality of life to Norway, followed by Australia. The US, which has high income but also widespread poverty, drops from third to sixth position.

For Ireland, the report will add fuel to the 'Brussels versus Boston' debate. All our economic indices are clicking the right way, we're earning more than Germans, Japanese and Britons, yet the report shows that so much is not right.

Our life expectancy is not what it should be, our society has huge inequalities and massive illiteracy, and we have failed to improve our showing on the Human Development Index, the main indicator of quality of life around the world.

If progress were measured on economic wealth alone, then Ireland's surging GDP would earn it a place in the world's top 10. Instead, because of the above failings, we languish in 18th place, just behind Germany and ahead of New Zealand.

In this respect, Ireland takes after the US, which has the second-highest per capita income after Luxembourg, but ranks only 12th for educational enrolment and 24th in life expectancy.

So have we pursued economic growth at the expense of a more rounded development and an improvement in the quality of life that touches all bases? Or will the rising tide of economic success eventually lift all boats and thereby improve our ratings?

As the Government will inevitably point out, not all the data used in this report are up to date; given the mass of statistics gathered from all over the globe, this would be almost impossible. Ireland's continuing economic surge and falling long-term unemployment is arguably not fully reflected in the report, which is, however, based on official figures.

The links between cause and effect are apparent from this report. Cigarette consumption in Ireland is higher than elsewhere, and life expectancy is lower. We spend proportionately less on health and have fewer doctors, so we shouldn't be surprised at the current crisis in the health service.

Ireland is ranked as a 'leader' on a new index measuring technological innovation and achievement, and Dublin features as a leading global hub for technology. However, our ranking of 12th, behind countries such as Finland (1st) and South Korea (5th), comes as something of a disappointment. Ireland is the 12th-largest exporter of high-tech products, behind the US, Japan and Germany.

Globally, the report contains mixed news. Countries such as Egypt, Indonesia, South Korea and Portugal have achieved large increases in the Human Development Index during the 1990s. However, in eastern Europe, the former Soviet Union and 20 African countries, the index has been falling.

When world leaders attending last year's UN Millennium Summit made high-flown promises to eradicate global poverty by the year 2015, they could hardly have expected that their goals would go off course so quickly. Yet in dozens of countries, the report finds, promises to cut child mortality and provide safe drinking water are well behind schedule.

The report is decidedly technology friendly, and asserts that developing countries could reap huge benefits from genetically-modified organisms. GMO risks can be managed, it believes.

Martha Christie models a gilded helmet by Róisín O'Doherty and a neck choker by Chi-Whi Ng.
Photograph: Joe St Leger.

'Ignoring technological breakthroughs in medicine, agriculture and information will mean missing opportunities to transform the lives of poor people,' the UNDP administrator, Mr Mark Malloch Brown, says.

Even old technologies frowned upon in the West may be essential for developing countries. DDT, for example, is a pollutant with severe environmental consequences, but in some developing countries it may provide the only affordable means of tackling malaria, the report suggests.

13 JULY 2001

E-Day Is Near, But Please Don't Mention The Euro

Frank McNally

Your euro-questions answered …

Q. Is the arrival of the euro any reason to panic?

A. No. Public concern has been heightened unnecessarily by business terminology, in particular the suggestion that next January, some 50 billion euro coins will be 'rolled out' across Europe. This would be an alarming prospect, especially for a small flat country like Luxembourg. In reality, the coins will be issued in the traditional way, over the counters of banks, etc.

Q. Will we have more than one currency in circulation here at any time?

A. For a short transitional period, yes. From 9 February, 2002, however, only the euro will be legal tender. Blank restaurant receipts will retain their status as hard currency indefinitely. But if you're forging these after the changeover, it's important to remember to use euro amounts!

Q. Will the euro end the confusion caused for holidaymakers by those infernal local currencies they seem to have everywhere on the continent?

A. Yes. The effect should be particularly noticeable in northern Europe, where countries

The Taoiseach, Bertie Ahern, speaking to members of the media, as he leaves the Four Courts in Dublin, after being awarded £30,000 libel damages against Mr Denis O'Brien of Cork. Photograph: Eric Luke.

occur with higher frequency. In the past, no sooner had you got the hang of the Dutch 'guilder' than you had to convert your money into the Belgian 'walloon' and so on. It was impossible. The Italian lira will be missed though, at least by humourists.

Q. Will unscrupulous traders seek to take advantage of public confusion about the new currency?

A. Most large organisations are expected to commit themselves to a code of fair practice. Indeed, bodies as diverse as the National Maternity Hospital and the Divine Word Missionaries have already signed up, and the public is urged to shop with these where possible. Individual operators may take advantage, however. Members of the public should be particularly aware of chancers stopping them in the street late at night looking for the 'bus fare home'. For example, '85p' does not convert to '€1.50', whatever they suggest!

Q. But won't some businesses be badly affected?

A. Yes. So-called 'pound shops' face a major dilemma. They can become 'euro shops', with drastically reduced profit margins. Or they can convert to euro 1.27 shops, which would preserve existing margins, but would have a big promotional downside. It's a tough choice.

Q. Since all prices in euros will appear to be higher, won't this have a psychological effect on consumers?

A. Yes, possibly. A helpful comparison, however, is with temperature. We measure this in both celsius and fahrenheit, and it can be cheering to learn that the temperature is in the 'eighties' (fahrenheit) rather than the 'twenties' (celsius). Also, it's worth recalling that after the move to decimalisation in 1971, prices in the 'new money' seemed to be lower. And remember what happened then? No? Me neither.

Q. The dollar is arguably the strongest currency in history. But didn't it start out as a European monetary unit?

A. Yes it did. In 1518, a nobleman in the Bohemian town of Joachimsthal minted silver coins popularly known as Joachimsthaler, soon shortened to thaler. By the 17th century the thaler was a unit of currency throughout central Europe. In Sweden, it became the daler. In 1720, a copper daler was equivalent in value to a silver daler, but it weighed 250 times more and could only be transported by horse and cart! The currency travelled when European settlers brought it to America, where it was eventually transformed into the modern dollar, via a complex laundering operation organised from a Chicago warehouse.

Q. Apart from the last detail, which you made up, you read all that in a book, didn't you?

A. *Europe: A History*, by Norman Davies.

Q. Will anything be the same again after 'E-day'?

A. Yes, this: You'll be running for your bus on a wet Monday night in February, and you'll clamber aboard just in time to realise you have nothing smaller than a €20 note. After stuffing this down the 'exact fare' chute, the driver will give you a change ticket, which will now also be in euros. You will fold this away carefully in an inside pocket, as you always do. But what chance is there that you'll ever get around to reclaiming the value from the Dublin Bus change-ticket office? No chance at all, that's what. The office may not even exist, for all you know.

14 JULY 2001

With All Due Respect, Your Honours, This Is A Mess

Fintan O'Toole

One of the first things a lawyer learns is that if you think judges have made a mistake, you address them 'with respect'. If you think they've got it totally wrong, the code is 'with great respect'. And if you think they've lost the plot, the appropriate phrase is 'with the greatest respect'. In that sense, Thursday's Supreme Court judgment in the Sinnott case deserves the greatest respect.

When it emerged that an unprecedented seven judges would hear the State's appeal against the Sinnotts' High Court victory, it seemed clear that a landmark judgment was on the way. The widespread assumption was that the court was moving to draw a line beyond which the State's neglect of its most vulnerable citizens could not go.

Here, after all, was a young man who had been deprived of almost the entire primary education to which he was constitutionally entitled. Of all the issues on which people with disabilities have suffered appalling neglect, education is the only one that has explicit roots in the Constitution, making it the key to a whole set of other rights.

By taking a clear and strong stance on Jamie Sinnott's human rights, the court could begin the process of restoring the State to its basic function of serving the needs, not just of the 350,000 citizens with disabilities, but of all of those whom the system has failed.

The court delivered a landmark judgment all right. It made it absolutely clear that the judicial arm of the State will join with the legislative arm in pushing away those who come looking for the right to the education they need.

No one doubts that the judges applied the law conscientiously. What is clearly open to question, however, is whether they applied it imaginatively, with a sense of moral purpose, or in a spirit of deep respect for the humanity of the people with intellectual disabilities whose fate they were deciding.

The most remarkable thing in the seven judgments is the absence of any real attempt to address the actual life of Jamie Sinnott, and of many others with autism. They are not like other litigants. They are not individuals dealing with the State. In a very real sense, the State itself determines their individuality.

Carers and teachers who work with autistic people will say that they become different people when they are getting proper schooling. With appropriate education, their individuality can function. Without it, they retreat into an unreachable private world.

Faced with the question of what rights these people have, the court itself retreated into a private world of narrow reasoning. Instead of asking what a primary education actually means for a person with autism, it largely confined itself to the question of what primary education meant to the framers of the Constitution. Even there, it came up with an incoherent and internally inconsistent set of answers.

The key reason for rejecting Mr Justice Barr's High Court ruling in favour of the Sinnotts was that the phrase 'primary education' had a fixed meaning that didn't extend to meeting the basic educational needs of a citizen regardless of age. The individual judgments, however, completely undermine this reasoning. For the judges themselves could not agree on what the fixed meaning of the term is.

Both the Chief Justice and Mr Justice Geoghegan said that for a normal child primary education might be regarded as extending to the age of 12. Ms Justice Denham and Mr Justice Murphy put the age at 14. Mr Justice Murray put it at 12 or 14. And in any case all of them, with the exception of the Chief Justice, then went on to extend it — in the case of children with disabilities — to the age of 18 and no further.

What they actually came up with, therefore, was a right that applies up to either the age of 12 or the age of 14, and that can be extended in special circumstances by another four or six years. In other words, a right that is inherently flexible. The concept that seems to explain their ruling, the clear constitutional meaning of 'primary education', turns out to explain nothing.

Equally incoherent is the notion of normality that runs through the judgments. On the one hand, the judges all accepted that the situation of a child with intellectual disabilities was not normal. This is why, in their view, the right to primary education extends in their case to the age of 18, while for

Early morning pilgrims make their way up Croagh Patrick, Co. Mayo. Photograph: Joe St Leger.

normal children it stops some years earlier.

On the other hand, however, they then go on to apply a rigid notion of normality to these same children. Their right to education stops at 18 because that is the normal age at which childhood ends. The result is an intellectual mess in which people with autism are partly normal and partly abnormal.

What is truly remarkable, however, is that in spite of all the contradictions within and between their judgments, six of the seven judges came up with a set of principles which happened to coincide precisely with what the State wanted.

This is remarkable because, as the Chief Justice pointed out in his largely dissenting opinion, the State's case was itself an utterly incoherent one. On the one hand, by not appealing the damages awarded to Jamie Sinnott for the breach of his constitutional rights up to the age of 22 (i.e. including four years beyond the age of 18), the State was implicitly accepting that the High Court was right to award those damages.

On the other hand, it was explicitly arguing that the High Court was wrong. This, as he put it, involved 'a feat of mental legerdemain' of which he himself was incapable. Unfortunately, this sleight-of-mind proved well within the capacity of his fellow judges.

The unalterable fact, however, is that the Constitution means what the Supreme Court says it means. The belief that has been around since the High Court judgment in the O'Donoghue case in

1993 — that the judicial arm of the State would make up for the neglect of the legislative arm — has proved to be definitively wrong.

This leaves citizens with a clear choice: either accept that our collective values should remain stuck in the 1930s when the Constitution was drafted, or force the political system to introduce laws worthy of a civilised democracy.

18 JULY 2001

Saints and Scholars Make Way To Businessmen

On Wall Street by Conor O'Clery

Journalist Thomas McConville from Portadown (my great grandfather) wrote a column from Wall Street for the *Ulster Observer* of 12 December, 1862. He described the brokers and dealers he encountered there as 'attenuated Yankees with compressed lips, and cold sharp noses, and dyed beards, who flit along this noted street from ten o'clock in the morning till five in the evening'.

'Yankee' was the Dutch nickname for English settlers and in those days referred mainly to the WASP establishment, which included figures like Andrew Carnegie, J.P. Morgan, William Duer, Alexander Hamilton and Jay Gould who controlled the big securities houses and merchant banks.

If Thomas McConville were to visit Wall Street today he would find that while the compressed lips and cold sharp noses of the old 'robber barons' are still in evidence, there are now many Celtic faces and a good sprinkling of Irish surnames among the movers and shakers.

It is well known how the Irish in America started at the bottom and worked their way up from the building sites to Tammany Hall and into the boardrooms, but it is less appreciated just how successful they have been of late in the banks and brokerage houses.

'It's almost an oxymoron, Wall Street Irish,' said Christopher 'Kip' Condron, president and chief executive of AXA Financial Inc, in a keynote speech as the main recipient of Irish America's Wall Street Top 50 Awards last year.

'If we were recognising the 50 top Irish poets in New York or the 50 top Irish tenors, it would feel more comfortable. It's out of character for the Irish to be successful at money-making ventures.' Most of the top 50 Irish on Wall Street 75 years ago 'would have been runners or clerks', he added. That is true, but a small number of brash, risk-taking Irish did make it big early on in the bastion of the Yankees.

One was Edmund Lynch, a seller of soda fountain equipment, who joined Charles Merrill in 1914 to set up Merrill Lynch, today the largest securities firm on Wall Street.

Then there was Joseph Kennedy, father of JFK and a prominent bear market operator who was famously snubbed as an Irish upstart by the most prominent Brahmin banker of them all, J.P. Morgan Jnr. Despite his reputation as a stock manipulator, President Franklin Roosevelt made Kennedy first chairman of the Securities Exchange Commission in 1933, with a mandate to police the very behaviour that made him wealthy.

This was 'sort of like putting a vampire in charge of a bloodbank', said Mr Condron, though Kennedy's administration of the SEC turned out to be highly successful, according to Charles Geisst in his *Wall Street, a History* (Oxford, 1997).

Another famous Irish character on Wall Street in the 1920s was Mike Meehan, a flamboyant speculator who was eventually expelled from the New York Stock Exchange for rigging share prices. And people still recall 'Sell 'em' Ben Smith, an overbearing and aggressive Irish-American trader who ran through a brokerage house in the crash of '29 yelling 'Sell 'em all, they're not worth anything', hence the name which stuck to him ever afterwards.

The Irish on Wall Street today are an altogether more civilised crowd, to judge from the highly respectable turnout on the top floor restaurant of the World Trade Centre last Wednesday for the fourth annual Top 50 Wall Street awards, organised by the founding publishers of Irish America, Niall O'Dowd and Patricia Harty.

The fact that the Irish, from North and South, have arrived on Wall Street was evident from the executive titles of the award winners, with names like Dunn, Keating, McDonough, Meehan, Morrissy, Murray, O'Neill, Tatlock and Wyant — and those were just the women of Irish origin among the city's top financiers being honoured.

The main honouree this year was Denis Kelleher, who joined Merrill Lynch as a messenger boy on the first day he arrived as a penniless immigrant from Co. Kerry in 1958, and went on to found Wall Street Access, a major discount brokerage for investment professionals.

Thomas McConville would find today that being Irish on Wall Street is in fact a positive advantage, as the Irish have acquired an aura of business confidence and ambition, thanks to the Celtic Tiger, to add to their much-trumpeted qualities as patriots, playwrights and poets.

'The secret of Denis Kelleher's success,' said Kip Condron as he introduced the Kerryman last week, 'is that he came with a brogue and conned everyone into thinking he was intelligent and exciting'.

Patricia Dunn, global chief executive, Barclay's Global Investors; Susan Keating, president and chief executive, Allfirst Financial; Kathleen McDonough, managing director, Ambrac Assurance; Colleen Ann Meehan, senior portfolio manager, Dreyfus Corporation; Dolores Morrissey, chairwoman, chief executive, Mutual of America Investment Corporation; Eileen Murray, managing director, Morgan Stanley Dean Witter; Mary Lynn O'Neill, managing director, Bear Stearns; Ann Tatlock, chairman, chief executive, Fiduciary Trust, and Margaret Wyant, founder and managing director, Isabella Capital.

An Irishman's Diary

Kevin Myers

The problem with *The Irish Times* — as I see it, y'know — is that it's so totally middle aged. Y'know what I mean? I mean, it's like, not in touch with young people, y'know? So, here in An Irishman's Diary, we're like, going to change all that, right? Starting with the subject matter, okay? I mean, the stuff you normally get here, that is SO not cool. And, like, the writing, it's so old-fashioned it's weird.

Here's my point, right like, I was out with Ultan and Siofra in the Chocolate Bar the other night. We were just hanging out, hitting the Red Bull and vodka, you know? And we were talking about newspapers, and Siofra, she's like, omigahd, I don't BELIEVE the things you get in that funny column in the middle of *The Irish Times*. Yawnsville or what? I mean, like, you'd expect something totally cool, who's clubbing where, who's hot, who's not, stuff about the movies, Hollywood, et cetera, relevant stuff, not that crap about boring old Northern Ireland — though I think Gerry Adams is SO cool — and what else, like Irish history and that sort of stuff. That is SO not interesting, okay?

And Ultan, he's like, Yeah, right, it's so not interesting that's it's unreal, bla bla bla. How totally weird can you get, bla bla bla. And I'm like, nodding my head, because I can't believe what I'm hearing, because, hey, I've been thinking stuff like this for, like, ever, only privately, and now here are two best mates saying the identical same things. I mean, that's so unreal, y'know, it's spooky. And I'm like, I DO NOT BELIEVE WHAT I'M HEARING, GUYS, THIS IS SO TOTALLY WEIRD. I thought I was the only one who thought like that, right?

So this is, like, a new leaf. okay? We're so totally after a young audience in *The Irish Times* that's it's not funny, and it starts here. We are going to be so cool here, guys, that you could catch a cold. This'll be the place to chill out, take it easy, find out what's going on, y'know?

I mean, did you hear about Fionan and Emma, they had a bust up, right? Jason told me, and I was like, OMIGAHD, that is unbelievable, because, you see, they'd been going round for like ever — right? — a majorly serious item. But Fionan had the hots for Aoife, okay? He took her to her debs when Roddy — who was her ex, but they were still best mates, and they'd go clubbing et cetera — got sick, I mean wasted, right, after dropping a tab too many, and his parents grounded him, bla bla bla.

That's when Fionan stepped in, and Emma SO didn't mind. I was like, YOU CANNOT BE SERIOUS, FIONAN is such a hunk — right? — and she was like, It's totally cool, Aoife and me have been bestest friends since way back when. And she sort of had a point, okay? I mean, they went to the Gaeltacht together, you know, and all sorts of other stuff, bla-de-bla-de-bla. But in her place, right, I wouldn't have let him go to the debs, not with Aoife, she is SUCH a tramp. She is SO not to be trusted.

Anyway, Fionan and Aoife went to the debs, and got totally rat-arsed, completely smashed, and at the end, at the very end, — right? — they start snogging. I mean, I guess they thought nobody could see them, but like it was SO obvious that everyone could, like right there, out in the open. I was there with a crowd from St Humphrey's and didn't see it at first, but Una came up to us and she was like, I CANNOT BELIEVE WHAT I'M SEEING, GUYS, THIS IS SO TOTALLY AMAZING.

And we, like, look, and there they are, like really getting stuck into one another; okay? And I was like, WOW, because it was totally unreal. But next day, like, no-one said anything, and we were like, that's cool, it's all blown over, et cetera et cetera, but obviously it hadn't, because Fionan and Emma have split up, and Fionan's with Aoife now, and Emma, you won't believe this, YOU WILL NOT BELIEVE THIS, she's started going out with Ultan, okay?

I am totally serious, guys. Una saw them in the Porsche his old man bought him for his 18th birthday, and she texted me there and then, and I was like, DA-DA, because I thought all along that Aoife had the hots for Ultan, they were at that charity ball last year, and she was SO obvious it was like WEIRD. Now they're an item, and I'd sussed it from the start. Wicked.

But hey, since then the scene has moved on, you know? Way cool. You'll never believe who I saw in the Shelbourne the other day. She walked into the bar wearing a see-through blouse and this little miniskirt, tiny, and I'm like, ohmigahd, it's Julia Roberts. She was like trying to pick up this guy, and he was such a babe, and he was like having none of it. He was like, Sorry, get real, like, you're way too old for me, and she was like GAGGING for it, and he was like, OH PUL-EASE. He was so not on for it, it wasn't true. You know who he was? He was that way cool person who writes An Irishman's Diary. What's his name?

Letters to the Editor July 2001

C of I and Drumcree

Sir, — Here we go again. As one who grew up in the Diocese of Cape Town in the 1940s and 1950s when Archbishop Geoffrey Clayton and then his successor Joost de Blank led the fight against racial discrimination, I read Canon Charles Kenny's outpouring of Anglican angst over Drumcree (Rite and Reason, 26 June) with a sinking heart.

It is simply not enough to support resolutions in synods, nor to have ever more reports from various working parties; one actually has to do something.

311th annual 12 July march in Dunmurry, Northern Ireland. Photograph: Jason South.

Why leave it to the primate? It is far too late for this year, but there is no reason why Canon Kenny and his fellow-Catalysts should not start planning for 2002. Perhaps they ought to pack the congregation, stand outside with placards, march down and present the RUC with an address of support. There are many other actions they could take.

In the longer term there is a need to educate — remember, in a lot of parishes the incumbents have been Orangemen for generations — as well as to create a replacement for the Orange Lodge, which in rural Protestant communities is often the only social venue, while playing in the band is the only youth activity. That is no doubt why members of the order are so often the pillars of the congregation.

Also, the other denominations must be involved, because this is not just an Anglican problem or even a

Northern Irish one. — Yours, etc., T.B. Hinchliff, Barnaboy, Rossnowlagh, Co. Donegal. 3 July 2001.

Poverty In Ireland

Sir, — I am shocked by the contents of the UN Development Report on development reviewed in your paper, placing Ireland 16th out of 17 Western countries, with 15.3 per cent of our population living in poverty. As one of the many people happy to return to Ireland after years working abroad to bring up our three children, I have to ask myself: what kind of country have I brought them back to?

It is clear that 'quality of life' is only for some. This country has the highest economic growth rate in the Western world, many have never had it so good, and the rest never got near it. Maybe the government

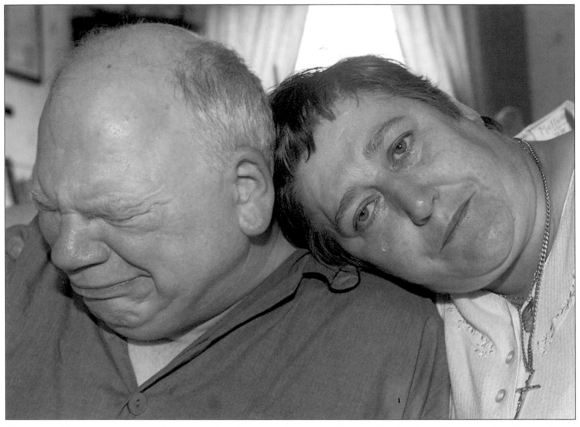

Christine Curran comforts her brother-in-law Francis who suffers from cerebral palsy, after a pipe bomb attack on their Barnfield Grange home in Derriaghy just outside Belfast. Photograph: Pacemaker Belfast.

could stop slapping itself on the back long enough to read the report? — Yours, etc., Rachel Widdis Cambay, Cabinteely, Dublin 18. 12 July 2001.

The Sinnott Judgment

Sir, — After the disgraceful conduct of the Government in the Sinnott case I wish to declare publicly that I am not represented by the 'Ireland' that appealed to the Supreme Court. — Yours, etc., Philip Hassell, Harcourt Street, Dublin 2. 14 July 2001.

Ordination Of Women

Sir, — In the re-ignited controversy over the ordination of women to the Catholic priesthood, Elizabeth Roddy writes of wondering, speculating and thinking about

various aspects of this contentious issue (4 July).

I too have done a share of wondering about the question. In particular, I wonder why, if the Holy Spirit is genuinely calling some women to serve in the ordained ministry, the same Holy Spirit doesn't appear to grant the same insight to his vicar on earth, the successor of Peter.

After all, did not God the Son reassure Peter and the other apostles that he would be with his beloved Church, guiding it all the days, yes, to the end of time? — Yours, etc., Mrs. D. Bourke, Lee Road, Cork. 14 July 2001.

A Question Of Money

Sir, — Apropos of D. K. Henderson (12 July), where is the evidence that Humpty Dumpty was male? —

Yours, etc., Oliver McGrane, Rathfarnham, Dublin 16. 18 July 2001.

Ordination Of Women

Sirs, — Mrs D. Bourke (14 July) wonders why, if the Holy Spirit is calling some women to be priests, He hasn't told the church. The Lord works in mysterious ways. Could it be that by calling far fewer men he might be suggesting that Peter's successors cast out into the deep and throw their net wider? — Yours, etc., Patricia Daly, Home Farm Road, Drumcondra, Dublin 9. 21 July 2001.

Disturbing Photograph

Sir, — I would like to state my objection as a parent of three young children to your front-page photograph (20 July), showing the clothes of Niall Murphy, the five-year-old who drowned along with his sister Trisha on Trá Mór beach in Belmullet, Co. Mayo, the previous day.

I found the photograph upsetting and an unnecessary and insensitive intrusion into the tragic deaths of the children as well as the grief of their family.

I know a good picture is worth a thousand words. But I felt this particular picture was cold, lacked compassion and was sensational, which I felt would further compound the grief of the Murphy family as well as other families who have had children die in similar circumstances. — Yours, etc., Patrick Gates, Ballybough, Dublin 3. 24 July 2001.

John Reaney, Kinvara, Galway, with Carna Boy, winner of Class 6 for three-year-old stallions at the Connemara Pony Show at Clifden, Co. Galway. Photograph: Eric Luke.

6 AUGUST 2001

Laissez-Faire Housing Blighting Countryside

Frank McDonald

The shocking statistics from last year are already well known: of the record total output of 50,000 new homes throughout the State, 36 per cent were single houses in the countryside. And how the Government can reconcile what is happening on the ground with its declared commitment to 'sustainable development' is a mystery.

The all-time record 18,000 'one-off' houses built in rural areas last year consumed 2,700 hectares (6,480 acres) of agricultural land and resulted in the loss of an estimated 540 kilometres (337 miles) of natural hedgerows to create new boundaries, set back from the roadway to provide safer sightlines and turning radii for motorists.

Last year's output of bungalows or two-storey houses in the countryside came on top of 10,000 built in 1997, 11,000 in 1998 and 14,000 in 1999. In total, for those three years, rural housing consumed 5,250 hectares (12,600 acres) of land, assuming an average site area of 0.15 ha (0.36 acres).

At the same time, nearly all of Ireland's small villages have experienced significant population decline over the past 15 to 20 years.

In effect, what we are seeing is the creation of 'doughnut' villages, whose physical form may remain intact, but whose hinterland is the area where development is concentrated.

These 'worrying trends', as Department of the Environment planners call them, are highlighted in a paper produced for the National Spatial Strategy, which is to offer a blueprint for more balanced regional development.

One of the key objectives of the paper was to compare various policies already in place with 'what is unfolding on the ground'. It also asks how the Government's 1999 White Paper on Rural Development, which favoured maintaining dispersed rural communities, can be reconciled with the Sustainable Development Strategy of 1997.

After all, as the planners note, rural housing is predominantly and increasingly car-dependent, with consequential increases in greenhouse gas emissions, as well as generating more pressure on rural roads and more demand for parking in towns.

The paper also contains a serious health warning about the implications for groundwater protection of adding new septic tanks to rural landscapes at an average rate of more than 13,000 every year.

The planners note that a recent sample survey by the Environmental Protection Agency of 1,200 group water schemes found that 42 per cent were polluted by faecal coliforms or other contaminants.

This level of contamination, caused by agricultural run-off as well as septic tanks for housing, indicated that groundwater protection measures were 'totally inadequate'. Thus, the planners recommend that still-pristine sources need to be fully identified and monitored, with appropriate spatial policies developed to protect them. 'This issue is one of the more pressing ones relating to dispersed rural settlement,' the planners said.

They correctly identify as one of the main driving forces for urban-generated rural housing the fact that farmers can sell sites for 'many multiples' of their agricultural value. Today's housing market has intensified this trend, as well as the tendency to deceive planning authorities that new houses are for sons or daughters.

The debate about urban-generated housing in the countryside is a 'battlefield of hearts and minds' between the interests of individuals on the one hand and sustainable development principles on the other. Controls borrowed from Britain had been resisted by the 'indigenous enthusiasm for a laissez-faire approach to rural housing.'

According to the paper, 'one of the fundamental issues that underscore the rural housing question is that society in general has not perhaps come to terms with the profound and irreversible changes that have occurred in rural Ireland over the past 30 years or so' — notably the fact that many landscapes had been suburbanised.

The planners say 'further work' is needed to refine the Government's 1999 White Paper on Rural Development, which stated that 'planning policy should, as far as possible, facilitate people willing to settle in rural areas', while being sensitive to the need to protect 'beauty spots', natural habitats and the rural environment.

What needs to be done, as the paper says, is to 'disentangle the issue of urban-generated housing from the broader issue of how to breathe new life into the rural settlement structure' — for example, by introducing measures to unlock the potential of

villages to satisfy 'the legitimate ambitions of people seeking a rural lifestyle'.

6 AUGUST 2001

Emotional Response to Photograph

Readers' Report by Mary O'Brien

Far more readers complained about the photograph on the front page on 20 July than about any single item that has appeared since I started in this job eight years ago. More than 150 people sent e-mails, phoned or wrote letters to object to the image of

The clothes of Niall Murphy, 5, at Trá Mór, Belmullet, Co. Mayo, where he and his sister Trisha, 15, were drowned. Photograph: Keith Keneghan, Phocus.

the shoes and clothes of Niall Murphy who, with his sister, had drowned tragically in the sea off Belmullet in Co. Mayo.

Many of those I spoke to were clearly upset. They said they couldn't help thinking how they would feel if it had been their children who had drowned and they were looking at this photograph.

Most referred to the trauma of the family of the drowned children, and said that by publishing the photograph *The Irish Times* was adding to their appalling distress. Some callers had lost children in tragic circumstances and told us we couldn't possibly imagine the hurt and upset the photograph had caused them, not to mention the family of these particular children.

Others were sad that their newspaper had been insensitive, that publishing the photograph showed a lack of integrity. They wondered whether tabloid values were now acceptable to *The Irish Times*. Had we, they asked, succumbed to market forces and were we now resorting to sensationalism to enhance sales?

Several readers felt tricked by the photograph. They said they had been fooled into associating it with happy summer days on the beach with the children. They were subsequently shocked and appalled when they realised what it was in fact illustrating. Two readers asked if the photograph had been 'set up'. Most assuredly not, they were told.

As a leading article said a few days later, the decision to publish the photograph was not taken lightly. Only after discussion among the senior editorial staff on duty was it decided that the

Model Jill Goldthorpe wears a black and cream, polka-dot flowing bias-cut skirt and shell top from the 'Gold by Michael H' range, in front of a canvas entitled 'Liquid Hills' by Paul Swan at a photocall in the Bridge Gallery Dublin, for the Irish Fashion Group's Spring/Summer 2002 Collection. Photograph: Bryan O'Brien.

powerful image would convey the reality of the tragedy in a way that words could not.

And, in so doing, it would reinforce the message that water is extremely dangerous at this time of the year when so many children enjoy lakes, rivers and the sea.

A few callers agreed there might have been some justification in publishing the photograph if it saved one life but they doubted it would. The overwhelming impression left by the photograph, they said, would be the insensitivity of *The Irish Times* in publishing it.

Having looked again at the decision, in light of all the complaints, the newspaper's view remains the same. Such a shocking image in a place of such beauty and tranquillity can only result in greater vigilance. In the words of the editor, the newspaper did not set out to cause hurt and if it did then of course it is regretted, but if the image saves one child's life this summer, it will have been justified.

A postscript to some of the calls referred to the page-five report and another photograph on the tragedy, which appeared on the same day. Unfortunately, the page also contained a large advertisement for our own website which showed two happy people swimming in the sea. This was a most unfortunate juxtaposition which, regrettably, was not noticed until it was too late.

Generally, in cases of tragedy, someone will check the advertisements on the page. For instance, in the case of an aircraft crash, an ad for an airline on the same page would be deemed inappropriate. In this case, the advertisement should of course have been moved but, as callers readily accepted, there was no question of showing any disrespect to the bereaved Murphy family.

Following a reference to political correctness in this column last month, we received a further complaint which asked us to publish an apology for a headline that did not meet fully the requirements of political correctness. The headline read: 'Down's children do better in normal schools'. The report referred in every instance to 'children with Down's syndrome', which is the phrase the writer felt should have been used in the headline.

The fact is that a headline cannot contain all the words of a normal sentence. The skill of the headline writer lies in using the minimum number of words to reflect accurately the content of the report. In this case, I don't believe they could have done better without making the headline too long and unwieldy and in the process cutting into the space allocated to the report.

In the same column last month, I referred to the acceptability or otherwise of the word 'idiot' in a crossword. I took the view that provided the clue reflected its current meaning of 'silly ass', there was no reason not to use the word. Those words came back to haunt me. A couple of weeks later, to my acute embarrassment, 'idiot' appeared in a crossword with the clue reflecting the old, outdated and unacceptable usage which refers to people with mental disabilities. Quite rightly, several crossword solvers contacted us to voice their concern. I could only apologise and promise that we would try not to let it happen again.

Readers' Report appears on the first Monday of the month. Readers may contact the Readers' Representative's Office by e-mail: readersrep@irish-times.ie or by telephone: (01) 675 8000 from 11 a.m. to 5 p.m. Monday to Friday.

7 AUGUST 2001

Unionists Waiting For IRA Arms Destruction Date

Gerry Moriarty

Yesterday we learned that the 'how' of putting arms beyond use was established. Next on the agenda is the 'when' and, with the usual caveats, there were some signs that there could be movement on that vital front soon.

A 'hugely historical breakthrough' was how the Sinn Féin president, Mr Gerry Adams, described the statement from the Independent International Commission on Decommissioning (IICD). And indeed it was: but there are many Doubting Thomases in the unionist camp, so expect much semantic analysis in the next couple of days.

Gen John de Chastelain after meeting an IRA representative learned the methodology of how the IRA could put its arms beyond use. The IRA representative described himself as 'P. O'Neill', Dr Ian Paisley told us after his meeting yesterday with the general.

Whether or not this was a pseudonym, Gen de Chastelain was none the less sufficiently moved to write: 'Based on our discussions with the IRA representative, we believe that this proposal initiates a process that will put IRA arms completely and verifiably beyond use.'

We don't know when that would happen. And that was where unionists placed their spotlight yesterday. The Ulster Unionist Party leader, Mr David Trimble, expressed satisfaction with the 'how' but he too wants to know 'when'.

He didn't close any doors however, accepting that the IRA initiative was 'significant' but withholding a definitive response until the IRA delivers more substantively. One was struck by how calm and collected he was after his meeting with the Northern Secretary, Dr John Reid, yesterday afternoon.

It was significant that in his press conference he also focused on the SDLP and whether it would sign up to the policing proposals. He appeared to be signalling that should the IRA deliver on arms he would also require commitments that the SDLP would join the proposed Policing Board.

Were this to happen he could argue that for the first time a significant portion of the nationalist population supported the policing arrangements for Northern Ireland, which in turn might allow Mr Trimble to persuade unionists to at least tolerate the difficult policing and other aspects of the British-Irish blueprint.

But those in the staunch No wing of unionism, when they had analysed the brief statement from the IICD, saw it as illusory and worthless. Such was the response from Dr Paisley and others.

Hardline UUP MP Mr Jeffrey Donaldson was also unimpressed. He referred to the decommissioning legislation. Arms must be 'rendered permanently unusable and permanently unavailable', he said. 'Actual decommissioning is our bottom line,' he added. He wanted the evidence, and there were many more like him yesterday.

But was the Taoiseach, Mr Ahern, signalling that the IICD could be issuing another statement shortly that deals with that missing element?

One has to be careful in interpreting comments from Mr Ahern but none the less he appeared to be strongly hinting at forthcoming action. 'It is a historic breakthrough,' he told RTÉ. 'Other things have to happen out of it, admittedly, but I'll be confident that that will happen.'

Mr Ahern believed that the IICD statement was sufficient to allow the political process to continue. 'And hopefully over the next number of days, perhaps the outstanding issue of the commencement of that process hopefully will also move on, and that will allow us to get on with the full implementation of the Good Friday agreement, which brings in all of the other issues of policing, demilitarisation and the stability of the institutions.'

Mr Ahern at least appeared confident that this wasn't just manoeuvring by republicans or a cynical attempt to switch the emphasis from what the IRA will do next to whether the Ulster Unionists will accept the word of the general — to engage in the blame game, in other words.

It may also have been significant that the British government published a further 'decommissioning scheme' yesterday, which gives the IICD, at its own request, more flexibility on how arms might be put beyond use. While the criteria remain that weapons are to be 'permanently unusable and permanently unavailable' there is some shift in language from 'decommissioning' to 'putting arms

The Minister for Public Enterprise, Mary O'Rourke (left), and Catherine Woods, wearing a creation by Keith Houston, after the announcement of Taispeántas 2001, an opportunity for young designers to show their work. Photograph: Pat Langan.

beyond use', possibly in deference to the symbolic sensitivities of republicans who object to the D-word.

One neutral but informed insider posed a succinct question yesterday: 'Is this move by the IRA a substitute for the IRA putting arms beyond use, or a prelude to the IRA putting weapons beyond use?' While the IICD was confident the IRA had initiated 'a process that will put IRA arms completely and verifiably beyond use' could it take '10 years, 20 years, or 40 years' before that starts? he asked.

Answering his own question, he said the general and his colleagues on the commission had their credibility to maintain. Gen de Chastelain was hardly going to be a 'dupe' or 'patsy' to some sharp but meaningless wordplay from republicans.

Another source close to the centre of operations said it was implicit that for politics to work actual movement on arms must start relatively soon. 'There are two effective deadlines,' he said. 'There is the 22nd of February next when the remit of the IICD runs out, and, perhaps more importantly, there is next Sunday, 12 August, when the British government could be forced to suspend the institutions or call fresh Assembly elections,' he added.

What the IRA does next, and when it does it, will determine whether or not the British government must trigger some mechanism to suspend the institutions. It could do so for a day and then reactivate them to allow the Assembly and Executive to continue for another six weeks, which might be necessary to resolve outstanding matters.

But, if in the next day or so, the IRA made a move on decommissioning — putting concrete caps on two or three of its arms dumps, for example — then it just might be possible to call a special meeting of the Assembly by the weekend to re-elect Mr David Trimble and Mr Seamus Mallon as First and Deputy First Minister.

To quote one senior source: 'If we can get the "when" question answered quickly, then I think what will be on the table from the IRA will be pretty irresistible, even for unionists.'

(A week later, the IRA withdrew its offer following suspension of the Northern Ireland Assembly by Dr Reid.)

9 AUGUST 2001

More Casualties Feared As Slowdown Bites

Jamie Smyth

Gateway's plans to close its European head-quarters in Dublin will almost certainly mean the loss of 900 jobs.

It will also heighten fears among the 50,000 people employed in the high-tech sector that further job losses and company closures could be on the way. Gateway is a flagship IDA Ireland investment and its decision to close its Clonshaugh facility is evidence the Republic will not be spared from the slowdown in the global technology industry.

Gateway's departure will mean the largest loss of employment in the technology sector since Seagate pulled out of Clonmel in 1997, making 1,400 staff redundant.

Gateway's Dublin operation was established in 1993 to manufacture and supply personal computers and services to the Europe, Middle East and African regions.

It was at the centre of Gateway's strategy to expand into a global business and received more than £20 million in Government grants.

However, in common with Xerox, which recently made 370 employees redundant in Dundalk, Gateway is fighting for survival and is prepared to take radical action to return to profitability.

Mr Mike Maloney, managing director Gateway Ireland, confirmed last night that the company was proposing to exit the UK and Irish markets to concentrate on the US market.

'The company will not survive by just selling personal computers. It is restructuring itself to develop and sell more services and solutions,' he said.

Analysts believe Gateway may completely exit the Europe, Middle East and African regions where it has failed to claim sufficient market share.

Mr Sami Pohjolainen, research manager with technology consultancy IDC, said Gateway had slipped out of the top 10 in the UK and was now placed just 10th in Ireland.

The company had encountered stiff competition in Europe from vendors such as Dell, which enjoyed much greater economies of scale than Gateway due to its supply chain management.

Despite introducing big price cuts, Gateway's sales in the past quarter declined 46 per cent in the European region, prompting it to review its entire operation.

Mr Maloney said no Gateway customers would lose out from the company's decision to pull out of the area because it would continue to operate some form of technical support facility.

The IDA is currently negotiating with Gateway to try to encourage the firm to keep these technical support operations in Dublin.

It is understood Gateway is keen to outsource this function to another company and transfer some of its 250 support staff to the new firm. A final decision by Gateway on the closure is expected to be made following a 30-day consultation period with employees. Gateway management admitted

Arnout Cator, a Gateway employee who has twice been made redundant by Gateway at the Gateway factory in Clonshaugh, Dublin, after the company announced the closure of its Irish and UK operation. Photograph: Frank Miller.

last night that it is unlikely the decision will be reversed.

Although the company had already hinted it may pull out of Dublin, yesterday's announcement will increase the fears of workers about job security right across the technology sector.

IDA Ireland said yesterday further job losses in the technology sector and even closures are likely over the next few months until there was an upturn in the sector. 'We're in the middle of a steep industry downturn and I don't think we have seen the last bad news,' said Mr Martin Cronin, a director of IDA Ireland.

The telecoms and personal computer industries have been hit hardest by the current slowdown as corporates and individuals put off new equipment purchases to save cash.

Telecommunications equipment maker Lucent said yesterday it would enter discussions with trade unions across Europe about job losses this week.

Redundancies among the 900 staff at the company's European headquarters have not been ruled out. The company expects to make between 15,000–20,000 redundant worldwide.

Almost all the major personal computer manufacturers have operations in the Republic, including Dell, Compaq, Apple Computers, IBM and Hewlett Packard.

Already Dell has shed staff through voluntary redundancies and fears are growing that Compaq, which is reviewing its Irish operations, may announce job cuts.

Last night the Tánaiste said there remained a strong labour market despite the recent downturn in the US technology sector. However, she also outlined that the Government could review the migrant work visas system if the situation changed.

She said she was hopeful that with the help of the relevant State agencies, alternative employment opportunities could be made available for the Gateway staff.

21 AUGUST 2001

A Historic Decision

Editorial

'I want to say to young people in the nationalist community: here is an opportunity. Here is the mechanism now through which policing can be changed and changed forever more.' To hear Mr Séamus Mallon utter these words yesterday as his party announced its acceptance of the British government's plan on police reform is to realise what a major milestone has been passed in Northern Ireland's affairs. For the first time in its history, cross-community accord on policing is within reach.

The SDLP's agreement to nominate members of the Policing Board is a welcome and courageous endorsement of the latest package worked out between the parties and the two governments. Effective and legitimate policing is a *sine qua non* of a more just and stable society in Northern Ireland. Without a universally-accepted police service the influence of the paramilitaries will continue.

That may well be an element in IRA and Sinn Féin thinking. The SDLP's decision may signify a significant realignment within nationalism. Sinn Féin has rejected the police reforms on the grounds that they do not fully implement the Patten report, thus breaking the united front with the SDLP and the Government which has been so marked a feature of the recent peace process. Irrespective of that, the Police Board is expected to go ahead with support from the Ulster Unionist Party. Its

endorsement by the North's Catholic bishops was also welcome and timely.

The Sinn Féin rejection is regrettable, given the intense efforts to bring all parties along with this package which addresses policing, demilitarisation, decommissioning and the stability of the new institutions. It is to be hoped that in time the party will come around to accepting that the implementation plan can indeed 'comprehensively deliver on the spirit and substance of the Patten report,' as the Taoiseach, Mr Ahern, put it. The SDLP's detailed justification of its decision yesterday, is a reminder of the long-drawn-out nature of the negotiations involved. They will continue in a different setting on the Policing Board, from which, in due course, Sinn Féin may well regret excluding itself. It took those who opposed the Treaty in 1922 some years to accept the Garda Síochána.

Now that this milestone has been passed, attention will return to the other elements in the package drawn up by the two governments after the Weston Park meetings last month. The most important of these is that a start be made to decommission arms held by the IRA. The realignment of political forces represented by yesterday's decision, coming alongside Sinn Féin's embarrassment over its links with the three men arrested in Colombia, might tilt the balance against working the agreement. That would be an historic mistake. It can best be avoided by a start to decommissioning.

28 AUGUST 2001

Romania Right To Try To Regulate Adoption

Pádraig O'Morain

For a time yesterday it was easy to see the Mihaela case as a battle between the cold-hearted, bureaucratic Romanians and the big-hearted, warm Irish.

Mihaela Torumbaru (4) from Romania with Briege Hughes from Dundalk after being told she can remain in Ireland for medical attention. Photograph: Tom Conachy.

The plight of a Romanian child being returned to an orphanage because of a visa mix-up touched people in a way that, say, the deportation of Romanians who come here to better themselves, and to support their children, does not.

Mihaela has endured a lot, at the age of four. Abandoned at birth, she is being reared in an orphanage and is severely disabled. The day two years ago when she was seen by Mrs Briege Hughes in the orphanage was a lucky day for her.

In bringing Mihaela to Ireland four times and arranging medical treatment for her, Mrs Hughes has done a great deal more than most of us can boast. In a fairly arbitrary and cruel world, people like Mrs Hughes provide the saving grace.

But to see the events of yesterday as a triumph for Irish open-heartedness over Romanian bureaucracy would be to take an unjustifiably simplistic approach. The Romanians have, after all, allowed Mihaela to come to this country four times and, so far as we know, there were no difficulties on the first three occasions.

Her return to Romania, had it happened yesterday morning — and had a ticket error and a TV3 camera not intervened — would not necessarily have been permanent. Mrs Hughes was told that the commission which oversees the orphanage would meet on 4 September to decide if it would allow her to return for medical care.

September 4th isn't far off, a week from today. To insist on dragging the child back for that one week seems like the height of bureaucratic silliness.

But the Romanians, one observer said, are 'damned if they do and damned if they don't'. When adoption was fairly unregulated after the communist government fell, there was scope for abuse, and the Romanians were criticised for it.

A year ago Romanian measures to eliminate abuses were praised by UNICEF. Since then, however, a European Parliament report by Baroness Emma Nicholson has again criticised the adoption process as open to abuse by those who gain financially from it.

Romania, anxious to join the EU, has responded by banning foreign adoptions until next summer. It has also been trying to improve its childcare policies in general so as to make it unnecessary for its children to be adopted abroad. Yesterday the Irish group, Parents of Adopted Romanian Children, said it wished Romania well in this endeavour.

In a context in which Romania has to be seen to be doing the right thing, can we complain if its authorities are unhappy that a child came here on an exit visa for a holiday and is then, it appears, staying for medical treatment which, presumably, could take months to complete?

We don't know how the child came to be on a holiday visa and we might wish the authorities in Mihaela's region had handled the issue with a somewhat lighter touch.

But we cannot have it both ways. Romania is entitled to act within the law to regulate its childcare services, just as we are entitled to act within our laws to regulate ours.

(Following publication of this commentary by Pádraig Ó Morain, it emerged that Mihaela had been living with a foster mother in Romania.)

29 AUGUST 2001

Bjonkers?

Brian Boyd

Cork The Bitch's Arse. And that was because of singing Tina Charles's 'I Love To Love' in the playground. But just because people have long hair and listen to Jimi Hendrix, that doesn't make them hippies, you know. The most exciting place on the planet is your kitchen. Singing in a blizzard while bumping into horses. Or even the Brooklyn Bridge, but only at rush hour. Listening to Sparks doing 'This Town Ain't Big Enough For The Both Of Us'. Being a Muslim but pretending to be a Catholic.

This is the way Björk talks. Loose, elliptical non-sequiturs overlap with gnomic micro-philosophies that in turn collide into syntax error and semantic acrobatics. And it's how she says it: Nordic vowels and consonants meet up and exchange tongues with sarf London glottal stops. And it's how she looks as she's saying it: screwing up her Inuit eyes, wiggling her turned up nose around and constantly patting her lightly freckled Slavic cheekbones, as if she's checking they're still there.

Björk is not of us. The sui generis left-field chanteuse even looks like an artist's impression of herself. Put her behind a microphone, though, and her other-worldliness evaporates as quickly as an Icelandic summer. That kinder-banshee voice: cloud bursts of yelps and yowls that swoop and soar all over the vocal register. Sylvia Plath in the key of life.

No *Bell Jar* here, though, this is more like 'Live at Three': 'Finding paradise in your kitchen,' says Björk, having an attack of the abstract similes, as she tries to explain what her new album is all about. The first since 1997's near-impenetrable *Homogenic*, it was going to be called *Domestica* because, as she points out, 'the most exciting place on the planet is your kitchen. The album is all about worshipping the home and I wanted to make an album about the kitchen that was exciting and euphoric and action-packed. I was looking up something in the dictionary one day, because you know I'm still learning English, and I came across the word "vespertine" which means "things that come out in the night", like the owl or the Northern Lights. It's a pop album for yer arse.' Sorry? 'Yer arse, the place where you live.' Oh, your house. Got you.

The interview is taking place, at Björk's request, in the headquarters of the French Communist Party in Paris. It's a sleek Bauhaus edifice with what looks like a giant igloo out in front.

'We're here because of the politics,' she smiles as she pats her face and looks around the confer-ence room, 'and also because I wanted to do a gig in this building, but I couldn't. It's a great building and I wanted to do it here for purely... (makes five different attempts to articulate the word "aesthetic" and eventually gets it) reasons'.

Attentive and polite in a strangely formal way, she has a wonderfully inventive take on the English language. Searching around for words to describe her new work, she frequently gives up on logic and reason and says things such as 'it's like butterflies going in your ear' or 'it's a lot like chocolate'. Trying to highlight the fact that *Vespertine* is an album of modern chamber music, she says 'it's like when it's snowing outside and you're drinking cocoa inside or even it's a bit like when your grandmother calls because she's sick but you just put on some lipstick'. The grandmother/lipstick dilemma, I know it well.

Little wonder she wanted to, figuratively, go home and lock the doors with *Vespertine*. A few years ago, just as she was due to be anointed as the most important female artist of her generation, two incidents of celebrity psychosis pushed her to the brink. In 1997 a crazed white supremacist in Florida, Ricardo Lopez, discovered her home address and sent her a letter bomb.

An obsessive fan, he wanted to kill her because of her then relationship with the black drum 'n' bass star, now Eastenders actor, Goldie. After posting the bomb, which didn't detonate, Lopez filmed himself on video blowing his brains out with a pistol. 'Rather strangely', she now says, 'the letter bomb didn't surprise me. It made me make the choice of whether I wanted to be a celebrity or not to be a celebrity. I chose not to be.'

A few months after the letter bomb, she arrived in Bangkok airport to be doorstepped by a journalist, Julie Kaufman. Björk snapped. She punched, kicked and wrestled Kaufman to the ground — all captured on live TV and gleefully replayed in any Stars Behaving Badly-type filler show. 'I just flipped,' she says. 'She wanted to do an interview and I told her not now, we'll do it

Lorna Felton from Oughterard, Co. Galway, at the Galway Races on Ladies Day.
Photograph: Bryan O'Brien.

tomorrow, so then she started pushing my son (Sindri, who was 11 at the time), trying to get an emotional reaction out of him for the cameras.'

'You know, people think I'm mad and eccentric. But I have to live with two of me — the myth of me and the real me. There are events that happen once or twice a year and people join up the dots and create this alternative persona ... anyway, I thought enough was enough. I left where I had been living (London) and went to Spain and then to Denmark before deciding to go home to Iceland for good. Back there I just picked up a tent, went out to the countryside and starting writing the songs for *Vespertine*. I just wanted to meet different people, make music, live a mobile life.'

If *Homogenic* was, as she puts it, 'a bit too much like a volcano', *Vespertine* is a soothing balm. Soft and diaphanous, a tinkly harp sound and celestial choirs snuggle up to the delicate beats and undulating melodies. 'It was just that thing of connecting again with the music. I always have this dream of me just walking along in the middle of a snow blizzard and bumping into horses and I'm just singing. Now, where I live (New York) I walk across the bridges, especially at rush hour and sing really loudly. I'm a freak. I could talk about and listen to music 24 hours a day. Music is the be-all and the end-all of everything for me. Like, I went to Greenland for two weeks holidays and on my second day there I was putting up ads in the local shops looking for singers I could work with. I travelled around from village to village meeting all these amazing Inuit singers. There are 16 of them on tour in Europe with me now. It's their first time outside of Greenland and they're ..., (waves her arms around to indicate a state of extreme excitement).

An only child who was brought up in a hippy commune just outside Reykjavik — 'Well, they had long hair and listened to Jimi Hendrix but that doesn't necessarily make them hippies' — her amazing vocal ability was discovered by a teacher who heard her singing Tina Charles's 'I Love To Love' in the school playground. She was

Cecilia Smiga as Donna Elvira in Mozart's **Don Giovanni**, *part of Dublin Corporation's Opera in the Open series, at the Civic Offices, Dublin. Photograph: Joe St Leger.*

immediately whisked down to the local radio station, instructed to sing it again live and shortly before her 11th birthday she released her first album (in Iceland only) which featured covers of Beatles and Stevie Wonder songs. At 16 she joined an avant-garde musical collective, Tappi Tikarras (roughly translated as 'Cork the Bitch's Arse'), before tasting international success with The Sugarcubes — fey indie popsters (recommended listening: their *Stick Around For Joy* album). It was only when she moved to London in 1991 and went solo that she really flexed her creative muscles, writing and co-producing her own work. Lyrically, she was a revelation.

While Noel Gallagher was exhorting us to 'roll with it' and Damon Albarn was writing about 'living in a very big house in the country,' Björk — whose first language isn't even English (she writes in Icelandic and translates herself) — was evoking

Emily Dickinson and Sylvia Plath, most notably on the excellent 'Hyperballad' (off *Post*) where she writes about how she lives on top of a mountain and on waking every morning the first thing she does is walk to the edge of the mountain and throw little things off, things like 'car parts, bottles and cutlery, or whatever I find lying around … it's become a habit, a way to start the day'. Later in the song, she writes, 'I'm back at my cliff, still throwing the things off … I follow with my eyes, 'til they crash, imagine what my body would sound like slamming against these rocks … '

Unlike Madonna, who only seems to select her collaborators/producers if they've already been endorsed by *Face* magazine (William Orbit, Mirwais), Björk forces the artistic agenda herself. The techno duo, Black Dog; the Berlin noiseniks, Atari Teenage Riot, and the riotously brilliant film-maker, Chris Cunningham, have all been brought in from the margins due to her work with them.

Unable to classify her as a 'bitch' or 'control freak', sections of the male media fall back on the 'barking mad' line to undercut her talent and ability. 'Oh yeah, the mad and eccentric angle,' she says, 'well, that's just people trying to explain me away.' And she pats her face again.

Vespertine is released this week on One Little Indian.

30 AUGUST 2001

Population Has Reached Its Highest Level In 120 Years

Jane Suiter and Joe Humphreys

The population of the Republic has reached its highest level in 120 years following a dramatic decline in emigration.

Figures from the Central Statistics Office show the population rose to 3.84 million for the year ended April 2001, the highest level since the 1881 census.

And for the first time on record, the number of people emigrating annually from the State has fallen below 20,000.

Published yesterday, the figures show net migration (in this case a surplus of immigrants over emigrants) reached a historic high of 26,300 in the year to April 2001. The number of emigrants was estimated at 19,900 and immigrants 46,200, a record proportion of whom were from countries outside of the EU and US.

Mr Gerry O'Hanlon, a director of the CSO, said the figures showed 'we are no longer an emigrant country'.

He predicted the population would continue to rise by between 40,000 and 50,000 a year for the foreseeable future, breaking the 4 million barrier in 2005–06 and reaching 4.6 million in 2031.

Economists anticipate the growth will put renewed pressures on the housing market, particularly in Dublin. However, public services such as health, education and the welfare system are not expected to suffer additional strains, in the short term at least, as the majority of returning emigrants and new migrants are of working age.

Mr Danny McCoy of the ESRI noted that many migrants had equity as a result of selling their homes abroad. 'That will support the housing market into the future.'

'Despite the increase in the absolute population level, the increasing number of migrants is simply making up for the falling birth rate.'

He said births were now below replacement ratio. As a result, there would be little if any additional pressure on schools or hospitals at the moment. He added that Ireland was still relatively under-populated, at about one-fifth the density of the UK.

The growth in population continues a trend which began in 1961, when the number of people in the State fell to a record low of 2.82 million.

As well as showing changes in migration, the

Workmen put the finishing touches to one of a series of nine enormous prints measuring 9.3 meters by 6.2 metres, by controversial Austrian Artist Gottfried Helnwein, as part of the Kilkenny Arts Festival. Photograph: Jason South.

figures record a natural increase in the population — stemming from a greater number of births than deaths — of 25,700 for the year ended April 2001. This was the largest such increase for over a decade.

The figures show that in the year up to March 2001, there were 55,000 births and 29,300 deaths, 1,100 more and 600 fewer respectively than in the same period last year.

On migration, the figures indicate that the flow of returning Irish nationals is slowing, although they continue to be the largest immigrant group, making up 39 per cent of the total. This is well below the 1999 level of 55 per cent.

The fastest growing area of immigration is from countries outside the EU and the US. In the year ended April 2001, there were 12,300 immigrants from such countries. This compares with 4,200 in 1996.

US nationals accounted for 2,800 of last year's immigrants, UK nationals 7,000 and other Europeans 5,800.

The figures are based on information provided by the CSO's Quarterly National Household Survey, along with official statistics on asylum applications, visa issues and other indicators.

The CSO stressed the figures may be revised following the next national census, which was postponed due to the foot-and-mouth crisis and is due to take place next year.

Relations and family friends carry the coffin of Bernie Cahill, Chairman of Aer Lingus, onto the Bere Island Ferry from Castletownbere, West Cork, watched by the local Lifeboat crew who escorted the ferry to Bere Island. Photograph: David Sleator.

Letters to the Editor
August 2001

Deaths On The Roads

Sir, — Like many others on our Island I am shocked by the wave of deaths on our roads. As a driver I have become more aware and probably more alert.

Over the past few days while driving to and from work, I have noticed four bus drivers talking on mobile phones while driving their buses and countless drivers of large articulated lorries driving with their left hand on the steering wheel, while holding their right elbow to the wheel and their phone to their ears. I've also noticed many taxi/hackney drivers using mobile phones while carrying passengers.

Last night I was at the junction of Clonshaugh Road and Oscar Traynor Road, waiting to make a right turn, with the onward traffic coming from the Clonshaugh Industrial estate. In the line of traffic to my right there were approximately eight people trying to move in the traffic while talking on their mobile phones.

I am quite sure that it is not only speeding and drunk driving that causes road deaths. Surely people should be banned from using mobile phones, especially when in control of public service vehicles or articulated lorries — to start with. — Yours, etc., Pauline Hatch, Dublin 17. 8 August 2001.

Gateway Closure

Sir, — Now that the IT sector is officially in decline and layoffs are occurring in high-tech factories around the country, I suppose the public-sector employees who insisted on matching the pay and conditions of their private sector couterparts wil be handing in their notice and joining us in the nearest dole office or airport. — Yours, etc., Shane Robinson, Harbour Court, Courtmacsherry, Co. Cork. 14 August 2001.

Sir, — Be aware that we never had a Celtic Tiger economy. We had a Titanic economy. It's going down in the same way. And the Irish are very at home with that. — Yours, etc., N. Quinn, Sandyhill Gardens, Dublin 11. 14 August 2001.

Doors On Dublin Buses

Sir, — When I left these shores some 15 years ago looking for work abroad, there was much discussion in the newspapers regarding the strange phenomenon of Dublin buses and the drivers' refusal to open the centre doors.

Indeed it was one of the first things that I noticed when arriving in England, waiting in vain to disembark from the front doors of a bus in south London only to be greeted by a baffled driver looking at me as if I was mad! 'What's the problem mate? Use the middle doors like everybody else.'

Needless to say I learnt my lesson that day and over the years travelling around Europe one soon gets accustomed to getting on the bus at the front, and getting off at the back. Curious to note then that on my return to Dublin the arguments regarding Dublin bus centre doors not opening still abound. — Yours, etc., Arthur Fortune, Shankill, Co. Dublin. 24 August 2001.

Death of Donald Woods

Sir, — It was with deep regret that Trócaire learned of the death of Donald Woods, a man committed to justice in Ireland as well as in his native South Africa.

Much of his work in apartheid South Africa was in supporting a free press, which he saw as essential to the struggle. After the dismantling of apartheid and the accession to power of the ANC, his commitment to the honesty and integrity of journalism remained. He feared that the emergence of a truly free and independent press would be compromised under a new regime. In this, he was a credit to his profession.

Writing to Trócaire in 1998 to mark the agency's 25th anniversary, Mr Woods said the training of new African journalists was 'essential to the continuation of the present transition process, and for the future development of a healthy civil society in our new democracy'.

Trócaire's partnership with this anti-apartheid activist dates back nearly 25 years. In 1977, as editor of the Daily Dispatch, Mr Woods launched Trócaire's education pack on his country. He later asked Trócaire to provide him with a typewriter, on which he wrote his book on Steve Biko which was later turned into Richard Attenborough's acclaimed film Cry Freedom. In 1983, he attended Trócaire's 10th anniversary celebrations and delivered our annual Maynooth lecture — just one of hundreds of speeches he delivered after he fled South Africa. Over the years, Trócaire funded his training work with young journalists.

He was very fond of Ireland and took part in a number of reconciliation projects in the North. The last time we met was at an arts centre in Armagh last year when he was in Northern Ireland to meet and encourage groups working to promote reconciliation.

Mr Woods's belief in justice, the personal sacrifices he made as an expression of solidarity with the oppressed, and his untiring commitment to his profession were an inspiration to a generation of journalists and activists. May he rest in peace. — Yours, etc., Justin Kilcullen, Director, Trócaire, Blackrock, Co. Dublin. 29 August 2001.

A fiery blast rocks the World Trade Centre after it was hit by two aeroplanes, 11 September, in New York City. Photograph: Allsport UK.

12 SEPTEMBER 2001

'Oh My God, People are Jumping' They Screamed

Eyewitness in New York by Conor O'Clery

The first bang came at 8.50 a.m., shaking the windows of my 42nd floor office which has a clear view of the two World Trade Centre towers three blocks to the south-east.

I looked out and saw a huge ball of flame and black smoke billowing out of the north-facing side of the nearest tower.

As the smoke cleared a massive hole 10 storeys high became visible just below the top 10 floors and flames could be seen encircling the building behind its narrow slit-like windows.

Ten minutes later a passenger plane appeared from across the Hudson River heading straight for the second tower.

I didn't notice it until the last minute.

It was tilted so that the flight path took it straight towards the second tower.

It hit and simultaneously a gigantic ball of flame emerged from the east side of the second tower as if the plane had crashed right through the heart of the 110-storey building.

Debris fell in chunks onto West Side Highway followed by a blizzard of shards of glass and paper where ambulances and fire engines were beginning to congregate.

Flames began to leap from the side of the Marriott Hotel just across from where the tiny white Greek Orthodox church stands incongruously in a car park.

People by this time were streaming from the bottom floor of the World Trade Centre, which stands on top of a shopping mall and wide marbled corridors containing airline offices, shops and a subway station.

Some 50,000 people work in the seven-building complex and many would have been in their offices by now.

Tourists would have begun arriving to queue for the lifts to the top of the tower with its famous window on the World Restaurant and wonderful views over Manhattan.

But they would not have been taken up to the 107th floor observation deck until it opened at 9.30 a.m.

Watching through binoculars I could see people hanging out of the windows beside and above where the fires were raging.

One man waved a white cloth as he clung to a window strut.

Then a body fell from a window above him with arms and legs outstretched and plummeted some 100 storeys onto Vesey Street.

Two other people fell in the succeeding minutes.

I ran down to the streets where office workers and traders, still wearing their red jackets, were milling around.

Some women were screaming 'Oh my God, people are jumping, oh my God.'

Some of the residents of my building, where many members of the financial district live, were sobbing uncontrollably. I returned to the office.

As I watched, the top of the second tower suddenly fell outwards onto West Side Highway, the main thoroughfare along the western side of Manhattan which passes right by the World Trade Centre.

Massive jagged pieces of the tower the size of houses crashed onto two fire engines and onto rescue workers on the roadway.

A huge cloud of dust and ashes rose from the impact, enveloping the Embassy Suites Hotel across the highway and the 50-storey buildings of the World Financial Centre which house Merrill Lynch and stands between the towers and the Hudson River promenade.

I shifted my eyes upwards to the first tower that had been hit and was still standing, and saw that several more people had appeared in the upper storeys where they had smashed windows.

The man with the white cloth was still there,

*The remains of the World Trade Centre stand amid the debris, following the terrorist attack on the building.
Photograph: AP Photo/Alex Fuchs.*

hanging precariously by one hand with his body out over the abyss.

I wondered why there was no attempt to rescue them by helicopter as part of the roof of the 1,350-foot building was clear of smoke.

But then the tower began to sway slightly and two people fell in quick succession from the windows as if unable to maintain their grip, falling down onto West Side Highway into the dust and smoke from the first collapse.

Then the tower simply slid in on itself, imploding with a huge roar, leaving the lift-shaft like a stump of a blasted tree with twisted metal arms.

This time the clouds of dust and smoke were so huge they enveloped the whole of southern Manhattan.

Thousands of tons of rubble fell onto Tobin Plaza, where open air concerts are sometimes held and onto the annex housing Borders giant book store.

A westerly breeze kept it about a hundred yards from my building. As it cleared, the scene around the towers was like one from a war zone, which it truly was.

The roadway and pavements and bicycle path, all the streets, cars, fire engines, pavements, traffic lights, awnings and police vehicles, were coated with dust. The green park between my building and the towers where kids play American football had been transformed into a grey field, as if covered with a toxic snow.

About 20 cars in the open air car park between it and the disaster scene were on fire.

As the dirty grey and brown smoke cleared around midday I could see that the Marriott Hotel had taken the full force of the falling tower.

All its windows were shattered and long strips of jagged metal hung over the awning.

The wide, covered pedestrian bridge from the mezzanine level of the financial centre and the

Winter Gardens, with its palm trees, was a twisted mass of wreckage.

Out on the streets again, people who had been standing aghast in Battery Park by the river were now streaming uptown on foot.

'Go north, head north,' shouted a police officer. The police and firemen remained mostly calm but their faces reflected the horror of the certainty that they had just lost many comrades.

Before the collapse dozens of firemen and police had rushed into the twin towers to try to help with the evacuation.

What had become of them? It was too horrible to contemplate.

Or to think of the thousands of people trying to escape from both towers, executives in suits, receptionists at polished desks, secretaries, traders, messengers, choking in their offices or racing down smoke-filled emergency stairwells below the destruction line.

It was just 10 minutes before nine when the first plane crashed into one of the towers and the offices were undoubtedly all either doing business or preparing for another working day.

The two gift shops at the top and the food court would have been almost ready to open up.

In the mall below, thousands at that time of day criss-cross through the wide corridors past designer stores and coffee shops and newspaper vendors.

Shocked and weeping people trotted down Greenwich Street and west Broadway and Broadway with their hands to their eyes, obeying the arm-waving police officers, and fleeing in the direction of uptown.

Others crowded onto the cross-Hudson ferries at the harbour surrounded by the financial centre buildings.

The ferries had borne workers from the New Jersey shore to their work in the financial district just two hours before. The clothes of those caught in the explosion of dust were coated with grey, some had dust-covered hair and eyebrows.

Between midday and one o'clock there were three more muffled bangs from the vast area still hidden by thick acrid smoke as more sections of the two towers collapsed.

As the smoke drifted eastwards further scenes of immense destruction came into view: The twisted metal and piles of rubble and crushed dust-shrouded emergency vehicles which filled Vesey Street and West Side Highway.

There among the rubble, coated with dust, were many bodies, some of those who had jumped, and some of firemen caught beneath the heavy, deadly cascade of falling concrete and metal.

Another plane appeared overhead, causing a frisson of panic but it turned out to be a military jet, arriving one assumes to shoot out of the sky any further suicide pilots. It was too late to save downtown Manhattan.

12 SEPTEMBER 2001

'We Saw Our Neighbour's Faces, All Frozen In Shock'

Eyewitness in New York by Elaine Lafferty

This is how we live now. We will hear the screams of our neighbours as the air fills with smoke and debris, as the unthinkable happens — the two tallest buildings in New York crumble down upon us, like toys, like cheap props in a bad movie.

We will watch as our fellow Americans, as US presidents are fond of calling this citizenry, emerge from the catastrophe of downtown Manhattan.

Their faces, all of them, regardless of race or ethnicity, are now a ghostly light grey, covered with the thick layer of ash that is enveloping this city.

Some of those faces are streaked with blood. All of the faces are frozen in shock.

This is how we live now.

We began our new lives at 8.47 a.m. yesterday when a plane streaked across the Manhattan

People make their way through debris near the World Trade Centre in New York. Photograph: AP Photo/Gulnara Samoilova.

skyline, as planes do all the time. But this one was different. Marco Ponti knew it immediately.

'I was walking up West Broadway and I looked up and saw this two-engine commercial airliner. He was low and fast. I looked at a lady walking a dog next to me and I said to her that this guy was too low. Then I heard him go full throttle and he crashed into the building. It was suicide. There was no engine sputtering,' he said.

Mr Ponti ran upstairs to the building where he works, 11 Beach Street, about eight blocks from the 110-storey World Trade Centre, the twin towers, one of which was now in flames.

Some 50,000 people work there, Mr Ponti knew. He grabbed some friends and they went downstairs to watch the fire.

That was when the second plane hit, some 18 minutes after the first.

'Confetti just came down, papers flying out of the windows. There was a fireball.' Another co-worker stood at the window of the same building and watched as the second plane hit. She is too frightened to have her name used.

'I can't describe it. It was like I saw the outline of the plane in the building. And this fire,' she said.

David Russell, president of American Flight Group, a private airline company and a former high ranking military official, knew immediately what had happened.

'This is a highly sophisticated operation,' he said. 'This kind of organised attack is the responsibility of a foreign government, not a lone knucklehead.'

Within minutes the streets of New York were filled with people fleeing downtown. The city was instantly transformed. It was like a strange parade, a procession of refugees dressed differently than we are accustomed to seeing — three piece business suits, briefcases clutched tightly, women in power suits and heels, all of them seemingly trying to talk into cell phones.

The north-south streets were filled. Seventh Avenue, known as the capital of the fashion district, even Second Avenue on the east side. The Brooklyn Bridge, a symbol glistening over New York's East River, looks like it is the scene of a strange religious pilgrimage as pedestrians walk to their homes.

They have no choice; the subways have been shut down, the Holland and Lincoln Tunnels closed. Roads are blocked, trains stopped. All the airports in the US are shut down. At Newark Airport in New Jersey, officers with machines guns are stopping cars.

'I am concerned about what is in the smoke,' said one man walking along the West Side Highway.

Lines began to form outside payphones as both land-based telephone lines and mobile lines began to fail with overload. Lines began to form at bank teller machines as people went into crisis mode.

'I don't know what to do,' said one woman, sweaty and eyes filled with tears as she entered her apartment building in Greenwich Village.

'My boyfriend works in Times Square. Will they hit there? I just went out to buy water.'

As the morning unfolded, even as the shock of the two planes hitting the World Trade Centre sank in, more news emerged. There were four planes hijacked in the US altogether. Some were still in the air.

Then the further news came. A plane had hit the Pentagon. Another plane had crashed in Pennsylvania.

Greta Van Susteren, a CNN employee, and her husband was sitting on a plane delayed on the tarmac in Washington, DC, heading to New York, when the first plane hit. It soon became apparent they were going nowhere. They returned to their car which they had left on the roof-top parking lot.

'We saw a plane near the Pentagon and then heard this "boom",' she said. She was unable to get back into Washington, DC because the roads were closed.

As the phone lines became useless, people began emailing. This one from a woman who lives downtown.

'F16s have been flying around here all morning. Every time I hear one I run to the window to make sure it's one of ours. When the first building collapsed, as we watched from my window, we could hear the screams of the people down there. That's how loud the screams were.'

People became glued to their televisions as the story unfolded.

American Airlines identified the planes that crashed into the Trade Centre as Flight 11, a Los Angeles-bound jet hijacked after takeoff from Boston with 92 people aboard, and Flight 77, which was seized while carrying 64 people from Washington to Los Angeles.

In Pennsylvania, United Airlines Flight 93, a Boeing 757 en route from Newark, New Jersey, to San Francisco, crashed about 80 miles south-east of Pittsburgh with 45 people aboard.

United said another of its planes, Flight 175, a Boeing 767 bound from Boston to Los Angeles with 65 people on board, also crashed, but it did not say where. The fate of those aboard the two planes was not immediately known.

Evacuations were ordered at the UN in New York and at the Sears Tower in Chicago. Los Angeles mobilised its anti-terrorism division, and security was intensified around the naval installations in Hampton Roads, Virginia.

Disney World in Orlando, Florida, was evacuated.

President Bush ordered a full-scale investigation to 'hunt down the folks who committed this act'. Word was that the President was hunkered down in a bunker in Louisiana.

The White House, the Pentagon and the Capitol were evacuated along with other federal buildings in Washington and New York.

Authorities in Washington immediately began deploying troops, including an infantry regiment.

The Situation Room at the White House was in full operation. Authorities went on alert from coast to coast, US and Canadian borders were sealed, all air traffic across the country was halted, and security was tightened at strategic installations.

'This is the second Pearl Harbour. I don't think that I overstate it,' said Senator Chuck Hagel, a Nebraska Republican.

By early afternoon, New York hospitals were all ready to help the wounded.

Outside St Vincent's hospital on Seventh Avenue, white gurneys were positioned outside the emergency entrance, waiting for ambulances to arrive.

Doctors and nurses stood on the pavement, their hands in blue rubber medical gloves, ready for the wounded, but strangely idle at this moment. Police had the streets cordoned off from onlookers and volunteers seeking to donate blood.

Ambulances did come. But even though some 152 people were admitted, there was no sense of the hospital being overwhelmed. The gurneys stood mostly empty, white sheets catching the autumn breeze.

Deborah Glick, a local elected state official, stood outside St Vincent's. She had been up early campaigning; this was election day in New York, the city prepared to elect a new mayor.

'I was at the subway stop campaigning for my candidate,' said Ms Glick. 'Now I am trying to figure out where to give blood.' The election was called off. The city was in suspension.

By noon, the two damaged buildings had collapsed, erasing what had seemed a permanent feature of the New York skyline, even though the World Trade Centre had only been there since 1972. In its place, the sky held only a plume of grey smoke, a cloud reminiscent of a volcano.

I remember when I used to work in the World Trade Centre, many years ago, on the 107th floor. I remember when my ears would pop as you were sucked up in the high speed elevators, usually around the 70th floor.

I remember last May, standing on the observation deck at night with my friends from Ballymacoda, Co. Cork. My friends looked through the telescopes on the roof.

The lights of the city glistened below, and you could see the Statue of Liberty on the horizon. From the top of the World Trade Centre it always seemed as if Americans could see everything.

That, like the illusion of safety, national security and immunity from the hatred that inflames those willing to die for their cause, was a cruel illusion.

13 SEPTEMBER 2001

FBI Seek Men Who Took Flight Lessons

Elaine Lafferty in New York

Barbara Olson was planning to fly from Washington, DC to Los Angeles on Monday. But Tuesday was her husband's birthday and she wanted to celebrate with him on Monday evening. So she decided to postpone her flight for a day.

Ms Olson and her husband were well known in the US, at least in political circles. With her long blond hair and verbal gift for slamming liberal politicians, the former federal prosecutor had become a regular on the television talk show circuit, particularly on CNN's *Larry King Show*. She also authored a critical book on Hillary Rodham Clinton. Her husband, Mr Theodore Olson, was a well-known lawyer who helped President Bush get elected. Today he is Solicitor General of the US.

Tuesday morning Ms Olson was up at the crack of dawn as she hurried to catch American Airlines Flight 77 that left Washington, DC's Dulles Airport at 8.10 a.m.

A little over an hour later, Ms Olson used her mobile phone to call her husband in his office at the US Justice Department. 'We are being hijacked,' she said. The line went dead, but she called again.

She described how the hijackers had used knives and box-cutters to hijack the plane. She described how they had herded the flight crew and passengers into the rear of the plane. She was, by all accounts, calm. But she also sought advice from her husband.

'What do I tell the pilot to do?' she asked him. The line went dead.

By then, of course, after 9 a.m., Mr Olson already knew about the two aircraft that had crashed into the World Trade Centre in New York. But like everyone else, he did not know exactly what was going on. He also did not know that other husbands, wives and parents had received similar phone calls.

Mr Peter Hanson was a businessman who was flying from Boston with his wife and two children. Mr Lee Hanson, Peter's father, lives in Easton, Connecticut. Shortly before 9 a.m. he received two mobile phone calls from his son. Mr Hanson told authorities Peter had called twice in short calls that cut off.

In the first call, Peter said a flight attendant had been stabbed. In the second, he said his plane was going down. That plane crashed into the World Trade Centre at 8.45 a.m.

'He called to his parents' home, and so in that way they were so together in that moment,' the Rev Bonnie Bardot told a memorial service held on Tuesday night in Easton.

A flight attendant aboard the second jetliner that struck the World Trade Centre managed to call an emergency number from the back of the aircraft, American Airlines said.

The woman reported that her fellow attendants had been stabbed, the cabin had been taken over and they were going down in New York. That plane crashed into the World Trade Centre at 9.03 a.m.

Ms Alice Hoglan lives in San Francisco. She told KTVU-TV that her son, Mr Mark Bingham (31), called her from aboard United Airlines Flight 93 that left Newark Airport en route to San Francisco.

'We've been taken over. There are three men that say they have a bomb,' Ms Hoglan quoted her son as saying.

That plane crashed at 10 a.m. some 80 miles south-west of Pittsburgh, Pennsylvania. There are reports that it was headed to the presidential retreat in Camp David, Maryland.

By 10 a.m., when the plane went down in Pennsylvania, most people knew what was going on. The fact that the US was the target of an orchestrated full-scale terrorist attack was made clear — as if there might have been any doubt after New York — when a plane smashed into the Pentagon. Mr Olson soon learned that his wife had been aboard that plane.

Last night, the White House said it initially targeted the White House and the presidential jet, Air Force One. But, at the last minute, it veered instead towards the Pentagon.

As the planes, some of whose pilots are believed to have been trained in the US, were crashing on the east coast, all flights in the US were halted and ordered to land at the nearest airport.

A man aboard one of those flights listened to the news as he got off the plane and learned that two of the planes had originated in Boston. He had boarded in Boston also, and he recalled getting into an altercation with several Arab men in a parking lot structure as they were getting into a Mitsubishi rental car.

He called police and described what he knew.

From that call, authorities were led to a rental car left at Logan Airport in Boston. Inside they found a *Koran*, a video on how to fly a commercial airliner and flight instruction materials in Arabic.

At least five Arab men have been identified as suspects, and the investigation appears to be focussed on Florida and Boston. Two of the men, whose passports were traced to the United Arab Emirates, were brothers, one of whom was a trained pilot, a source told the *Boston Herald*.

Hijacked United Airlines Flight 175 flies towards the World Trade Centre twin towers shortly before slamming into the south tower as the north tower burns. Photograph: Reuters/Sean Adair.

At least two other suspects flew to Logan yesterday from Portland, Maine, where authorities believe they had travelled after crossing over from Canada.

The FBI interviewed a Venice, Florida, couple about two men who stayed at their house for a week in July 2000 while the men were taking small-plane flight training at Venice Municipal Airport.

FBI agents 'informed me that there were two individuals that were students at Huffman Aviation. My employer and (the) FBI told me they were involved in yesterday's tragedy,' said Mr Charlie Voss, who was interviewed with his wife, Ms Drew Voss, at their home by a Florida newspaper.

The couple accepted the two men as house guests as a favour to the company, Mr Voss said. The men, who stayed just a few days, trained at the airport and came to the house to sleep, he said.

The FBI was also seeking search warrants in Broward County in southern Florida and Daytona Beach in central Florida. A car was towed by authorities at one of those locations.

The government believes the hijackers were trained pilots and that three to five were aboard each of four airliners that crashed on Tuesday in the worst terrorist attack ever in the United States, said Justice Department spokeswoman Ms Mindy Tucker. She said the conclusion was based on information gathered from the phone calls made by passengers on the planes.

'It appears from what we know that the hijackers were skilled pilots,' said Ms Tucker.

A flight manifest from one of the flights included the name of a suspected supporter of Mr Osama bin Laden.

And US intelligence intercepted communications between supporters of Mr bin Laden, discussing Tuesday's attacks on the World Trade Centre in New York and the Pentagon, Senator Orrin Hatch told the Associated Press.

'They have an intercept of some information that included people associated with Osama bin Laden who acknowledged a couple of targets were hit,' Mr Hatch said.

Law enforcement officials told AP that early evidence suggested the attackers may have studied how to operate large aircraft and targetted transcontinental flights with large fuel supplies to ensure spectacular explosions — and maximum destruction.

The farewell phone calls from passengers and at least one flight attendant on the four targeted flights described a similar pattern: hijackers working in groups of three to five, wielding knives, in some cases stabbing flight crews as they took control of the cockpit and forced the planes toward their targets.

As the US mourned, attention focussed more on Boston and Florida and the attempt to find the men responsible for this day of infamy.

17 SEPTEMBER 2001

Refugees Facing Desperate Plight

Miriam Donohoe at Jalozai refugee camp on the Pakistan/Afghan frontier

Sami Javed sobbed quietly as he surveyed the heartbreaking scenes of human desolation around him.

Two of his young children died from dehydration and lack of food here in Jalozai Camp for Afghan refugees in Pakistan's north-west frontier province. Sami, who fled his homeland's brutal civil war in May, is not alone in his loss.

The mortality rate in this makeshift refugee camp has doubled in the last month with up to 14 deaths a week now being reported by aid agencies.

An estimated 50,000 refugees are located in Jalozai Camp 25 km east of Peshawar.

Half have been living here for several years and their conditions are somewhat bearable.

But as the civil war in Afghanistan has escalated, thousands more have arrived here, putting huge pressure on already stressed resources.

Between 30 and 100 new families are arriving here every week.

These refugees are living in deplorable condi-tions. They do not have enough to eat and disease is rampant. Their homes are makeshift tents.

Now Pakistan is bracing itself for thousands more Afghan refugees as they prepare to leave their country, fearing a strike by the US following the attacks last week in New York and Washington.

When I arrived yesterday, I was greeted by pictures of malnourished children with their blank-faced and helpless parents trying to survive.

Many of the children were covered with abscesses and had other infections on their faces and bodies as they roamed around the filthy site, a breeding ground for infection. One little boy I saw was completely covered with sores. But he still managed to smile despite obvious pain.

Other little children had bloated stomachs and sunken eyes, sure signs of malnutrition. There is a constant shortage of fresh water.

Five minutes after arriving, a UNHCR water tank delivered a fresh supply and the people living here flocked to fill plastic bottles and saucepans. This lorry comes with water five times a day.

Rations of wheat are distributed to families every morning. One woman, whose husband died in battle in Afghanistan, here with her four daugh-ters and two sons, showed me her ration bag, which carried the International Islamic Organisation logo.

'This is not enough for me to feed my family. We are hungry,' she cried.

She explained she was also ill. The woman took my hand and placed it on her stomach. I could feel a huge tumour the size of a tennis ball through her clothes. She said she has received no medical treatment.

The staple diet in recent weeks has been bread, which the desperate refugees make with their wheat rations and water.

A little boy pulls at my T-shirt. His name is Khaee and he is six-years old. He looked half that age. He has been here for six months but says he would prefer to be at home in Afghanistan. 'I am hungry all the time.'

In an open tent, Kimeia is lying on a dirty mat on the ground. She is very weak and says she has been ill for several weeks. Both her legs are very swollen. 'Something must be done. We are a for-gotten people here. We will all die if we do not get help,' she said as her three children played quietly.

The only income people in Jalozai Camp earn is the equivalent of 25p a day for spinning cotton thread from wool. It seems every adult in the camp is involved in this painstaking activity.

According to a UN Integrated Regional Information Network for Central Asia Report, posted on their website last Friday, the mortality and malnutrition rates among children at Jalozai will increase due to deteriorating hygiene, lack of clean water and food.

The report says the number of children enrolled in a feeding centre in the camp had increased from 550 three weeks ago to 800 last week, with the figure expected to increase further.

Dr Amin Oman, who works in a medical clinic in Jalozai, is quoted in the report as saying that children do not have the balanced diet needed to help their growth. Of the children seen at the clinic every day, 80 are malnourished.

Yesterday, *The Irish Times* and RTÉ reporter Mr Tony Connelly and cameraman Mr Michael Cassidy were among the first news organisations to gain access to the camp in recent times. Pakistani authorities have refused permission to journalists to visit because they said it was 'too sensitive' at this time.

One aid worker said relief destined for the camp is being taken by the Pakistani authorities. With the help of a local guide we were driven into the camp by a back road and were warned to be discreet. We were advised against going to the newest part of the camp where we were told con-ditions were even worse because of heavy security.

After 30 minutes, the police approached and told our guide they would like to question us as we should not have been there. After some negotiating we were allowed to leave.

As the US shapes up for an attack on Afghanistan, conditions at Jalozai will probably get worse as more refugees flee to safety. After 23 years of war, first against the Russians and then years of civil strife, these brave but trodden people are possibly facing their biggest battle yet.

Over the weekend, thousands of Afghans have gathered at the Pakistan border in the hope of leaving before a US attack on their homeland.

The Pakistan government is reported to have deployed additional forces to prevent the displaced people from entering the country. An estimated 5,000 refugees have reached the border at Torkham but Taliban officials have baton-charged the crowd and pushed them back, according to one newspaper report.

One woman told yesterday of the ultimate indignity. Relatives only get material about five metres long to cover their dead. It is not enough.

These people don't want to know about the terrorist, Osama Bin Laden, or America. Their only concern is survival. These are the forgotten victims of Afghan's civil war. And with the threat of a new attack on the country edging closer and closer, these refugees may soon be joined by thousands more of their weary country people.

18 SEPTEMBER 2001

Dow Jones Becomes New Casualty

Conor O'Clery

Thousands of traders, brokers, analysts and executives, who make the world's biggest Stock Exchange hum with activity, returned yesterday to Wall Street to do business for the first time since Tuesday, 11 September.

An emotional and sombre procession of commuters, some wearing surgical masks, poured in

Emergency personnel continue rescue efforts amid the wreckage of the World Trade Centre towers in New York. Photograph: AP Photo/Ruth Fremson.

from the subway stations and the Staten Island ferry, running for the first time since two hijacked airliners ploughed into the towers of the World Trade Centre.

They passed through police checkpoints where they were asked for two forms of identification, and paused to gaze in awe at a devastated landscape, where the very shadows are different now the 110-storey twin towers of the World Trade Centre are gone.

Streets had been cleaned of debris but financial workers and the people who work in the restaurants, bars, newspaper kiosks and concession stores which service the skyscraper canyons around Wall Street, had to cope with cables laid across streets and an acrid smell from the ruins three blocks away.

They looked startled at the National guardsmen in camouflage lounging with semi-automatic rifles on street corners, and lingered to read the home-made posters with the smiling faces of the disappeared who haunt the streets of downtown.

At 9.30 a.m. traders gathered on the New York Stock Exchange floor as chairman Mr Richard Grasso emerged on to the famous balcony with Mayor Rudolph Giuliani, Treasury Secretary Mr Paul O'Neill, Senator Hillary Clinton and other dignitaries, to pay tribute to the 'fabulous men and women who are crawling through the rubble even while we speak.

'These wonderful men and women who put their lives on the line allow us to do what we do,' he said, before giving way to a female US Marine major who rendered the patriotic anthem, 'America' to a hushed exchange.

Some traders clutched Stars and Stripes and bit their lips as she sang the words, concluding, 'From the mountains to the prairies, God Bless America, my home sweet home'.

After a two-minute silence, followed by a huge cheer for the rescue services personnel who were given the honour of ringing the opening bell, the usual pandemonium broke out.

The expected sell-off began, making the Dow

Jones the third big casualty of the strike on the Trade Centre.

But the infrastructure of the world's biggest exchange, which normally executes trades worth $43 billion a day, survived the catastrophe more or less intact. Screens were up, phones and Internet worked. Brokers were able to place orders and the system connecting brokers to clearing houses appeared to work.

'It's good to be back in business, we're going to stick our thumb in the eye of the murderers,' said Mr O'Neill at the NYSE building where an American flag was draped over the entrance.

At ground zero nearby, rescuers continued to sift through the wreckage of the World Trade Centre, but hope of finding survivors has evaporated.

On Sunday, rescuers reached a train platform 80 feet below the centre's remains but found no survivors.

As the tension drained from the city after its nightmare of last week, City Hall, court houses and other government buildings reopened their doors.

'The life of the city goes on, and I encourage people to go about their lives,' said Mayor Giuliani.

The Wall Street subway station remained closed, and only subways on the east side of downtown Manhattan were running. A new ferry service carried passengers across the East River from the borough of Brooklyn. Streets were closed to vehicles and some thoroughfares were barricaded.

Some places downtown had trouble with telephone and electric services and there were telephone problems at police headquarters.

The city telephone giant, Verizon, suffered severe structural damage.

Newspaper vendor Mr Dhiren Shah was able to resume business after losing about $1,000 over the last week. 'It's terrible', he said, 'we feel like we are missing the landmark of New York.'

Mr Dennis Goin, president of Goin & Co., brokerage firm, planned to sleep at his office near the Stock Exchange. He was prepared for a difficult day.

Firefighters raise a flag in the afternoon on Tuesday, 11 September 2001, in the wreckage of the World Trade Centre towers in New York. Photograph: AP Photo/Thomas E. Franklin.

'You might be calling to people who you might call once a month, and when you place that call, you might be told that Joe isn't here anymore,' he said.

22 SEPTEMBER 2001

A Love Letter to Manhattan

Nuala O'Faolain

On Saturday nights, if you live near Houston Street in the Village, you might as well not try to sleep. Until near dawn the kids drive along the street, east to west, west to east, whooping and hollering and beeping the horns of their cars. They're partying, for no better reason than they are where they are. In Fun City.

I know, because I spent the past three winters in various rented rooms in lower Manhattan, writing my first novel and then trying to think of a second. Writers can live anywhere, but I chose there as the place to attempt a late career change, because New York is a city created by the optimism of generations of immigrants, and I hoped the optimism would rub off on me. I chose it because, to my mind, it was more than fun, it was a joyous place, the Paris of our time, stylish, frivolous, affordable, and wonderfully hospitable to dreams. It is the one place I know where personal transformation is the general goal and applies to everyone of any age and gender and class, from the boy from a dusty crossroads in Guatemala who delivers the groceries, to the face-lifted and tummy-tucked women who cruise Tiffanys efficiently while their husbands wait at the bar of the Harvard Club.

Manhattan is not monumental and self-important, like Washington, and it doesn't manufacture, like Chicago, and it isn't intellectual, like Boston. Its industries are the light ones — publishing, fashion, advertising. It knows it is light, and it sends its own light New Yorkness up. Twice when I was there the place indulged itself in mass hysteria when first a hurricane and then a blizzard were forecast. It is true that the peddlar streets around Chinatown were weirdly empty of fake-Prada handbag sellers for a day, and the sky went black and a hot wind whipped along buildings I had never seen barricaded before. But that was as bad as it got.

Afterwards, there wasn't the slightest embarrassment at the over-reaction to the weather warnings, or any apology.

Manhattan had been playing a game called frightening itself. It never seriously believed the Apocalypse was coming. But now, butterfly Manhattan is pinned under the nets of vicious forces, though viciousness is wholly alien to its spirit.

The island narrows to the width of three fields, down where the Trade Centre towers stood. It has a unique atmosphere, that district, where you can almost touch one side of the city from the other, and there are glimpses of vistas as watery as Venice, and the stocky buildings are lightened by brisk, marine breezes full of sparkle and light. At night its narrow streets are taken over by dimly gleaming seabirds who come down to scavenge the fast food wrappers the office workers leave behind when they pour out of their offices and hurry home.

The beginnings of the city are here, at what was once the tip of a scrub-covered peninsula where the slow sheets of water from the East River and the Hudson River succumb to the bright expanse of the great harbour. I lived down there for a while, a block from the ferry to Ellis Island in one direction: two blocks from the World Trade Centre in the other.

I was lent a place high up in an ornate building which was once offices and is now apartments for singles working across the way in Wall Street — a short, curved street that follows the line of the log wall the first European settlers put up to defend their settlement against the people they dispossessed. Their native enemies slipped up and down along the trail they'd made in the wilderness, a trail that the Dutch settlers called Burgh Weg, which became the word, Broadway. On the floor above me, young men and women in expensive sports gear toiled on the treadmills in the gym, where clerks in celluloid collars once stood at their ledgers.

Investors were trying to make the financial district into a neighbourhood, but it hadn't really caught on. The place lost all its urbanity in the evenings. The bars and cafés closed when the offices did. Even the sex club closed early. Chauffeurs dozed in their limos outside expensive drinking clubs waiting for the last broker or banker to come out, wiping his lips, to be driven to the suburbs. The streets were empty and very quiet. But because the island is so narrow at that point and so many subway lines enter Manhattan there, just below the surface, the moaning and clanking of the trains filled the air all night long. It was as if huge demons were trapped down there, under the earth on which the skyscrapers stood.

There was a notice in the bookshop at the foot of the World Trade Centre building one day. A man who'd written a book on the birds of Manhattan would lead a bird-watching tour from there, all welcome. The 10 or so of us who showed up were a typically motley, eccentric, socially inexplicable group of New Yorkers. One old man had a solar tepee on, and some of the others wore sturdy shoes and carried binoculars, though we were following the walkways and piazzas directly under the towers, and looking for our birds in the plantings in pebbledash troughs and dank beds that divided the expanses of concrete. Several of the birdwatchers had water bottles fixed to their belts, though I don't suppose we were ever more than a hundred yards from refreshments. But the repartee was loud and funny, and as we mooched along towards Battery Park we actually did see more than a dozen different kinds of bird pecking at the thin grass, or going about their bird lives under the municipal laurel bushes, behind the roller skaters and cyclists and baby buggies and the courting couples entwined on graffiti-covered benches.

What bird, someone asked, is the official bird of New York?

No one was sure.

It should be the bluebird, a woman said dreamily, because the bluebird is the bird of happiness.

Don't you believe it, honey, a woman in full makeup, wearing a long lace dress and a huge backpack, said. No one ever came to this city to be happy.

But they did. Where we were walking — a stone's throw from where bloodstained dereliction now begins — is tearstained land, but the tears were tears of joy. That's where the immigrant ships tied up, before there were entry controls. That's where the blacks and the Irish fought it out for waterfront jobs — tough jobs, but better than anything they could have, ever, where they came from. Europeans escaped the limitations they had been born into, when they walked down the gangways and out into the pullulating, raucous, no-holds-barred city. I went to Manhattan for that — to be an immigrant. I wanted to try something new in a city that was created by wave upon wave of adventurers trying something new. I lived most of the time in a bedsitter on 3rd Street. But I used to go back to the bottom of the island because I loved the way you can see the layers of experience the city is composed of down there. I might have been in the vicinity of the Trade Centre towers to use the central Post Office beside them, or to mooch around Century 21, the greatest designer discount store in the world. There were always Irish voices in there, calling to each other about La Perla bras in an unfortunate red, or Moschino jeans for half nothing, but only in dwarf or giant sizes. Walking home from south to north I would be following the immigrant trail again, towards a new life, a welcomed future.

I have two sets of friends who live very near where the towers were — lived, they've been evacuated now. On the night of the last presidential election there was a party and the windows were open onto Chambers Street because our hostess is English so smoking was allowed, and our cheers and laughter must have disturbed the druggies and the homeless having a sit-up sleep in the all-night burger bars. At some point, the exhausted presenter on one channel announced that the whole thing was a mess and it might be days before we knew who had won the presidency.

Okay — I'm going home, I said, finishing off my wine. I'm happy, and I want to stay that way. And I walked home, humming.

I set my course so as to keep in view the Chrysler building, ahead of me in midtown, because its scalloped roof is so beautiful. Just as I always kept the WTC towers in view when I walked south. Often, the clouds were lower than the top floors. At evening time, especially, the ranks of lights high up in the dark, behind moving shreds of cloud, were lovely, glimmering, silver things. And there was a pink neon furled umbrella on the façade of the second tower. It was vaguely amusing. I have friends who have a newsstand/cafe on Hudson Street. The husband strolled out his door and looked up after he heard the first bang. He is a gentle man, a music lover, a man who agreed that the two of us could leave the Met after just one act of *Tristan and Isolde* because it was so overwhelmingly moving. He stood on the pavement outside his building, and witnessed his fellow human beings as they jumped to their deaths. They jumped past the pink umbrella. When will he be whole again?

When will my friend who works in J.P. Morgan in Wall Street be untroubled again? She can't ever go back there, she says: the smell of death got into her that day. My friends in publishing are mainly Jewish. How long will the US protect Israel, they must be asking themselves, if this is the price it is asked to pay? And is there anywhere at all in the world they can be unafraid? My best friend asked me a few months ago whether I thought it was safe for her to go to the Jerusalem Book Fair. Now, Jerusalem is everywhere that beautiful, formerly sanguine, young woman walks.

I made some money from my book, and with it I arranged for semi-permanent access to the innocent high spirits of Manhattan. For the price of a house in, say, Crumlin, I put a deposit on a space in a warehouse just beside the Holland Tunnel. The idea was that by next year, maybe, the warehouse would be turned into apartments. Whenever I thought of the winter months I might be going to spend there, I imagined walking the lively streets and hurrying in from the sharp, blue-skied cold to talkative meals in restaurants, and then the payoff being able to do hard work because of being so carefree.

Now, I can imagine nothing.

My plan, of course, doesn't matter at all in itself. But I mention it because it matters that the gift of hope, which has been Manhattan's gift to millions throughout its existence, and was its gift to me, has been snatched from its grasp. It matters that the spectrum of intangible things I valued Manhattan for is the very spectrum that has disappeared. The myth that Manhattan had of itself has been murdered. Its harmless obsessions with fashion and celebrity and being where it's at, have been massacred along with everything else. A society that never imagined itself being anything but envied — that could not imagine being hated — must now find dark and uncertain ways of being.

I take it that there is dust everywhere on the building I was going to have my space in. There must be dust all over lower Manhattan. Consider what must be in that dust, since hardly any whole bodies have been found. If ever I look down at a smudge on my hand there, I'll know what I'm looking at. But — leave Manhattan? Turn away from it? Would you turn away from a beloved woman because she had been brutally raped? Wouldn't the love still be there, though now it accommodates pain and division and sadness?

I'm an old hand — I knew that here we have no abiding city. I knew that there are really no Fun Cities. But it is sorrow of a new kind, for those who loved Manhattan's sassy self-belief the way one would love it in a child, to see that suffering is turning the child, even as one looks on, into a wary adult.

Julianne Clifford-McCourt, daughter of Ruth Clifford from Cork, Ireland, who died on board one of the planes that hit the World Trade Centre.

Index